# IRISH WRITERS
# AND
# SOCIETY AT LARGE

# IRISH LITERARY STUDIES

# "IRISH WRITERS AND SOCIETY AT LARGE"

edited by
Masaru Sekine

## Irish Literary Studies 22

1985
COLIN SMYTHE
Gerrards Cross, Bucks.
BARNES AND NOBLE BOOKS
Totowa, New Jersey

Copyright © 1985 by Masaru Sekine, David Burleigh, Joan Coldwell,
Maurice Harmon, A. Norman Jeffares, Brendan Kennelly, Declan Kiberd,
Alasdair Macrae, Augustine Martin, John Montague, A. C. Partridge,
Ann Saddlemyer, Frank Tuohy, George Watson, Robert Welch

First Published in 1985 by Colin Smythe Limited
Gerrards Cross, Buckinghamshire

**British Library Cataloguing in Publication Data**

Irish writers and society at large.—(Irish literary studies,
ISSN 0140-895X; v. 22)
1. English literature—Irish authors—History and criticism
I. Sakine, Masaru     II. Series
820.9'9415     PR8711

ISBN 0-86140-226-X

First published in the United States of America in 1985 by
Barnes & Noble Books, 81 Adams Drive, Totowa, N.J. 07512

**Library of Congress Cataloguing in Publication Data**

Irish writers and society at large.
(Irish literary studies, ISSN 0140-895X; 22)
Includes index
1. English literature—Irish authors—History and criticism—Addresses,
essays, lectures.
2. Literature and society—Ireland—Addresses, essays, lectures.
3. Ireland in literature—Addresses, essays, lectures
I. Sekine, Masaru, 1945–     . II. Series
PR8718.I7 1985     820'.9'89162     85-7351

ISBN 0-389-20580-X

Produced in Great Britain
Set by Action Typesetting, Gloucester
and printed and bound by Billing & Sons Ltd., Worcester

# CONTENTS

# INTRODUCTION

This collection of essays is published to mark the establishment of IASAIL–JAPAN, a branch of IASAIL, the International Association for the Study of Anglo-Irish Literature. IASAIL–JAPAN held an Inaugural Conference at Waseda University, Tokyo, in September 1984. Guests present at this conference were the founding Chairman of IASAIL, A. Norman Jeffares, the founding Secretary, Brendan Kennelly, the present Chairman, Heinz Kosok, and a former Chairman, Ann Saddlemyer. Other guests included Joan Coldwell, Declan Kiberd, John Lawlor, and Frank Tuohy. This volume includes some of the papers given at the conference as well as essays especially written to celebrate the founding of IASAIL–JAPAN by other distinguished authors and critics engaged in the study of Irish literature. It will be followed by a volume of essays on Irish drama to be published later in 1985.

The Japanese branch of IASAIL was established through the work of a founding committee, whose members were Reiji Fujimoto, Taketoshi Furomoto, Okifumi Komesu, Kenichi Matsumura, Osamu Osaka, Tetsuro Sano, Masaru Sekine and Hiroshi Suzuki. This committee received support from Hiro Ishibashi, a Vice-Chairman of IASAIL, Yukio Oura, the Chairman of the Yeats Society of Japan, and Iwao Mizuta, the first Chairman of IASAIL–JAPAN. Hiromichi Matsudaira played an invaluable part in the administrative work leading up to the launching of the association.

The aim behind the creation of IASAIL–JAPAN was to encourage Japanese scholars engaged in the study of Anglo-Irish literature, to provide opportunities for them to meet each other and to furnish occasions for the establishment of further contacts with other scholars throughout the world, in order to exchange ideas and enrich the study of Irish literature in Japan and to make the Japanese interest in and contribution to Irish Studies more widely known.

In the past links between Ireland and Japan suffered from the geographical and cultural distances dividing the two countries.

In the twentieth century, however, a change came about with the interest that Ireland's greatest poet, W. B. Yeats, developed in Japan, in the ideas of Zen philosophy and in the traditional Japanese Noh theatre. The former affected Yeats's thought and poetry, the latter was more obviously reflected in his dramatic work. He wrote *Four Plays for Dancers* in which he was influenced by the stylised form of the Noh, which he called the Noh stage of aristocratic Japan. He obtained the assistance of a young Japanese dancer, Michio Ito, in the production of the first of these four plays, *At the Hawk's Well*. Ito, incidentally, was in Europe in order to learn current European dance techniques, and had not been trained in the Noh theatre, so it is dubious how much help he actually gave to Yeats in his pursuit of Noh aesthetic ideals. Yeats at one time toyed with the idea of living in Japan as a Professor. He was deeply impressed by the continuity of Japanese culture and when Junzo Sato, then resident in Oregon, gave him his centuries-old family sword he found this an inspiring symbol of the spiritual force of Samurai tradition.

Yeats's work began to be studied in Japan, originally by a small group of scholars, among them Professors Hojin Yano and Shotaro Oshima. Professor Oshima's contribution to Japanese studies of Anglo-Irish literature in general was remarkable. He was the author of many books and articles on the subject, among them the elegant study *W. B. Yeats and Japan* (1965), written in English. He visited Ireland on many occasions (calling on Yeats at Riversdale) and founded the flourishing Yeats Society of Japan.

The studies begun by a handful of scholars are now deeply rooted in Japanese academic life, and interest extends beyond Yeats, Synge, Lady Gregory and other figures of the Irish Renaissance back as far as Jonathan Swift, and even further back, into Irish writing in Irish. While such classic writers as Wilde, Shaw, Joyce and Beckett are studied in detail, attention is also being focussed on younger contemporary writers.

IASAIL-JAPAN's foundation demonstrates the growing enthusiasm aroused in Japan by past and present Irish writing.

Waseda University                              Masaru Sekine
Tokyo, 1985

# ACKNOWLEDGEMENTS

The publishers wish to thank the following publishers for permission to publish material quoted in this volume.

to Faber and Faber Limited to publish extracts from the following
    Brian Friel's *Faith Healer;*
    Seamus Heaney's *Preoccupations, Wintering Out, Death of a Naturalist, North, Sweeney Astray, Station Island* and *Field Work;*
    Louis MacNeice's *Collected Poems;*
    Paul Muldoon's *Mules;*
    Tom Paulin's *A Strange Museum* and *Liberty Tree;*

to The Dolmen Press to publish Works by John Montague from his *The Dead Kingdom* and *The Rough Field;*

to Oxford University Press to publish poems from Derek Mahon's *Poems 1962–1978* and *The Hunt by Night;*

to Macmillan, London & Basingstoke, and The Macmillan Company, New York, to quote the poems of W. B. Yeats.

IASAIL–JAPAN Series
ISSN 0267-6079; v. 1

# DEAD AND GONE: THE FICTION OF JENNIFER JOHNSTON AND JULIA O'FAOLAIN

DAVID BURLEIGH

> *Puritan Ireland's dead and gone,*
> *A myth of O'Connor and O'Faolain.*
> John Montague—*The Siege of Mullingar* (refrain)

Women novelists, unlike women poets and playwrights, have a long and distinguished tradition in Anglo-Irish literature. Indeed, in depicting the lives of the ascendancy, the Anglo-Irish in the sociological sense, from Maria Edgeworth at the beginning of the nineteenth century down to the still-living Molly Keane, women writers have tended to predominate. This essay discusses the work of two younger living authors, Jennifer Johnston and Julia O'Faolain, whose work extends and enriches an already worthy tradition.

Though in many ways very different, as quickly becomes clear from even a brief examination of their books, some connections can be made between these two authors. Both are women, out of the same country and of the same generation. Both, too, are children of formidably famous literary parents (the playwright, Denis Johnston and the short-story writer, Sean O'Faolain). This background echoes, at least superficially, that of Maria Edgeworth, whose father was a writer, though not of fiction, before her.

In the world that Jennifer Johnston sets before us, there are a great many elderly men, whom we usually encounter in the advanced stages of decrepitude. They are accompanied, if they are married, by middle-aged women bitter over the loss of their beauty. Their sons are soft and ineffectual, their daughters spirited but naive. There is usually a housekeeper, who has a brusque manner that conceals a heart of gold. There is often a gardener too, to look after the extensive grounds. Yet with these stock and rather unpromising characters, Jennifer Johnston has

1

created a series of short novels, wryly observed and tersely written, that are intensely moving.

Her first book, *The Gates* (1973), was in fact the second published. It is not, however, a practice run, but a remarkably accomplished book, which instantly establishes the manner of composition and announces the themes of her work. It tells the story of Minnie MacMahon, whose parents, an Anglo-Irish gentleman and an ordinary shop-girl, died when she was four. Minnie, now nineteen, has just finished her education in England, and left the home of an uncle there to return to that of another in Ireland, which she prefers. Uncle Frank, affectionately called 'Proinnseas' by his niece and 'the Major' by others, lives with his housekeeper in a 200 year old house beside the sea in Donegal.

The first notable theme is one of change and decay. This is developed in the opening pages of the book, while Uncle Frank waits for Minnie at the railway station, which is due to be closed down soon. Indeed railway stations seem to have a particular fascination for the author and recur in her other stories. The house itself is run-down, and Uncle Frank almost penniless, although he employs local people to work for him, thus fulfilling an expected social role. Among these are the Kellys, a rough family of poor Catholics. As the story proceeds, Minnie becomes involved with and attracted to the eldest Kelly son, Kevin. With him, she plans to sell the gates of the house to some visiting Americans. When the deal is completed, however, Kevin runs off to England with the money.

The impulse behind Minnie's involvement with Kevin, like her return itself, is that she prefers Ireland to England, and consequently the Irish to the English. There is a movement towards reconciliation, integration (it is suggested that Minnie's mother was a tinker), which is defeated by circumstance. Ironically, though Minnie dislikes England, she is still coloured by it (she says things like 'starvers' for 'starving'), and this sets her apart from Kevin quite as much as the violence of his home life compared to the tranquillity of hers. Their plan, as she sees it, is to start a garden that will bring life, and money, back to the old house. Let down, Minnie discloses the truth to her uncle, and is reconciled with him instead.

The position of the Anglo-Irish, at home neither in Ireland nor in England, displaced persons in the new Irish state, is caught early in the novel:

Just off the road leading to the Major's house, the Protestant church crouched like a little old lady, embarrassed at being found some place she had no right to be, behind a row of yew trees. The other end of the village, on a slight eminence, a semi-cathedral, topped by an ornate gold cross, preened itself triumphantly.[1]

A theme of loneliness and isolation, then, is also introduced here. Besides belonging to the Anglo-Irish as a social class, Minnie is an orphan, and her uncle is old and unmarried. Finally they achieve a respectful understanding of each other. Jennifer Johnston usually allows some measure of redemption to her characters at the conclusion of each book.

The story is briefly and sparely told. Much of the book consists of dialogue, for which the author has a brilliant gift. There is little figurative language—the old men, of whom there are two in this book, are described as birds, and the Catholic family are compared, rather unfortunately, to dogs. The only major short-coming is to be found in the portrait of the visiting Americans which is, to say the least, rather stereotyped. The same charge has been made about the author's portrayal of the Kelly family, though with less justice.

This first novel has been dwelt on because it seems to contain the germs of the books that were to follow. Thus we find that the next two novels are also concerned with military men and with old age, though separately. *The Captains and the Kings* (1972), the second of the author's novels (though the first published) is a story about friendship. Charles Prendergast, an elderly widower, estranged from his daughter, lives alone in a large house. His only help is the alcoholic and rather spiteful gardener, Sean. Charles himself is a younger son, his life having been overshadowed by his elder brother Alec, who died in the war.

Charles is haunted, by the legend of his dead brother, and by his own mother's cruel rejection of him. He is dismayed by his own weakness, and withdrawn because of it. When he forms an innocuous friendship with a young Catholic boy, Diarmuid Toorish, from the nearby village, this is complicated by events beyond his control, and understood as pederastic. Disaster ensues, the only saving graces being the very civilised attitude adopted by the priest at the end of the novel, and the fact that the old man has the good fortune to die before the police come. The boy's parents, Mr and Mrs Toorish (subliminally, perhaps, 'boorish'), behave abominably.

What matters, however, is that Charles, a dry passionless man who has been a baffled observer all his life, finds a warm human contact before it is too late. In the throes of his misfortune, he realises, and has the courage to say: 'I loved the boy. Do love. Yes'.[2] It is a very delicately related tale. It is also remarkably frank, when we remember that Forrest Reid's planned novel on the same theme remained unwritten because he was too frightened of the subject.[3] And that was only fifty years ago.

Jennifer Johnston's third novel, *How Many Miles to Babylon?* (1974) is also concerned with male companionship. Though set in a different period, with a different permutation of characters and events, it picks up very directly from many of the places where *The Captains and the Kings* leaves off. It is a story about soldiers in the First World War, and it is notable that Alexander Moore, the central character, has the same Christian name as Charles's elder brother in the previous book. It is also a story about loyalty and love, again with a suggestion of homosexuality about it.

Alexander Moore is the only child of a kind-hearted elderly father and a beautiful, embittered mother. Alec is confused as to what is expected of him, and how he can measure up to it. 'They all wanted me to become a man. I found it hard to grasp exactly what this entailed',[4] he writes later. At the outbreak of war, he declines to join the other young men of the neighbourhood who are going off to fight. His mother, demanding sacrifice, reveals to her son that his father is not the old man. In this way, she exerts her will and forces Alexander to go. At the same time, Jeremiah Crowe, a local Catholic lad of the same age with whom Alec enjoyed a secret friendship as a boy until forbidden by his mother, joins up, though for quite different reasons.

Johnston skilfully evokes both the world of officers and fox-hunting men, and the horrors of trench warfare. She provides a third character, in the person of an Englishman named Bennett, whose presence helps to emphasise the differences between the Anglo-Irish and the English—outside Ireland, all the Irish are the same. Alec, cloudy, uncertain, wanting only to get away from his family, is eventually galvanised into clear and irrevocable action when, Jerry having been condemned to death for desertion, Alec despatches his friend personally rather than head a firing squad as he has been ordered. As a result, Alec too must die.

Earlier in the novel there is another scene in which a senior

officer, Captain Glendinning, deals expediently with a seriously
wounded soldier who is beyond help. This event serves as both
echo and inspiration in the story. The novel is written as a
journal while Alec waits himself for execution. This is not an
original technique, but it creates the requisite feeling of tension
in the reader while the story unfolds. When the climax
approaches, we realise that Alec has achieved a deeper and
more terrible expression of his humanity, as opposed to the
manliness demanded of him, than anything his parents could
have imagined.

*Shadows on our Skin* (1977) ventures for the first time inside a
working class, and Catholic household. The setting is again
contemporary and the background that of the Ulster 'Troubles'.
Joe Logan, a young Derry boy who, like the earlier Diarmuid,
is unhappy at home, makes friends with a young woman
schoolteacher. Joe's family have some connection with the IRA.
When it is discovered that the teacher's fiancé is a British
soldier, there is a quick reprisal and the novel closes with her
departure. Though the nature of the dialogue and the situation
are different, we meet again a strong mother, this time a
forbearing one like those in O'Casey, and an old, sickly father.
The portrait of the boy is very fine indeed, and the family
relations are acutely observed. As always, the story is deftly
told.

For all its skill, however, *Shadows on our Skin* sits
uncomfortably beside the author's other books, though it is
difficult at first to see why this is so. It is probably because the
placing of the story against a background of the 'Troubles' gives
the book a documentary air. Despite having been nominated for
the Booker Prize, this book stands up least well among the
author's works to re-reading. It is also, of course, outside the
upper-middle class territory that she obviously knows and
understands more deeply.

As if to confirm this judgment, Jennifer Johnston withdrew
again to more familiar terrain in her next novel, *The Old Jest*
(1979). Here she takes up a story hinted at in the book that
preceded it. Nancy Gulliver, who describes herself as 'a
somewhat haphazard person',[5] is, like the schoolteacher in
*Shadows on our Skin*, an orphaned girl from Wicklow. Nancy,
however, still lives there, with a spinster aunt and her senile
grandfather. It is the summer of 1920 and Nancy has just left
school. The Great War has just ended, but the Irish Question is
not settled. It is the time of the killing of Michael Collins and the

hunting of political suspects, one of whom Nancy finds she has ingenuously befriended.

There are several humorous portraits in the book—the Miss Brabazons, with their precious Daimler, Joe Mulhare, who looks like a rabbit—which lighten the atmosphere. And anyway trouble is mostly what the members of the household read about in the newspapers, and politics are only what Nancy and the man she has befriended, whom she nicknames Cassius, talk about in a general way. But the dialogue in this book shows a new richness and resonance, taking on, as it does, the nature of philosophical exchange. This is particularly true of Nancy's conversations with Cassius, where we hear the voices of two loners, the young and the old, innocence and experience. These form the substance of the book.

By contrast, description of action is spare and minimal, mere stage directions. The shooting of Cassius near the end of the book is rendered very matter-of-factly:

She walked through the soldiers and up towards the blocks of stone, then she stopped and looked back. He had thrown his bag on to the sand and was fumbling in his pocket for the gun. He took it out and looked at it for a moment, and then threw it down beside the bag. Then they shot him. Two. Three shots. Running.[6]

That is all, no embellishment. And afterwards the old man, a retired general, chants abstractedly, 'Where is death's sting? Where grave thy victory?'[7] But Nancy's world has been shattered.

Death, victorious or otherwise, is the subject of *The Christmas Tree* (1981), in which we travel the entire journey towards it in one of the author's most powerful and affecting novels. The structure of the book is similar to that of *How Many Miles to Babylon?* Constance Keating, like Nancy Gulliver and Minnie MacMahon before her, wishes to write. Now, aged forty-five and dying of leukaemia, she is composing an autobiographical sketch which is in fact the story we are reading. This is a daring and candid book, which vividly conveys a sense of the protagonist's physical decline.

Constance has already foregone a university education and left her home in Ireland to live in London and be alone. She has failed as a writer and recently decided to have a baby before she becomes too old. Informed of her illness after the birth, she suddenly decides to return home, still alone, and die in her father's house, resisting help. Her sister takes care of the baby, whose father is a Polish Jew whom Constance met on holiday. Constance wishes the father to have the child, and the novel consists of her recollections as she waits for Christmas to come, for the baby's father to arrive, and for death. The last part is written, convincingly, by an orphan girl brought in to help.

Again there is a restrained and precisely factual approach to action, accompanied by the new and deeper veins of richness in dialogue. Perhaps the best parts are the short exchanges Constance has with each of her parents, and the longer ones with her Jewish lover. The love affair is short-lived, and it is the only instance of a satisfactory sexual liaison in all of Jennifer Johnston's novels. Two names recur from the preceding book— Bridie, the name of the housekeeper, and then the orphan girl, and the surname Barry, which is Cassius's real name, and also that of Constance's brother-in-law. Quotations from the Bible and Shakespeare are woven into the text.

Refrains from nursery rhymes, or songs, or poems, can be found in many places in Jennifer Johnston's six novels to date (a seventh is announced but unavailable at the time of writing). These add a special cadence, a poetic and legendary quality, to the stories. Johnston also frequently uses the presence of birds as a counterpoint to a happening or a conversation. Crows stirring in trees, pigeons on a windowsill, swans over a lake, a seagull on a roof—sometimes they move with events, but more often they are indifferent. The terseness of the prose is invigorating.

The particular strength of Jennifer Johnston's work, beyond the technical skill of her writing, lies in her ability to keep the reader consistently morally engaged. Her protagonists—the bereaved, the orphaned, the outcast—are all spirits struggling to enlarge themselves. The urge that moves them is a very unclear one, without a plan or a vision, only the push of some inner will. But when they break through the constraining matrix, often traumatically, clarity is achieved. Those that are able to go on, do so with better understanding, and the final effect is uplifting.

★

Julia O'Faolain differs in many ways from Jennifer Johnston. She is a more rumbustious writer, with a broad, discursive mind, and her fictions, of varying length, cover a much wider range of geographical and social locations. The world that she deals with is basically a three-cornered one. It stretches from Ireland (with some connections across the Irish Sea in Britain), to continental Europe (mainly France and Italy), and then to the United States (in particular, California).

With one significant exception, Julia O'Faolain's settings are all more or less contemporary. And her work is most commonly occupied with a theme of personal love, or, more specifically, the physical expression of it, with male and female sexuality. Cultural, religious and political concerns are introduced where they intrude upon areas that are private and sexual, but it is the latter which seem to interest the author most. The O'Faolain referred to in John Montague's poem used as the epigraph of this essay, is Julia O'Faolain's father, Sean.

In the title piece of the author's first published volume, We Might See Sights! and other stories (1968), the protagonist, a girl called Madge, goes with her friend Bernie to visit a cave. But first Madge has to end another relationship with a girl who, according to Madge's mother, is socially unsuitable. The rejected companion is described thus:

Rosie had blonde, naturally curly hair, abundant as an aureole and alive with lice. She had a mouthful of bossy teeth and foamy laugh.[8]

This is an extremely vivid picture, rhythmically stated, showing how Julia O'Faolain's strong sense of language is present right from the beginning.

Her friendships rearranged, Madge goes off with Bernie and the latter's mentally defective baby brother to explore the cave. Here they catch sight of a couple making love. The girls withdraw but the defective child doesn't understand. Afterwards, Madge beats him in a rage of adolescent jealousy and frustration. Unreasonable urges, we learn, are lurking inside us, ready to burst out and seek expression, if not in one form then in another. Instances of sexual denial reappear in the author's work.

In another story from the same collection, also the title story from a later selection of these and other tales, Melancholy Baby (Dublin, 1978), lonely, selfish Aunt Adie, married but childless and sexually unfulfilled, tries to dominate her orphaned niece Gwennie: 'Like the poised claw of a crane, her affective energies remained in suspense'.[9] But these energies will not be refused and do fight their way out, with extremely unpleasant results for Gwennie. It is a recognizable and convincing, if not entirely new, way of looking at Ireland, about which the author writes with sardonic humour and, it often seems, a kind of smouldering anger.

The object of Julia O'Faolain's anger in her first novel, *Godded and Codded* (1970), about a young woman seeking sexual adventure in Paris, is middle class convention, with its supply of platitudinous prohibitions. Sally, the young woman, says of herself: 'I am like a leaky gas jet. I shall poison the air if my fumes are not lit'.[10] She then proceeds to shuck off the restrictive attitudes of her Dublin parents. The novel is written in a jaunty style suitable for a romp, and some of it is quite funny. But none of the characters seem either very real or very sympathetic, though they are shrewdly observed and entertainingly presented.

What the novel does do, however, is establish the theme of a female finding her independence. This is continued and expanded in the title story of another collection, *Man in the Cellar* (1974). Indeed, with this second collection, the focus of the stories shifts noticeably from questions of exploration, to those of continuation, from the making to the maintenance of marriage. Engaging and thought-provoking, they give life to a wide selection of personae and situations.

*Women in the Wall* (1975), Julia O'Faolain's next book, is a stunning departure, both chronologically and in its imaginative scope, from all the previous work. It is set in sixth century Gaul, after the collapse of the Roman Empire, a time of tribal rivalries and random violence. 'Gaul', we are told, 'was like a painted chessboard whose inks have run. Borders were vague'.[11] Partly historical reconstruction, partly invention, it is basically the story of a woman named Radegunda and the convent she founds when she leaves her husband, the King, to turn her back on the sensual world.

Giving up the world, however, for the 'reverse world' of Christianity, Radegunda is just as passionately physical in her search for spiritual union with God—she tortures and brands herself—as she was in bed with the King. A reason for atonement is suggested, as it is again when the illegitimate daughter of the convent's abbess, Ingunda, decides to become an anchoress and have herself closed up in a wall as a gesture of devotion. In the background there are political plots both inside and outside the convent. It is a very exciting story, the most compelling that the author has written, and a much livelier book than Helen Waddell's classic, *Peter Abelard* (1933), which deals with the Middle Ages at a later century.

Thematic consistency is maintained with Julia O'Faolain's other work through her examination in this novel of the consequences of the peculiar lives that celibates lead. A disapproval of celibacy was already implicit in the early stories, and here we find constant references to 'waste of life' and 'living death':

These women, who called each other 'Mother' and 'Sister' were neither, were so many stoppered bottles. Emotion fermented in them. Their tenderness was turned on a distant, inconceivable infant: the babe of Bethlehem, an image just persuasive enough to set the milk of human affection moving in their body ducts. They longed for reality. Any reality. [12]

They are, however, unable to see themselves in this way, and continue to mortify their flesh in endeavours to release the spirit. Despite O'Faolain's evident scepticism about religious practices, and a circumspectness in describing miraculous happenings, this is a very powerful book, wide and deep in its sympathies.

Vestigially medieval values, and unexpected and improbable acts of violence, persist down to the present in Ireland. Puritanism, too, though much undermined, still holds on in many quarters. It is not dead and gone, as John Montague, parodying Yeats's 'September 1913', would have us believe. But it is certainly dying. The current availability of books that were earlier banned is proof of that. But the social and political changes that have taken place have not produced a country that is rich with hope and opportunity. Reflecting this, Julia O'Faolain's Irish novel, parodying the opening line of Yeats's 'Sailing to Byzantium', is entitled *No Country for Young Men* (1980).

A complex and rich book, this novel is her most ambitious work so far. The main narrative describes an American filmmaker's attempts to extract secret information about the troubles of the 1920s from an elderly nun. The film is intended to raise funds to be sent to the North through an organisation called, wittily, Banned Aid. While the old nun struggles with her recalcitrant memory, the events of an earlier time are brought before us. The political past is thus cleverly, and comically, telescoped into the present, and we can watch both unfolding at the same time. Sidelights are cast along the way on other matters, such as American interference in Ireland.

The novel has a full gallery of characters, many encountered only briefly, but Julia O'Faolain always fixes them with a sharp eye. James Duffy, the ingenuous film-man, first encounters the Irish at a radio station in California:

There was an Orangeman from Belfast in a pair of bright new cowboy boots, a local priest whose cufflinks were slightly bigger than quarters, and a fierce, butch-looking girl from Ireland who turned out to have a remarkable knack for scoring debating points and keeping physical control of the mike. She spoke with the fluency of a mimeographed flyer ... [13]

The dialogue which ensues from a purported discussion between the priest and the young woman is hilarious, interleaved as it is with another conversation that James is having. The whole book contains a series of such vignettes which come together to create a broad portrait of a time and place.

The other crucial strand of the narrative is James's affair with Grainne O'Malley, in whose home the old nun is staying because they are distant relatives. Both Grainne and James are married, which means that their affair must be kept secret, though it doesn't succeed in remaining so. The difference in their backgrounds profoundly affects their sexual liaison. And the liaison itself affects the lives of Grainne's husband and son, and James's wife, who receives detailed letters chronicling its course which we are allowed to read. Contingent events precipitate the situation into one of crisis, while the attachment of James and Grainne to each other deepens.

Once more the theme is revealed to be an examination of sexual relations. In this novel, and the one succeeding it, there is a preoccupation with marriage: its uncertainties, its durability in a permissive age, its interracial possibilities, its adjustment to the changing social position of women. And those who stay outside it, celibates and virgins, especially if they oppose it in any way, are given short shrift by the author. Thus the crusading Jane, who runs a home for Battered Wives in which Grainne spends some time, is made to appear foolish. And the two acts of violence which occur in the book are both perpetrated by individuals who have denied, or been denied, any sexual experience. One is the stabbing of an American participant in the revolution, Sparky Driscoll, by the nun Judith Clancy in her youth, and the other James's tragi-comic murder at the end of the book by the gardener Patsy Flynn. Patsy of course was also involved in work for the IRA in his youth. A connection between sexual repression and acts of violence is strongly implied.

Purposelessness and disappointment colour the atmosphere of the newborn Irish State:

Already, men who had been straining up towards a bright, unbounded future found themselves talking of the past. A new order had begun. The whirling wheel of fortune had jammed.

But many young men could not accept that no more could have been got from the British. Change was addictive and anyway there were no jobs.[14]

This can be compared with what one of the minor characters in Jennifer Johnston's *The Gates* has to say. The speaker is an old man called Big Jim Breslin, who looks back from the present over the changes:

'And not all of them for the best, either. So few people care for anything, only themselves. The young people can't wait to get away. What sort of a country have we made that people don't want to live in?'[15]

Other transformations, such as the growth of middle class affluence and the spread of education, have also taken place by this time. One other parallel between the two writers, apart from a preponderance of weak men in their books (Julia O'Faolain has strong men too, but they usually play a secondary role), is that the instrument of James's downfall and death, a self-appointed avenging angel, Patsy, is an unmarried gardener. Charles Prendergast in Johnston's *The Captains and the Kings* is also the victim of his mean-minded gardener, likewise a single man.

One of the minor sub-plots in *No Country for Young Men* follows the inner thoughts and development of Grainne's son, Cormac. From his embarrassment at having to stay in the Battered Wives' home with his mother, to his horror over his mother's conduct with the American, we are provided with an amusing and understanding portrait of a young adolescent. Comparing Cormac with Jennifer Johnston's protagonist in *Shadows on our Skin*, we find that Julia O'Faolain's boy is a great deal more articulate, but this can be understood as a reflection of his class background.

Julia O'Faolain's next novel, *The Obedient Wife* (1982), is in a way complementary to the book it succeeds. It gives the other side of the story, that of the wife who must wait in America while her husband philanders in Europe, and the future of the marriage hangs in the air. The difference is that the couple in this case are not American but Italian, and also that, unlike James and his wife, they have a child, a boy. Son and mother bide their time in California, in an area of mud-slides, surrounded by people living lives quite different from their own, and threatened by all of this. Carla, the wife, has a dalliance with a priest which is handled with generosity. Cazz Dobrinski, a parasite and layabout who is one of their neighbours, is perhaps the most evil, and also the most memorable, character in the book. The American idiom is brilliantly caught. At the close of the novel, the family are reunited, and marriage survives, reassuringly but not very surprisingly.

One of Julia O'Faolain's particular talents as a writer is her ability to allow people to speak for themselves, in such a way that they often uncover or condemn themselves out of their own mouths. That we have the feeling that we are listening to the personae she adopts, and not to the author herself, is a measure of her skill as a novelist. Considering the range in the backgrounds of the people in her books, from politicians to gardeners, Irish, American and Italian, this represents quite a considerable achievement. It also means that she can sustain short stories in monologue form remarkably well.

In her third collection of short stories, *Daughters of Passion* (1982), we find examples of such monologues. The tales have varied settings, only two of the nine being concerned with Ireland. One of these is the story of the title, about three women, two of them Catholic orphans and the third a Catholic convert of Anglo-Irish stock, who have attended the same convent, then meet again in London and become involved with the IRA. The central character, Maggy, is in Brixton gaol on hunger strike as the story opens. She has planted a bomb and murdered a policeman, her reason for doing so not being entirely clear, though it appears to be another case of displaced passion. Julia O'Faolain makes splendid play out of the differences between the three women, whose fates are unexpectedly intertwined.

The other piece from this collection with an Irish setting is also a very fine one. 'And Why Should Not Old Men Be Mad?' (another title from Yeats) deals with an elderly bishop in a mental hospital and an old lawyer friend who comes to visit him. Written with great humour, it concludes somewhat in the manner of Chekhov's 'Ward Six'. The other stories pursue and extend themes of marriage and sexual relations. The author's prose in these later stories shows greater suppleness and repose, as do her sympathies, but with no diminishing in the tough intelligence with which the characters are drawn.

Though she has always been vivid and evocative, inventing fresh images to elucidate her meaning and please her readers, some passages in Julia O'Faolain's earlier books are jerky and difficult to read. In later work there is much less reliance on the stream of consciousness technique for representing inner thoughts. Sentences become longer and more fluid, alliteration is less clamorous, and there is a welcome decline in the use of exclamation marks. At its best, her writing has a refreshing ribaldry and a literate wit that make it continuously enjoyable to read. The author's cosmopolitanism is, of course, rare in Irish writing.

Without doubt *No Country for Young Men* is Julia O'Faolain's most substantial book to date. It is her most wide-ranging and complex work of fiction, and one of her most pleasurable. (A further novel is due soon). It takes an admirably cool and critical look at Ireland, though its mixture of realism and farce is not completely successful. Her most remarkable book is the earlier *Women in the Wall*, with its extraordinary imaginative reconstruction and gripping tale of an age which, though long ago, continues to resonate down into our own mad, knee-capping time.

It has not been the purpose of this essay to assess and place these two authors, Jennifer Johnston and Julia O'Faolain. It is too early to attempt that; but it is time to give some indication of the quality of what they have already achieved, and to express the hope that more and better may yet be to come.

## REFERENCES

1. Jennifer Johnston, *The Gates*. London: Fontana (1983), p.19.
2. Johnston, *The Captains and the Kings*. London: Fontana (1982), p.138.
3. See Brian Taylor, *Green Avenue: The Life and Writings of Forrest Reid*. Cambridge: Cambridge Univerity Press (1982).

4. Johnston, *How Many Miles to Babylon?* London: Fontana (1981), p.124.
5. Johnston, *The Old Jest.* London: Fontana (1980), p.50.
6. *Ibid.*, p.153.
7. *Ibid.*, p.158.
8. Julia O'Faolain, *Melancholy Baby and other stories.* Dublin: Poolbeg Press (1978), p.7.
9. *Ibid.*, p.34.
10. O'Faolain, *Godded and Codded.* London: Faber and Faber (1970), p.39.
11. O'Faolain, *Women in the Wall.* Harmondsworth: Penguin Books (1978), p.132.
12. *Ibid.*, p.182.
13. O'Faolain, *No Country for Young Men.* Harmondsworth: Penguin Books (1980), p.29.
14. *Ibid.*, p.226.
15. Johnston, *op. cit.*, p.61.

# THE BODKIN AND THE ROCKY VOICE: IMAGES OF WEAVING AND STONE IN THE POETRY OF W. B. YEATS

JOAN COLDWELL

'I have no speech but symbol'.[1] 'It is only by ancient symbols, by symbols that have numberless meanings besides the one or two the writer lays an emphasis upon, or the half-score he knows of, that any highly subjective art can escape from the barrenness and shallowness of a too conscious arrangement, into the abundancy and depth of Nature'.[2] Yeats spoke frequently of the symbolic content of his verse, and many critics have noted the resonance of key images such as birds, trees, tower, dance, rose, gyres, sun, moon and stars, and have explored their relationship to the poet's interest in the *Anima Mundi* and his use of visual emblems to stimulate the psychic process.[3]

From the large number of repeated symbols in Yeats's verse I choose two associated with his theory of the poetic process: the cluster of images connected with the weaving and sewing of cloth, and the many references to stone and rock. These are antithetical symbols—everything to do with weaving and sewing is in motion, the spindle whirling, the shuttle passing to and fro across the warp, the warm piece of cloth steadily growing, while stone is cold, static and unchanging. Taken together, in the kind of balance of contraries that Yeats, like Blake, saw at the heart of all things, they provide a key not only to Yeats's aesthetic theory but to the related concepts of love and patriotism.

Both weaving and stone have a long history as literary metaphors, going back to classical Greece and Rome, but they also come naturally to an Irishman in whose country weaving is a leading craft and for whom stone, whether as rocky outcroppings or as monumental evidence of ancient religions, is a familiar feature of the landscape. Thus Yeats, remembering his suggestion that Synge should go to the Aran Islands, that 'most desolate stony place', (*CP*, p.149) writes: 'my imagination was

16

full of those grey islands where men must reap with knives because of the stones'.[4] It is from the stony places that Yeats's imagination, like Synge's, reaps a harvest. The stony landscape and the theory of art as stone are ideas that take firm hold in Yeats's middle and later years; weaving is a simpler concept, perhaps more optimistically romantic, and it offers a symbol of poetry to Yeats throughout his career.

Metaphors of weaving are common in our critical vocabulary. We habitually speak of a tightly woven verse, of the thread of an argument, the texture of a poem, the spinning of a story. Originating with Sappho in the seventh century B.C., who sang of Eros as a weaver of stories, the metaphor became prominent in the odes of Pindar, who spoke of himself as a poet-weaver, 'weaving a many-coloured song for men who wield the spear', and, again, of weaving 'for the sons of Amythaon a many-coloured crown [of poetry]'.[5] One is reminded here of the many-coloured 'embroidered cloths' of heaven Yeats wishes to spread before his beloved and of the coat 'covered with embroideries' used as metaphor for his early mythological poems. (*CP*, p.142).

The focus of the weaving metaphor is on writing as a craft, 'this craft of verse' (*CP*, p.109), rather than as a matter of inspiration from the Muse. It is a process to be learned and developed , painstakingly, by trial and error. Thus, in 'Adam's Curse' (*CP*, p.88), Yeats speaks of 'stitching and unstitching' a line of poetry, which must seem like the result of a moment's inspiration even though it has been laboured over for hours. Similarly, in 'Coole Park, 1929', great works of poetry are described as 'Thoughts long knitted into a single thought' (*CP*, p.274).

J.M. Snyder suggests that the Greek poets' use of weaving as a metaphor for poetic song originated with the structural similarities between a loom and a lyre:

A Greek loom was a large upright device, consisting of two posts and a crossbar at the top, from which the strands of the warp were suspended and held straight by weights attached at the bottom; a Greek lyre (of any one of several types) had two arms and a crossbar to which were attached the instrument's gut strings, held in place by a fastener at the base of the soundbox. Attic vase paintings reveal that shuttles for looms and plektra for lyres were remarkably similar spoon-shaped objects.[6]

One might, I suppose, argue that there are likewise similarities between the loom and the Irish harp, though to my mind the visual force of the metaphor lies more in the way a rectangular piece of cloth grows on the loom as a rectangular poem grows line by line. Nevertheless, Yeats makes a fanciful story about the origin of the harp of Aengus, where the instrument is woven by the goddess Edain, who

> wove seven strings,
> Sweet with all music, out of his long hair,
> Because her hands had been made wild by love.(*CP*, p.471)

When weaving is suggested in Yeats's love poetry, it is usually associated with the woman's hair, sometimes in a fairly conventional way as in 'Your well-belovéd's hair has threads of grey', (*CP*, p.86) more often in a metaphor of entrapment, as in 'I am looped in the loops of her hair', (*CP*, p. 109) or in an image of a cosmos transformed by the poet's obsession:

> But know your hair was bound and wound
> About the stars and moon and sun.          (*CP*, p.81)

In the short poem 'His Bargain', imagery of spinning, weaving and the belovéd's hair are concise and complex:

> Who talks of Plato's spindle;
> What set it whirling round?
> Eternity may dwindle,
> Time is unwound,
> Dan and Jerry Lout
> Change their loves about.
>
> However they may take it,
> Before the thread began
> I made, and may not break it
> When the last thread has run,
> A bargain with that hair
> And all the windings there.          (*CP*, p.299)

We are indebted to A. N. Jeffares for tracing the reference to Plato's spindle to Book X of *The Republic*, where Necessity has a distaff from which all the universe revolves and before whose daughters, the three Fates, each man must make his choice of a way of life.[7] The poet's choice of a love overrides fate and necessity: he was bound in the lover's hair 'before the thread began' and will stay so 'after the last thread has run'. So too, in 'The Fool by the Roadside', the end of time is conceived as being

> When thoughts that a fool
> Has wound upon a spool
> Are but loose thread, are but loose thread.

(*CP*, p.247)

The end product of Irish weaving is taken by Yeats to symbolise the homespun genuineness of the audience he craves for his art. In 'The Fisherman', he visualises the 'wise and simple man' of his own race for whom he writes. The fisherman with 'sun-freckled face' wears 'grey Connemara cloth' (*CP*, p.166); similarly, the speakers in 'The Phases of the Moon' are clad in 'Connemara cloth worn out of shape' (*CP*, p.183). The contemporary poet who is in many respects Yeats's successor also uses woven cloth as a metaphor for the Irish, but in Seamus Heaney's case with a more overt political reference:

> O all the hamlets where
> Hills and flocks and streams conspired
>
> To a language of waterwheels,
> A lost syntax of looms and spindles,
>
> How they hang
> Fading in the gallery of the tongue!
>
> And I must talk of tweed,
> A stiff cloth with flecks like blood.[8]

For Yeats, the syntax of looms and spindles was far from lost. His poetic vocabulary includes technical words such as bobbin, spindle, spool and, remotest of all, pern. This latter word, perfectly familiar to old-style weavers and still well-known in cloth-making areas such as West Yorkshire and Scotland, has given commentators some trouble. Yeats himself thought it necessary to provide a gloss: 'When I was a little child at Sligo I could see above my grandfather's trees a little column of smoke from the "pern mill", and was told that "pern" was another name for the spool, as I was accustomed to call it, on which the thread was wound'.[9] After spinning, the yarn is wound onto the pern; one category of worker in the woollen mills was called a 'winder'. A reference of 1792 in the *Oxford English Dictionary* speaks of women spinning and men 'filling pirns'. Thus, Yeats envisages the dead Robert Gregory reversing the process, unliving, or in the terms of *A Vision* 'dreaming back', the accumulated experiences of a lifetime:

> He unpacks the loaded pern
> Of all 'twas pain or joy to learn . . .
> Knowledge he shall unwind          (*CP*, p.163)[10]

A pern is usually made of wood, wider at one end than the other and somewhat cone-shaped. Wool is wound from the spindle onto the pern, which then fits inside the flying shuttle as used on the large looms of the woollen mills. It is its visual appearance and its turning motion that connect it in Yeats's mind with his concept of gyres, whether as a description of a white gull's movement 'gyring down and perning there' (*CP*, p.216), or of himself vacillating between hatred and desire: 'Though I had long perned in the gyre' (*CP*, p.209). The antithesis here confirms the fact, suggested by the gloss quoted above, that Yeats uses pern very precisely to refer to the spool of wool as it lies within the shuttle, for only in that position can a pern move between the two sides of a loom, between hatred and desire.

This is the key to understanding Yeats's pern metaphor in its best-known context, 'Sailing to Byzantium':

> O sages standing in God's holy fire
> As in the gold mosaic of a wall,
> Come from the holy fire, perne in a gyre,
> And be the singing-masters of my soul.          (*CP*, p.217)

On one level of interpretation, the poet prays for timeless and divine inspiration to enter his soul in the downward spinning motion of the pern when it is taking wool from the spindle. At another level, the image powerfully conveys the idea of the reconciliation of opposites, the harmony of dualities, which is central to the whole poem. The shuttle makes a linear motion to and fro across the warp; within the shuttle, the spool or pern constantly gyrates. We have a visual image of the composing and the reading of a poem: the shuttle hand or eye moving across the lines of the page, the pern imagination gyrating and spiralling within. Circular motion within the linear: a poem 'cold and passionate as the dawn' (*CP*, p.167).

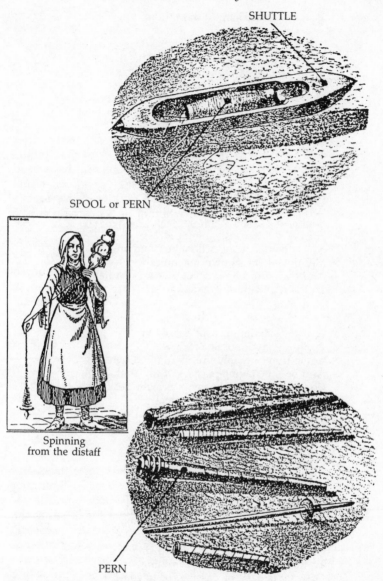

SHUTTLE

SPOOL or PERN

Spinning
from the distaff

PERN

Illustrations by Harold Blackburn from Phyllis Bentley's *Colne Valley Cloth*, The Huddersfield and District Woollen Export Group, Huddersfield, 1947.

### Sailing to Byzantium

#### I

That is no country for old men. The young
In one another's arms, birds in the trees
—Those dying generations—at their song,
The salmon-falls, the mackerel-crowded seas,
Fish, flesh or fowl, commend all summer long
Whatever is begotten, born and dies.
Caught in that sensual music all neglect
Monuments of unageing intellect.

#### II

An aged man is but a paltry thing,
A tattered coat upon a stick, unless
Soul clap its hands and sing, and louder sing
For every tatter in its mortal dress,
Nor is there singing-school but studying
Monuments of its own magnificence;
And therefore I have sailed the seas and come
To the holy city of Byzantium.

#### III

O sages standing in God's holy fire
As in the gold mosaic of a wall,
Come from the holy fire, perne in a gyre,
And be the singing-masters of my soul.
Consume my heart away; sick with desire
And fastened to a dying animal
It knows not what it is; and gather me
Into the artifice of eternity.

#### IV

Once out of nature I shall never take
My bodily form from any natural thing,
But such a form as Grecian goldsmiths make
Of hammered gold and gold enamelling
To keep a drowsy Emperor awake;
Or set upon a golden bough to sing
To lords and ladies of Byzantium
Of what is past, or passing, or to come.

                                             (*CP*, pp.217-218)

Contrast between motion and stasis, time and timelessness, underscores the tension in the poem between nature and art.

The gyrating pern and the disintegrating cloth of the scarecrow's tattered coat may be seen as a culmination of Yeats's weaving imagery; they suggest poetry's compound of spiritual inspiration and natural, earthly experience. The finished work of art itself is, in contrast, hard, motionless and unchanging: 'Monuments of unaging intellect': the reader brings the gyrating imagination to put the poem, as it were, into motion. Donald A. Stauffer suggests that the best short description of the mode of Yeats's great poems would be 'lyrical stasis';[10] nowhere is this better demonstrated than in 'Sailing to Byzantium', the lyrical aspect epitomised by the weaving process and stasis by the condition of monumental stone.

Before I turn to the variations on Yeats's symbolism of stone, I should point to the appropriateness of the weaving image in analysis of Yeats's poetry. 'Sailing to Byzantium' is a fine example of the carrying through of a thread of imagery. Each stanza has a reference to song, for instance, and old age is implicit in each. Even the simple word 'thing' is picked up and given the kind of significance it has at the beginning of Keats's *Endymion*: 'A thing of beauty is a joy for ever'. Of few other poems is it so appropriate to speak of the densely-woven texture, the richness of implication in such hyphenated words as 'salmon-falls' and 'mackerel-crowded'. Simultaneously, critics write of the 'stony clarity' of Yeats's verse, of its 'marmorean stillness'.[12] This was the quality so particularly admired by another Yeatsian disciple, Sylvia Plath, whose poetry is distinguished by what Richard Howard calls 'the lithic impulse', presumably by analogy with lithography, where an image is incised on stone. In Sylvia Plath's work, the attempt to make poetic form resemble the condition of stone is a transaction with the 'great Stasis' of personal annihilation.[13]

Like weaving, monumental stone has long been associated metaphorically with poetry. The *locus classicus* is in Horace's poem beginning *'Exegi monumentum'*: 'I have completed a monument more lasting than bronze and loftier than the royal structure of the pyramids, which no corroding rain, or violent north wind, can destroy or the innumerable succession of years and the flight of ages. I shall not wholly die, and a great part of me shall evade death'.[14] The idea is echoed in Shakespeare's Sonnet LV: 'Not marble, nor the gilded monuments/Of princes, shall outlive this powerful rhyme'. These literary antecedents surely reverberate in Yeats's 'Monuments of unaging intellect'.

Possibly the greatest inspiration for Yeats's symbolism of

monuments came from his travels in Italy and his readings in art history associated with them. Herbert J. Levine argues convincingly for the crucial influence on 'Sailing to Byzantium' of Ruskin's *The Stones of Venice* (a suggestive title in this context), a copy of which Yeats owned. [15] In 'Byzantium', visual images from such reading and travels—images of golden handiwork, the Emperor's pavement and marbles of the dancing floor—crystallize in an ideal of art so impersonal, non-subjective, that it is, like Keats's nightingale, 'all breathing human passion far above':

> A starlit or a moonlit dome disdains
> All that man is,
> All mere complexities,
> The fury and the mire of human veins.          (*CP*, p.280)

In 'The Tower', written close to the time of 'Sailing to Byzantium', the poet includes Italian Renaissance art, and Greek sculpture such as he had seen in the British Museum, among the high things of life, worthy of shaping experience in the 'translunar Paradise' after death:

> I have prepared my peace
> With learned Italian things
> And the proud stones of Greece,
> Poet's imaginings
> And memories of love,
> Memories of the words of women,
> All those things whereof
> Man makes a superhuman
> Mirror-resembling dream.          (*CP*, pp.223-224)

'Poet and sculptor, do the work'. (*CP*, p.399). Just as weaving was used to suggest the difficult craft of poetry, so is the painstaking work of a sculptor. Thus Yeats writes of Dante as one who 'set his chisel to the hardest stone', and

> fashioned from his opposite
> An image that might have been a stony face
> Staring upon a Bedouin's horse-hair roof.'          (*CP*, p.181)

In 'Lapis Lazuli', the chiselled object can be interpreted in much the same way as Keats's Grecian urn, where the 'foster-child of silence and slow time' serves as an analogy for the poem itself. The carved, static lapis lazuli stimulates imaginative movement:

perhaps the Chinamen may climb a mountain, maybe snow falls, or cherry blossoms. The incisions in the stone can be variously interpreted by the observer; so too the poem requires the active imagination of the reader.

Some of Yeats's most revealing images relating art to stone are those that form part of the eulogies to Major Robert Gregory, who

> understood
> All work in metal or in wood,
> In moulded plaster or in carven stone.          (*CP*, p.151)

In a classical affectation, Gregory as pastoral poet is one who played his pipes among the hills:

> And when he played it was their loneliness,
> The exultation of their stone, that cried
> Under his fingers.                          (*CP*, p.160)

Of the dead friend's promise as a painter Yeats wrote:

> We dreamed that a great painter had been born
> To cold Clare rock and Galway rock and thorn,
> To that stern colour and that delicate line
> That are our secret discipline
> Wherein the gazing heart doubles her might.
>                                   (*CP*, pp.150-151)

The 'stern colour' of 'cold Clare rock' is here identified as one of the sources of Yeats's poetic inspiration, 'our secret discipline' wherein renewal and strength are to be found. A poem to Lady Gregory, 'To a friend whose work has come to nothing', bids her find solace

> like a laughing string
> Whereon mad fingers play
> Amid a place of stone.                      (*CP*, p.122)

In an amusing passage at the beginning of the *Concordance to the Poems of Yeats*, Stephen Parrish invents a composite of the Yeatsian landscape based on the number of appearances of certain words: 'Yeats's landscape of images, we all agree, is a forest of trees (each with a mask hanging on the trunk), their branches alive with birds—a forest running along the edge of the sea, broken by an occasional house with a tower and rose garden, and overhead (though not all at once) the sun, the moon and the stars'.[16] There is one significant omission, surprising given the high number of its listings in the concordance, and that is of stone and rock. Yeats's landscape is stony: the poet sits 'on that old grey stone/Under the old windbroken tree', (*CP*, p.214) the wild swans at Coole are 'among the stones', (*CP*, p.147). The fishermen casts his line 'Where stone is dark under froth', (*CP*, p.167) and in Coole Park 'saplings root among the broken stones'. (*CP*, p.274). In the same image as in 'In Memory of Major Robert Gregory', we have 'I stumbled blind/Among the stones and thorn-trees', (*CP*, p.122) and 'I have been in the Path of Stones and the Wood of Thorns'. (*CP*, p.68). Yeats habitually associates his tower home of Thoor Ballylee with stone; set in 'an acre of stony ground', it has 'a chamber arched with stone' and a 'grey stone fireplace'. (*CP*, p.226-227). The ending of 'Ancestral Houses' pulls together, in a tribute to his wife and Lady Gregory, the stone tower of his home and the poem that celebrates it:

> And know whatever flourish and decline
> These stones remain their monument and mine.
>
> (*CP*, p.229)

The stream outside Yeats's tower, where the moor-hens dive, is the focus of a powerful symbol in the political poem 'Easter 1916'. The 'living stream', the steady flux of experience and growth, is 'troubled' by the passions of fanatics devoted to a single cause:

> Hearts with one purpose alone
> Through winter and summer seem
> Enchanted to a stone
> To trouble the living stream.          (*CP*, p.204)

The reference earlier in the poem to the 'wingèd horse', Pegasus, classical symbol of poetic inspiration, suggests that the enchantment to stone relates to the Greek myth of the Gorgon Medusa, mother of the winged horse. This once-beautiful woman had been turned into a monster whose hair teemed with snakes; those who looked at her eyes were turned to stone, 'changed utterly'.

The details of this myth were particularly relevant to Yeats's situation as the frustrated and rejected lover. Maud Gonne, who had seemed with her Ledean body to be a second Helen of Troy, grew in his imagination to have the petrifying power of Medusa. His heart's agony leaves him lying 'like a bit of stone ... Under a broken tree' (*CP*, p.250); his looking at her smile 'transfigured' him and made him incapable of action:

> But since I laid a hand thereon
> And found a heart of stone
> I have attempted many things
> And not a thing is done. (*CP*, p.249)

In his sardonic comment 'Men Improve with the Years', the poet envisages himself as turned to stone, 'A weather-worn, marble triton/Among the streams'. (*CP*, p.152) In a moment of bleak depression, this state seems more desirable than the fierce emotions once generated by the woman's face: now he would rather be 'Colder and dumber and deafer than a fish' (*CP*, p.109).

The frequent emphasis on the beauty of Maud Gonne's hair and her 'delicate high head' is an ironic reversal of the Medusa image, where hair and head are images of horror. It is these that have enchanted him and removed his life-force:

> since you were gone,
> My barren thoughts have chilled me to the bone.
> (*CP*, p.102)

It is in the poem 'A Bronze Head' that we find the most subtle relating of the Medusa myth to Maud Gonne. In contemplating Laurence Campbell's bronze-painted plaster cast of Maud's head at Dublin's Municipal Gallery of Modern Art, the poet finds all the force of this severed head in the eye, as earlier in life he had once thought her to be possessed by supernatural power, 'As though a sterner eye looked through her eye'. (*CP*, pp.282-283). Everything else but this eye is 'withered and mummy-dead'. The myth is further implied by the metaphor of Maud as a race-horse, a Pegasus 'at the starting-post, all sleek and new'. Thus the contradictory effect of his love is enforced by the inherent duality of the Medusa myth: Maud was a source of poetic inspiration and yet she also froze the poetry in him.

Artistic endeavour can itself sometimes be a Gorgon. Medusa and Pegasus are the central images in 'The Fascination of What's Difficult', the poet being turned to stone by the steady strain of working for the theatre, so that it seems as if Pegasus has been domesticated and turned into the humblest beast of burden:

> The fascination of what's difficult
> Has dried the sap out of my veins, and rent
> Spontaneous joy and natural content
> Out of my heart. There's something ails our colt
> That must, as if it had not holy blood
> Nor on Olympus leaped from cloud to cloud,
> Shiver under the lash, strain, sweat and jolt
> As though it dragged road-metal. My curse on plays
> That have to be set up in fifty ways,
> On the day's war with every knave and dolt,
> Theatre business, management of men.
> I swear before the dawn comes round again
> I'll find the stable and pull out the bolt.            (*CP*, p.104)

Similarly, in 'Coole Park and Ballylee, 1931', it is as if true poetry has gone from Ireland:

> all is changed, that high horse riderless,
> Though mounted in that saddle Homer rode
>
> (*CP*, p.276)

Of all experiences, the prospect of death is the most petrifying. A great number of Yeats's stone images relate to tombs and it is not surprising that the poet specified his own epitaph be cut 'On limestone quarried near the spot', (*CP*, p.401). In one of the finest of his many meditations on death, 'The Man and The Echo', the poet locates himself in 'a deep chasm one mile long and only thirty feet broad'[17] which lies on the south-west of Knocknarea, a tomb-like setting in itself. How significant this is, in contrast to the Dantean dark wood or the pastoral mountainside of classical convention:

> In a cleft that's christened Alt
> Under broken stone I halt
> At the bottom of a pit
> That broad noon has never lit,
> And shout a secret to the stone.            (*CP*, p.393)

In this dark night of the soul, in the 'cavern of the mind', the poet acknowledges his ignorance of what death holds:

> O Rocky Voice
> Shall we in that great night rejoice?

What do we know but that we face
One another in this place?

The Rocky Voice, the Echo, is Yeats's own voice, giving back to
him the thoughts of his own mind: 'Lie down and die' and 'Into
the night'. Like Hamlet, the poet rejects the suicidal bodkin, or
needle; like Lear he will continue to endure whatever suffering
may remain, to look on life with the gay glittering eyes of the
artist. The poem arrives at the resolution offered in 'The Gyres':

> Out of cavern comes a voice,
> And all it knows is that one word 'Rejoice!'          (*CP*, p.337)

At the very end of his life, in his last month, Yeats reverted to
the imagery of weaving in that most moving and gentle poem
'Cuchulain Comforted'. (*CP*, pp.395-396). The dead hero finds
himself in a traditional underworld; it faintly suggests settings
in Virgil and Dante, but it also has the visual effect of a surrealist
film: 'Eyes stared out of branches and were gone', shrouds
'muttered head to head/Came and were gone'. The famous
warrior here encounters his opposite, 'convicted cowards all':
no matter how 'violent and famous' and conditioned to the idea
of sudden death, man must acknowledge the coward in himself,
the part that will 'die in fear'. This contrast is enforced by the
strong physicality of the man, with his wounds and blood,
versus beings who are not even ghosts or shades but only
garments, the shrouds in which their earthly bodies were
buried. At the centre of the poem is the sewing image: the
'linen-carrier' shows Cuchulain how to 'Obey our ancient rule
and make a shroud'. In other words, the shrouds make
themselves, just as in Yeats's philosophy we all make ourselves
out of the opposites within; as in 'The Man and the Echo' 'we
face one another in this place'. In a recapitulation of the manner
of the earlier poems, sewing becomes a symbol of poetry:
labour, honesty and facing the stony truth leads to the golden
birds of Byzantium:

> 'We thread the needles' eyes, and all we do
> All must together do.' That done, the man
> Took up the nearest and began to sew.
>
> 'Now must we sing and sing the best we can,
> But first you must be told our character:
> Convicted cowards all, by kindred slain

'Or driven from home and left to die in fear.'
They sang, but had nor human tunes nor words,
Though all was done in common as before;

They had changed their throats and had the throats of birds.

### NOTES

1. W. B. Yeats, 'Her Courage', *Collected Poems*. London: Macmillan (1952), p.179. All subsequent quotations from the *Collected Poems* will be indicated by page references within the body of the text.
2. W. B. Yeats, *Essays and Introductions*. London: Macmillan (1961), p.87.
3. See, for example, Donald A. Stauffer, *The Golden Nightingale*. New York: Macmillan (1949); Harold Bloom, *Yeats*. New York: Oxford University Press (1970); and T.R. Henn, *The Lonely Tower*. London: Methuen (1950).
4. W. B. Yeats, 'Preface to the first edition of *The Well of the Saints*' (1905), *Essays and Introductions*. London: Macmillan (1961) p.299.
5. See Jane McIntosh Snyder, 'The Web of Song: Weaving Imagery in Homer and the Lyric Poets', *The Classical Journal*, vol. 76, no. 3 (February-March 1981), pp.193-196.
6. Snyder, p.195.
7. A.Norman Jeffares, *A Commentary on the Collected Poems of W. B. Yeats*. London: Macmillan (1968), pp.378-381.
8. Seamus Heaney, 'The Wool Trade', *Wintering Out*. London: Faber (1972), p.37.
9. Quoted by Jeffares, p.176. The *Oxford English Dictionary* spells the word 'Pirn', but Yeats used 'pern' or 'perne'.
10. Stauffer, p.62.
11. Seamus Heaney, 'The Makings of a Music', *Preoccupations*. London: Faber (1980), p.77.
12. Stauffer, p.62.
13. Richard Howard, 'Sylvia Plath: "And I Have No Face, I Have Wanted to Efface Myself...", *The Art of Sylvia Plath*, ed. Charles Newman. London: Faber (1970), pp.79-81.
14. Horace, *Carmen* 3, xxx (translation mine).
15. Herbert J. Levine, 'Yeats's Ruskinian Byzantium', *Yeats Annual No. 2*, ed. Richard J. Finneran. London: Macmillan (1983), pp.25-34.
16. S. M. Parrish, ed., *A Concordance to the Poems of W. B. Yeats*. Ithaca, New York: Cornell University Press (1963), p.vi.
17. Sheelah Kirby, *The Yeats Country*. Dublin: Dolmen (1962), p.27.

# THE ERA OF INHIBITIONS: IRISH LITERATURE 1920-60

MAURICE HARMON

Conditions in post-revolutionary Ireland were so uncongenial for the writer that it is remarkable, not so much that there was a decline in the quality and the volume of the literary output, but that any literature was written. Seldom in the history of any country can so many forces have combined to inhibit the creative processes. The *Playboy* riots were harbingers of a society and a set of cirumstances particulary unfavourable to the artist. Certainly the experiences of the next generation confirmed Synge's and Yeats's predictions that the money-grubbing Paudeens were taking over. By the mid-twenties, when O'Casey's plays were under attack, the social scene had changed so much, with such drastic shifts in the centres and directions of political and religious power, that the artist experienced considerable difficulties in his fight for freedom of expression. Synge was threatened by people without political power; O'Casey faced official opposition by a native, predominantly Catholic government. The era of inhibitions had been born and, if one is to measure the achievements and aspirations of its writers, it is well to know something of the adverse circumstances pressed upon them.

Most of the post-revolutionary writers had been born at the turn of the century. Their growth to manhood had paralleled and been deeply affected by their country's passage from colonial status to independence, as the age of paralysis witnessed by James Joyce in the twenty-odd years after the death of Parnell in 1891 gave way to a steadily quickening tempo of national resurgence. That revival took many forms—cultural, political, and military. The Gaelic League urged the claims of the Irish language as a mark of cultural identity. The Gaelic Athletic Association sponsored participation in national games, such as hurling and football. The Abbey Theatre mirrored a native heritage of myth and legend, of folk ways and native idioms.

The literature of the Revival, grounded in native tradition and raised to international level in the work of a host of first-rate artists, asserted the individuality of the Irish temperament. Unexpectedly, old Fenians, like Tom Clarke and John O'Leary, inspired a new generation with the integrity of the Republican spirit. Political movements, such as Sinn Fein, gathered momentum. And in the cities, under the magnetism of James Larkin and James Connolly, workers began to assert their rights to decent wages and decent home conditions.

In the first two decades of this century these and other strands of national renewal combined. They came to a head in the Tramway Strike and resulting lock-out of unionised workers in 1913, in the Easter Rising of 1916 and in the successful massing of public opinion and aims in the troubled years of the Anglo-Irish War of 1919-21. Inevitably, the young writers were caught up in the excitement of those stimulating and purposeful years. Their early poems and stories reflect their romantic and idealistic involvement with the national cause. Even Yeats, so sceptical about the valour of the age, so convinced that self-interest and timidity had overtaken the land, voiced his admiration for the nobility of those who rose in rebellion and gave birth to the terrible beauty of their sacrifice:

> MacDonagh and MacBride
> And Connolly and Pearse
> Now and in time to be,
> Wherever green is worn,
> Are changed, changed utterly:
> A terrible beauty is born.

But independence did not come without bitterness, without the loss of national unity. The glorious years of the fight against the ancient enemy, so sacredly celebrated in traditional song and story, gave way to fratricidal strife, and a civil war, which seared the country's soul. So those young men and women, born about 1900, raised on the excitement of resurgence, and stimulated by the promise of achievements to come once freedom was won, suffered the disillusion of national division. Joyce's bitter recognition of moral decay in the years after Parnell was repeated for them in the twenties. The wine of life had run sour and those who hoped to express the new Ireland in literature looked at it out of dazed and bewildered eyes.

The new Ireland was indeed strange and uncongenial, nor were the new writers specially qualified, either by personal experience or by the example of their predecessors, for the job of interpreting it. A whole range of new attitudes and subjects surrounded, defined, and challenged them. They emerged as writers at a time when the subjective, romantic attitudes of the Literary Revival were being replaced by a more realistic and more analytical approach. For a while Liam O'Flaherty, Sean O'Faolain and Frank O'Connor could recreate the wonder, as well as the violence and the drama, of men under arms, as O'Casey did. But they could not imitate Joyce's rejection of home, religion and country, despite their disillusionment. This younger generation of prose realists could not abandon what they had very often fought to establish. Joyce's detachment had been more easily won, since his experience of Ireland had not included the romantic nationalism of the 1916-21 period. The new writers differed also from their predecessors of the Revival period in the availability of subjects. Those pioneers, whose way had been prepared by the activity of poets, scholars, and translators in the 19th century, had drawn freely from a rich store of legend, myth, history, folklore, and literature. Writers now had to think what to write about, and to find ways in which to handle a reality that was not immediately exciting, heroic, or supernatural. Poems about fairies and leprechauns belonged to a romantic past, however recent, as did concepts of the noble peasant, and old symbols of national longing. Cathleen ni Houlihan, whose queenly beauty had once drawn willing service from her people, had become a 'ragin' divil' and an old lady who said 'no'.

Out of the turbulence of revolution had come a new society, in which the old Anglo-Irish Protestant aristocracy and middle class, alien in origin and loyalties, were replaced by a native bourgeois class. The loss of aristocratic leadership in matters of politics, government, and general taste, was not compensated for by the rise of a native, uncultivated Catholic middle class with a marked peasant background and little sense of civic responsibility, or by the rise to great influence of a locally unsophisicated Catholic Church. The predominance of de Valera in the political sphere encouraged a chauvinistic and isolationist mentality. Economic policies included tariff protection for native industry. Supporters of Gaelic literature and language, with governmental backing and encouragement, tried to protect Ireland from the influences of outside literatures. Pious groups, with the blessing of a short-sighted and puritanical Church, and the support of Catholic newspapers, such as *The Standard*, wanted to immunize the country from outside contacts. Censorship, both official and private, restricted freedom of expression, and of intellectual and imaginative growth. Significantly, de Valera's Constitution of 1937 mirrored the bourgeois mind. It was characterized not by bold affirmations of individual liberties, but by cautious qualifications of and restrictions upon just about every freedom it granted. The new society was, in short, not the kind of environment conducive to literary expression.

The writer himself was under suspicion. The Literary Censorship Act of 1929 marked the blending of moral and patriotic elements in a combined attack on what he represented. The Act had the effect of sanctioning the existing censorship by local groups and signalled the increasing influence of what they stood for. And, although it did not hinder the good writer from doing whatever his artistic conscience decreed, it did have the serious effect of cutting him off from his primary audience. It was also distressing to be officially branded as a menace to public morality, to find one's books excluded from libraries and pounced upon by Customs men. It made life awkward for the family who had to endure the malice and the gossip of the ignorant. And what wife could easily shrug off the general notion that she was married to a pornographer? Even the satisfaction of knowing that the Censorship Board constantly exceeded its powers hardly outweighed the daily irritation of being unjustly maligned. That sense of alienation endangered the artist most of all, since it tended to sour his outlook and to make it difficult for him to maintain a sane and healthy relationship to his material.

Significantly, the literature of the new society is surprisingly lacking in comedy and the general direction of each writer's development shows him struggling to achieve a balanced and detached point of view. Instead of comedy, one finds Austin Clarke's crabby and tormented poetry, Sean O'Faolain's misfit heroes and lonely outcasts, Frank O'Connor's pathetically confused half-lovers, and Liam O'Flaherty's giant-killing informers, martyrs, and assassins. For a country so apparently full of anecdote, so naturally and traditionally rich in imaginative life, it was indicative of the spiritual state of the national consciousness that the literature failed so frequently and for so long to express the lighter side. O'Casey's strained comedies, his burlesque and extravagance only confirm the general impression. The writer's world had in fact been diminished by the social upheaval of the revolutionary period. And so had his material.

He could now handle either the traditional, intellectually simple life of the small farm or the new, undefined life of the city. Of the two, he would be drawn instinctively to the familiar rural background, but that had already been overworked by the Abbey Theatre. Innumerable plays by such playwrights as Padraic Colum, Lady Gregory, J. M. Synge, T. C. Murray, Lennox Robinson and their successors had dealt with its basic themes—the hunger for land, the greed, the late marriages and the mixed marriages, the religious intensities, the small intrigues, the roguish characters, and the family feuds. But the alternative was strange. Urban conventions were embryonic and presented few clearly defined social patterns. Novelists, in particular, feel more at home with a dense social texture in which competitive pressures make themselves felt and personalities embody traditional forces. They can delight in unravelling the complicated, interrelated patterns that make up the whole scene. But the thinly-composed, one-class society of the new Ireland offered little excitement of that nature and it was precisely because it was new that novelists failed to express it.

Then too, writers after the revolution not only felt distate for their milieu, but suffered from the lack of congenial companionship. Death and exile steadily denied them the stimulus of suggestion and emulation. By the end of the thirties the leaders of the Revival had died—Yeats, Lady Gregory, George Moore, George Russell. James Stephens and Sean O'Casey lived in exile and, in 1941, in the midst of a world war that further isolated them through their country's neutrality, James Joyce died. They suffered also from the lack of criticism. There were no resident critics of real ability; because of the friendly smallness of the community, most observers of their work tempered criticism with kindness, at least in print. The temptation to leave for a more stimulating and more competitive environment was always present. Even the bombed cities of England, London, Liverpool, Manchester and others, often seemed more attractive than the overprotected Eden in which they had been born and reared.

Contact with the outside world was desirable for many reasons. Above all it helped the writer to keep in touch with contemporary thinking and contemporary literary methods. He badly needed to counter the intellectual and technical disadvantages of being made insular by his country's isolationist policies and trends. Europe also offered rich and varied examples of how writers related to particular environments and almost every Irish writer learned by European example. At the beginning of the period, the possibility of emulating some of the Russian novelists specially excited Irish writers, particularly Sean O'Faolaín and Frank O'Connor who were encouraged in that idea by Daniel Corkery. It was felt that the two contries had much in common in temperament, in their feeling for the land, and in their strong consciousness of national identity. But the differences soon outweighted the similarities. Most striking were the dissimilarities in the structure of the two societies. Russian novelists handled all levels and classes in an inclusive and generous manner. The Irish writer had no corresponding variety of experience or inclusive sympathy. His difficulties stemmed from the breakdown in Irish society. A Russian novelist such as Turgenev could achieve social significance by making his leading characters representative of successive attitudes taken by the Russian intellectual. In Ireland there was little of an intellectual tradition to refer to.

A European alignment had another drawback. If the Irish writer felt his isolation and frustration in a period of social confusion, so did his European, English, or American counterpart. His search for identity and a desirable image of life was part of a widespread anxiety. It was not only in Ireland that the traditional order had fallen apart, not only in Ireland that the artist was faced with fragmentation in social, moral and political values. Proust and Valéry, Mann, Rilke, and Kafka, as well as Yeats and Joyce, sought to construct a literay coherence at a time of universal incoherence. Their successors, reaching manhood in the twenties, were all faced with a similar set of circumstances, and the Irish writer found that Europe tended only to mirror conditions at home.

Still, the continuity of the literary tradition was maintained in Ireland. And, if there is a single vision within the period it is the vision of wholeness. Much of the period's literature is concerned with the problem of the effects of inhibition on the individual and on the country. Keenly aware of the forces that curtail freedom, the writers give imaginative portrayal to characters, situations, and themes that select, evaluate, and judge the moral consequences of an over-restrictive environment.

Thus the work of the poet Austin Clarke voices the spiritual state of an individual excessively hedged about by a dogmatic and conservative church.

> I count the sorrowful mysteries
> Of earth before the celebrant
> Has turned to wash his mouth in wine.
> The soul is confined to a holy vessel,
> And intellect less than desire.
> O I will stay to the last Gospel,
> Cupping my heart with prayer:
> Knuckle and knee are all we know
> When the mind is half despairing. ('Repentance')

Instinctively drawn to the Church, and honestly recognising its influence in his growth and development, Clarke attacks it for not being wide enough in its outlook to include men of his far-reaching intellect and complexity of temperament. At the same time he has spoken out vigorously against the insensitivity of contemporary middle-class values, protesting the cruelty of teachers, the inhumane treatment of unmarried mothers, the vulgarity of aeroplane pilgrimages to Lourdes, the casuistry of bishops, the shooting of political prisoners, and other evidences of a Church and State become smug and corrupted by too great power. His has, in fact, been the major poetic voice for a healthy group within the community anxious to remind the Church of its universal wisdom and to keep the State from ignoring the checks and balances of a democratic society.

To a lesser extent the poetry of Patrick Kavanagh also protests against those repressive voices that hamper individual growth.

> The tension broke. The congregation lifted its head
> As one man and coughed in unison.
> Five hundred hearts were hungry for life—
> Who lives in Christ shall never die the death.
> And the candle-lit Altar and the flowers
> And the pregnant Tabernacle lifted a moment to Prophecy
> Out of the clayey hours.
> Maguire sprinkled his face with holy water
> As the congregation stood up for the Last Gospel.
> He rubbed the dust off his knees with his palm, and then
> Coughed the prayer phlegm up from his throat and sighed:
> Amen.
> ('The Great Hunger')

His work at its best responds feelingly to the seasonal flowering of nature which contrasts so strongly with the withering of men and women into barrenness through a too faithful obedience to the Church's stern laws against sexual indulgence. On this subject he and Clarke attack the Jansenistic teachings of the clergy, which had had incalculable effects on individual dignity and marital normality.

Clarke and Kavanagh called attention to the consequences of repression and held out—by contrast—a desirable vision of wholeness. The short story writers had a similar vision. Dissatisfied with the undefined state of the new urban scene, they were attracted to the remoter western regions of the country, where they saw traces of a former coherence and of a simple dignity. Not that they were blind to or ignored peasant vices, but each, in some of his finest stories, paid tribute to the past heritage of the people. Frank O'Connor's story, 'Uprooted', for example, tells of the return of two brothers to their childhood home in the west. There everything speaks of what they have lost by seeking to make their lives in the Dublin and Wicklow region on the east coast. Familiar conversations, shy ways of peasant girls, sharply etched details of sky and land, the vividness of ocean—they see everything and hear everything with the heightened awareness of men separated from what they love. Feeling their loneliness and sense of alienation in the newer world of the east coast, they respond to the magic of the west:

His mother, the coloured shawl about her head, was blowing the fire. The bedroom door was open and he could see his father in shirtsleeves kneeling beside the bed, his face raised reverently towards a holy picture, his braces hanging down behind. He unbolted the half-door, went through the garden and out on to the road. There was a magical light on everything. A boy on a horse rose suddenly against the sky, a startling picture. Through the apple-green light over Carrignassa ran long streaks of crimson, so still they might have been enamelled. Magic, magic, magic! He saw it as in a children's picture-book with all its colours intolerably bright; something he had outgrown and could never return to, while the world he aspired to was as remote and intangible as it had seemed even in the despair of youth.

Liam O'Flaherty's 'Galway Bay' is, similarly, a hymn of praise to his people of the Aran islands. In the vital, heroic figure of a tough, cantankerous old man, making his last journey from the islands to the mainland fair, he suggests the proud values of their past, even as he records their disappearance before the advance of civilisation. Similarly, Sean O'Faolain, in 'The Silence of the Valley', evokes the breakdown of tradition in his account of the death of an old story-teller, the one man who could interpret between the past and the present. Such stories represent a widespread feeling of loss as Irish life moves inevitably away from its indigenous heritage and into the cosmopolitan world of this century.

That 'progress' could not be impeded and none of these writers shared the shortsighted view of the ultranationalists who sought to shelter Ireland from the forces of change. But their response to the urban scene was less warm than to the west. Many of O'Faolain's stories, for example, mirror the lonely state of the man without a congenial, imaginatively satisfying background. Occasionally, he sees his contemporaries as lost within the contradictory forces that converge on modern Irish life—the new, unassimilated ideas from the outside and the subconscious, atavistically powerful forces that lie within even the most seemingly sophisticated and urbanised Irishman. In a similar pattern, Frank O'Connor often focuses on the disruptive nature of outside attitudes and values on native behaviour and character. The literature, in other words, mirrors the uncertainty of the artist unable to find a place in his own society.

Looking back at the period outlined above, it is clear that Ireland has changed. A whole new generation of writers has emerged, men and women born about 1930 and since, whose lives have been shaped by forces of the post World War Two period, by the opening up of Ireland itself to outside influences both intellectual and financial, and by the renewal of violence in Northern Ireland. Unlike their predecessors in the generation of O'Faolain and Kate O'Brien they have not given their allegiance to political leaders or causes. Within their life-times leadership has passed from the 'dragon old men' who reflected the antagonisms and aspirations of the revolutionary period. Their most vivid memories are not of republican fighters such as Kevin Barry or Dan Breen, but of the gutted cities of Europe, the 'rose illumination of thighs' in Hiroshima, the futile heroisms of Cyprus or Algiers, the devastation in Korea or Vietnam. They have written of the horrors of the concentration camps and of the atomic destruction of cities. Not that Austin Clarke or Sean O'Faolain were indifferent to such calamities, but the young writers were aware of them from an early age. Their outlook from the beginning was cosmopolitan and they were sceptical towards local issues. John Montague's assertion that 'Puritan

Ireland's dead and gone/A myth of O'Connor and O'Faolain' was not the complete truth but it represented a new attitude. Thomas Kinsella's use of patriotic names once celebrated by Yeats was ironic: shopfronts bear the inscriptions 'MacDonagh & McBride/Merchants; Connolly's Commercial Arms...' His long, reflective poem 'Nightwalker' bitterly regrets the effects on cultural values when the ethic of commercial success becomes a national priority.

Their cosmopolitanism is seen in their openness to intellectual trends and to technical developments outside Ireland. They find settings for their work in England, continental Europe, North America, and elsewhere. Novelists such as Edna O'Brien, Julia O'Faolain, Brian Moore or William Trevor have an international dimension that is quite natural to them. To be an Irish writer it is not necessary to write exclusively about Ireland. John Banville has written of Copernicus, Kepler and Newton. Writers have largely turned aside from social preoccupations to concentrate on individual psychology. At the same time the 'backward look' that characterised Irish writers for Frank O'Connor is still a significant factor. Poets, novelists and dramatists explore the past in familial, racial, historical and cultural terms. This oscillation between Irish subject matter and non-Irish material is a sign of the strength and confidence of contemporary writers.

Conditions have improved. The Arts Council and other bodies provide grants and awards for writers and other artists. A number of new publishers, such as Gallery and Wolfhound, publish the work of Irish writers. The reading public has increased in numbers. More importantly, the writer is no longer generally regarded with suspicion. The censorship laws have been eased. John McGahern's novel, *The Dark* (1965) was banned on the grounds of indecency. His novel, *The Pornographer* (1979), was not, although it is sexually much more explicit. Similarly, Edna O'Brien's early novels, sensitive accounts of young girls growing up, were banned, but her later novels, often about adult sexuality, were not. In drama also there has been a renewal of energy and vitality. The meretricious comedies that satisfied popular taste in the nineteen-fifties have been swept aside by the innovative work of Brian Friel, Thomas Murphy, Thomas Kilroy, Thomas McIntyre and others. Samuel Beckett's plays had considerable influence in this development and the emphasis is on theatre of the senses rather than on verbal theatre. Novelists have also become less conventional in form and method. Whereas in the post-revolutionary period only Flann O'Brien could be regarded as an experimental modernist, now a number of writers, including Aidan Higgins, John Banville and Neil Jordan, write a modernist kind of fiction. In poetry there has been a remarkable renewal of energy. Some of this has been associated with the violence in Northern Ireland where several impressive poets have emerged, such as John Montague, Seamus Heaney, Derek Mahon and Paul Muldoon. In the South, Thomas Kinsella, Richard Murphy and several promising younger poets are at work. Just as the repressive and restrictive circumstances of the 1920-60 period inhibited the growth of the literature, so now the more liberal and open society, although undergoing profound psychological change, has resulted in a more dynamic kind of literature.

# ANGLO-IRISH LITERATURE: TREATMENT FOR RADIO

A. NORMAN JEFFARES

*This is a four part treatment of the theme:*
*it is reproduced by kind permission of the Australian*
*Broadcasting Commission*

## I

I have caused divers of them to be translated unto me, that I might understand them, and surely they savoured of sweet wit and good invention, but skilled not of the goodlie ornaments of poetry yet were they sprinkled with some pretty flowers of their own natural device which gave good grace and comeliness unto them, the which it is great pity to see go abused to the gracing of wickedness and vice which would with good usage serve to beautify and adorn virtue...

This is a passage from a prose work, *A View of the Present State of Ireland*, by the Elizabethan poet and administrator Edmund Spenser, describing Irish poets. These were bardic poets who spoke in Gaelic and composed their poetry in it. They were keeping alive the traditions of Ireland, they preserved the history of a largely aristocratic Gaelic civilisation. And Spenser thought their poems were very dangerous. They expressed, he said, 'a desire to maintain their owne lewd liberty, they being most desirous thereof' but this sensitive 'understanding' Christian poet had a simple suggestion for dealing with the Irish poets; they should he said, 'be put to death'.

This ruthless attitude of Spenser's may surprise some people who know him for his beautiful Christian romance, *The Fairie Queene*, that poetic hymn to virtue, that great imaginative work of high seriousness, full of wisdom in its depiction of good and bad characters. It has been called a 'gorgeous gallery of gallant inventions', filled with magnificent, richly decorative word pictures, with mellifluous, melodious word music.

Not so widely read now as it used to be, it is still the work by Spenser most likely to be read by people who grow up in

42

England. But in Ireland those who read Spenser are more likely to know *A View of the Present State of Ireland*. Spenser wrote it in 1596; born out of a personal knowledge of Ireland, it reflected what he thought he had learned about the country while serving in Ireland during Elizabeth the First's Irish wars. He worked as a kind of A.D.C. to the English Commander in Chief and then became a powerful bureaucrat, clerk to the Council of Munster. He was given land, a large estate in County Cork. He was part of the Elizabethan plantation of Ireland, the settling of English landowners, soldiers, farmers and labourers on confiscated land, from which the Irish inhabitants were forcibly ejected.

This Elizabethan period marked a flare-up in the constant insurrection which had greeted the English claim of sovereignty over Ireland since the days of Henry the Second. Spenser recorded the wretchedness of Ireland, its poverty, the terrible effects of famine; and he did all this with what now might seem a simplistic view: on the one hand England represented order, justice, religious truth and the glories of Gloriana's realm; on the other hand Ireland represented chaos, rebellion, savagery, false religion—and a refusal to accept English rule and English ways.

To remedy such a situation Spenser suggested the creation of four great garrisons to harry the Irish and reduce them completely. He knew what this kind of war would do:

The Irish will soon consume themselves and devoure one another. The proofs whereof I saw sufficiently ensampled in these late warres of Mounster; for notwithstanding that the same was a most rich and plentifull countrey, full of corne and cattell, that you would have thought they would have bene able to stand long, yet ere one yeare and a halfe they were brought to such wretchednesse, as that any stonye heart would have rued the same. Out of every corner of the woodes and glynnes they came creeping forth upon theyr hands, for theyr legges could not beare them; they looked like anatomyes of death, they spake like ghosts crying out of their graves; they did eate of the dead carrions, happy were they if they could finde them, yea, and one another soone after, insomuch as the very carcasses they spared not to scrape out of theyr graves; and if they found a plot of water-cresses or shamrokes, there they flocked as to a feast for the time, yet not able long to continue therewithall; that in short space there were none allmost left, and a most populous and plentifull countrey suddaynely left voyde of man or beast; yet sure in all that warre, there perished not many by the sword, but all by the extremitye of famine.

Spenser had no qualms, then, about eliminating Irish poets;

their desire for 'their own lewd libertie' justified such measures. Here was a confrontation, a confusion, a tension between two languages in one island, between two ways of living, two attitudes of mind, two legal systems, two religions—and two literary traditions. For, out of the tensions and extremes, has come the achievement of Anglo-Irish literature.

People often ask what *is* Anglo-Irish literature. There are histories of English literature in plenty, but very few of Anglo-Irish literature. And people ask why Anglo-Irish literature should have a history of its own. The answer is perhaps one of viewpoint. Anglo-Irish literature looks very different when you see it in the context of histories of English literature, because it tends traditionally to be absorbed in this larger context. Anglo-Irish authors are not seen, as they should be, as a part of a literary development, a literary achievement with its own action and reaction, an interplay of pagan and Christian sensibilities, of Gaelic as well as English elements, a background of Irish as well as English history.

The absence of minor Anglo-Irish writers from histories of English literature is obvious to the Irish reader but not perhaps to the English or American or Australian reader. And yet these minor writers are part and parcel of the process, the literary tradition, the cultural pattern to which the greater writers belong. In part, it is the process of Irish history, the long tangled skein of relations between Ireland and her larger neighbour. And, on the whole, the larger population always knows less about the smaller than the smaller knows about the larger. It is probably true, today, for instance, that the average Englishman knows more about the United States than the average American knows about the United Kingdom. The larger culture tends to look only at the highpoints of the smaller. Thus, for instance, American university students—and very many of them do study Anglo-Irish literature—tend to think that Anglo-Irish literature consists of Yeats, Joyce and, possibly, John Millington Synge. But these writers were formed upon Irish literary traditions as well as English; their roots go deep into the Irish past, into Gaelic traditions and culture.

What then is Anglo-Irish literature? And what is its total achievement? Perhaps the simplest answers are that it is writing in English by Irish authors and that it is a hybrid growth. In it there is the sense of order of the English, formed over the centuries with a linguistic and intellectual legacy from Roman and French conquests, expressed in a language which developed a written literature tempering imagination with classical control. Anglo-Irish literature, however, has also an Irish verbal exuberance, a flexibility arising from the complex richness of Gaelic grammer, syntax and vocabulary. It is largely an oral tradition deriving from spoken literature.

This element of traditional Irish culture took some time to enter into Anglo-Irish literature. But the subject matter, the condition of Ireland, soon did. Those who began to write effectively in English from the seventeenth century onwards were, however deep or shallow their Irish roots, colonial writers. Their problem was a colonial problem. They were largely members of a small Protestant garrison ruling the country after William of Orange and Mary replaced James the Second on the English throne. They controlled Ireland for the English and for themselves. But they never completely controlled it. Once the Catholic population was apparently quelled after the Battle of the Boyne, and enchained by the savage Penal Laws, the Anglo-Irish found that the Westminster government acted primarily in the interests of England. And they did not want to be treated as if they were a colony.

That was the political problem. There was the inevitable literary one: how does a colonial writer achieve success, lasting literary success? Ultimately it depends upon how far the author's writings have universal significance, how far they become international while drawing upon local matter.

The first writer to fulfil these conditions was Jonathan Swift. He presents a paradox, for he was classically educated at Kilkenny College and Trinity College, Dublin, and he rightly features in every history of English literature, master of satire that he is. And yet he is a very Irish writer, and by right of birth, for as he put it, he 'happened to be dropped in Ireland'. And he died there, too, buried in St. Patrick's Cathedral with a sonorous Latin epitaph he wrote for himself. Yeats produced a fine version of it in English:

> Swift has sailed into his rest;
> Savage indignation there
> Cannot lacerate his breast.
> Imitate him if you dare,
> World-besotted traveller; he
> served human liberty.

But Swift's more jocose side emerged in many of his poems, in 'The author upon himself', for instance:

> Swift had the sin of wit, no venial crime,
> Nay, 'twas affirm'd, he sometimes dealt in rhyme,
> Humour and mirth had place in all he writ,
> He reconcil'd divinity and wit.

And then there were jesting poems on his own death, for one of Swift's great virtues was his ability to be deeply serious without being solemn. He left his money to build, he said, 'a hospital for idiots and lunatics in the city or the suburbs'. This distinguished hospital, known as Swift's Hospital, is still in existence in Dublin, and Swift ended a poem on his death with these remarks on his gift:

> He gave the little wealth he had
> To build a house for fools and mad,
> And show'd by one satiric touch
> No nation wanted it so much.

Despite this wryly ironic comment on Ireland, Swift's writings are where a history of Anglo-Irish literature ought to begin, for Swift is the first great anti-colonial writer. He owed his anti-colonial ideas to William Molyneux, an M.P. of the Dublin parliament, who wrote a fierce attack in 1698 on England's treatment of Ireland. This is called *The Case of Ireland being bound by Acts of Parliament in England, stated.*

Here is an example of Molyneux's patriotic indignation; he was arguing that though the two countries, England and Ireland, had the same head of state, the king, they were separate in their jurisdictions; Ireland had its own parliament in Dublin and owed allegiance to the king but not to the English parliament in Westminster. Molyneux rejected any idea of colonial status for Ireland:

Have not Multitudes of Acts of Parliament both in *England* and *Ireland* declared *Ireland* a *complete Kingdom*? Is not Ireland styled in them all, the *Kingdom* or *Realm* of Ireland? Do these *Names* agree to a Colony? Have we not a Parliament and Courts of Judicature? Do these *things* agree with a Colony?

Swift was to echo these feelings. Before looking at him as a specifically Irish writer it is worth considering how most people would react to a mention of his name. Most people who know his work have probably come to him by way of *Gulliver's Travels*. The invention in it, the unusual, the fantastical nature of this story, delights young readers—and, then as they get older, they are delighted by the satiric view of mankind it provides. Gulliver, gigantic among the Lilliputians, then dwarfed by the Brobdingnagians, next in the mad world of Laputa with scientific invention run riot, and finally among the brutish man-like yahoos and the elegant, cooly rational horses, the Houyhnhnms, is part of the heritage of the English-reading world. The story of Gulliver is Swift's way of showing us ourselves from different angles, showing us how Gulliver the man seems to those with other scales of value, other ways of looking at life.

Fewer readers, probably, think of Swift's earlier *A Tale of a Tub* with its sardonic view of religious quibbling, its exposure of the hypocrisy which departs so far from the truth of Christianity with such a speciously logical use of argument. And then there is the superb imagination and lively wit of his *Battle of the Books*. These three books are Swift's major works, though modern readers, and critics too, are coming more frequently to admire his poetry, poetry which so shocked the Victorians with its frank scatology and four letter words. Now Swift's sheer sense of fun, his blunt realism, his horror at the filth and stink of the eighteenth century and the contradictions between its surface elegance and underlying falsification, appeal to us because of their intrinsic honesty. It was Swift's honesty which fired his forceful, biting wit, his deliberate use of highly successful literary shock tactics. Yet, if these writings were all we had of Swift, we might be tempted to leave him in the histories of English literature, or in treatises on satire, carrying in our minds a picture of his powerful, detached intellect contemplating the absurdity of human nature, the contradictions between man's pretences and his practice. Or, perhaps, we could think of him as the first truly successful political journalist, whose writings in *The Examiner* helped the Tory Government to end a war. But what are we to make of the man who cried 'Burn everything English but their coal'? Or what are we to think of Swift, then Dean of St. Patrick's Cathedral in Dublin, who wrote the *Drapier Letters* in a fine fury of indignation when it seemed the English parliament was about to foist a cheap, debased currency on Ireland. These *Drapier Letters* show us Swift's hatred of corruption. The first of these pamphlets addressed 'To the Tradesmen, Shopkeepers, Farmers and Country People in general of the Kingdom of Ireland' was signed M.B. Drapier. Swift invented this shopkeeper, and appealed through him to ordinary people to reject the proposed cheap coinage, Wood's halfpence. Swift argues that bad money drives out good. Here is an example of how he builds up an argument round a particular point, the effect of a debased, unacceptable coinage. He leads us on with apparent simplicity through a whole chain of developments, his imagination spurring on his intimidating invention:

Suppose you go to an ale-house with that base money, and the landlord gives you a quart for four of those half-pence, what must the victualler do? his brewer will not be paid in that coin, or if the brewer should be such a fool, the farmers will not take it from them for their bere [barley], because they are bound, by their leases, to pay their rents in good and lawful money of England, which this is not, nor of Ireland neither, and the 'squire, their landlord, will never be so bewitched to take such trash for his land; so that it must certainly stop somewhere or other, and wherever it stops, it is the same thing, and we are all undone.

The common weight of these half-pence is between four and five to an ounce; suppose five, then three shillings and four-pence will weigh a pound, and consequently twenty shillings will weigh six pounds butter weight. Now there are many hundred farmers, who pay two hundred pounds a year rent; therefore when one of these farmers comes with his half year's rent, which is one hundred pounds, it will be at least six hundred pound weight, which is three horses load.

If a 'squire has a mind to come to town to buy cloaths, and wine, and spices for himself and family, or perhaps to pass the winter here, he must bring with him five or six horses loaden with sacks, as the farmers bring their corn; and, when his lady comes in her coach to our shops, it must be followed by a car loaded with Mr. Wood's money.

Even the beggars, says Swift, will be ruined:

For when I give a beggar a halfpenny it will quench his thirst or so a good way to fill his belly; but the twelfth part of a half-penny will do him no more service than if I should give him thre pins out of my sleeve

And he ends the first letter by aiming it firmly at the mob:

N.B. The author of this paper is informed by persons who have made it their business to be exact in their observations on the true value of these half-pence, that any person may expect to get a quart of two-penny ale for thirty-six of them.

April 1724 saw the first pamphlet; the second Drapier's communication appeared in July, the third in August and the fourth one in October. Everyone knew who was writing them. Indeed Swift is still known as the Drapier in Dublin. The letters became more scholarly as they replied to semi-official defences of Wood and his proposed coinage and to a Report of the Privy Council. Finally this particular piece of corruption has proved to be the basis for an argument leading up to an appeal to the Irish to see what is at stake:

A people long used to hardships lose by degrees the very notions of liberty; they look upon themselves as creatures at mercy, and that all impositions laid on them by a stronger hand are, in the phrase of the report, legal and obligatory. Hence proceed that poverty and lowness of spirit, to which a kingdom may be subject, as well as a particular person. And when Esau came fainting from the field at the point to die, it is no wonder that he sold his birth-right for a mess of pottage.

And Swift reverts to Molyneux's view:

It is true, indeed, that within the memory of man the parliaments of England have sometimes assumed the powers of binding this kingdom by laws enacted there; wherein they were at first openly opposed (as far as truth, reason, and justice are capable of opposing) by the famous Mr. Molineux, an English gentleman born here, as well as by several of the greatest patriots and best whigs in England; but the love and torrent of power prevailed. Indeed the arguments on both sides were invincible. For in reason, all government without the consent of the governed is the very definition of slavery: but in fact, eleven men well armed will certainly subdue one single man in his shirt.

This is strong stuff—and it becomes stronger, for the Drapier remarks that if England, represented by Walpole, threatens to ram their half-pence down the throats of the Irish, they have the remedy wholly in their own hands. He has digressed a little, he says, in order to

refresh and continue that spirit so seasonably raised amongst you; and to let you see that by the laws of God, of Nature, of Nations, and of your Country, You are, and ought to be, as free people as your brethren in England.

Swift is every bit as indignant as Molyneux had been. There was deep personal feeling behind his argument:

Were not the People of Ireland born as Free as those of England? Is not their Parliament as fair a Representative of the People as that of

England? And hath not their Privy Council as great or greater share in the Administration of Publick Affairs? Are they not Subjects of the same King? Does not the same Sun shine on them? Have they not the same God for their Protector? Am I a Free-Man in England, and do I become a Slave in six Hours by crossing the Channel?

This rage finally overflowed in Swift's extreme *saeva indignatio*, the fierce anger of his highly ironic pamphlet—*A Modest Proposal*—in which he condemns landlords, the idle rich, the poor, the dissenters, the Papists, the absentees, the shop-keepers and the beggars. Assuming the *persona* of an economist, a reasonable, detached observer, he surveys the desperate situation of Irish poverty: since other expedients have failed he weighs up, coolly and pragmatically, the advantages of fattening up young children as human food:

I have been assured by a very knowing *American* of my acquaintance in *London*, that a young healthy Child well Nursed is, at a year old, a most delicious nourishing and wholesome Food, whether Stewed, Roasted, Baked, or Boiled; and I make no doubt that it will equally serve in a Fricasie, or a Ragoust.
I do therefore humbly offer it to publick consideration, that of the Hundred and twenty thousand Children, already computed, twenty thousand may be reserved for Breed, whereof only one fourth part to be Males; which is more than we allow to Sheep, black Cattle or Swine; and my Reason is, that these Children are seldom the Fruits of Marriage, a Circumstance not much regarded by our Savages; there-fore, one Male will be sufficient to serve four Females. That the remaining Hundred thousand may, at a year Old, be offered in Sale to the Persons of Quality and Fortune, through the Kingdom; always advising the Mother to let them suck plentifully in the last Month, so as to render them Plump, and Fat, for a good Table...
I grant this Food will be somewhat dear, and therefore very proper for Landlords; who, as they have already devoured most of the Parents seem to have the best Title to the Children...

Swift developed into a patriot almost despite himself. He had hoped to become a Bishop or at least a Dean in England, and when he finally returned to Dublin in 1714 as Dean of St. Patrick's Cathedral he regarded this appointment as a kind of banishment, and hoped to keep a resolution of 'never medling with Irish politics'. He did stay quiet for six years; but the situation was too much for an independent-minded intellectual: he saw with Molyneux's eyes that the industry, trade and commerce of his country were being actively hindered in the interest of the neighbouring, wealthier island.

Yet again we are reminded of the echo of Molyneux's angry queries—'Have we not a Parliament and Courts of Judicature? Do these things agree with a Colony?'—in Swift's fierce enquiry:

'Were not the People of *Ireland* born as *Free* as those of England? Is not their *Parliament* as fair a *Representative* of the People as that of England?...

Swift, however, was more than provincial, more than anti-colonial; he was universal in what he later called his 'perfect Hatred of Tyranny and Oppression'. He showed the way to later Anglo-Irish authors—and orators. When Henry Grattan was speaking on the Rights of Ireland in February 1782 he acknowledged Swift's ideas:

This brings the claim of England to a mere question of force. It is a right which Swift, I think it is Swift, has explained—the right of the grenadier to take the property of a naked man. I add, this man has now gotten back his arms, and begs to get back his property.

Grattan was referring to the Irish Volunteer movement which had backed his aims and was to make them viable. Grattan wanted the Anglo-Irish to become more than a garrison, more than a protestant ascendancy.

The question is, he said in another speech,

whether we shall be a Protestant settlement or an Irish nation. Whether we shall throw open the gates of the temple of liberty to all our countrymen, or whether we shall confine them in bondage by penal laws. So long as the penal code remains, we never can be a great nation. The penal code is the shell in which the Protestant power has been hatched, and now it has become a bird it must burst the shell or perish in it.

Successful in his campaign against restrictions on Irish trade, Grattan had begun to fight for legislative independence. And in April 1782 he succeeded in having various acts repealed. A triumphant speech reflected his hopes that the Irish Parliament in Dublin—it was known as Grattan's Parliament—would now create a united nation:

I am now to address a free people: ages have passed away, and this is the first moment in which you could be distinguished by that appellation. I have spoken on the subject of your liberty so often that

I have nothing to add and have only to admire by what heaven-directed steps you have proceeded until the whole faculty of the nation is braced up to the act of her own deliverance.

Grattan's vision was that of a statesman, but the members of the Dublin parliament did not match it. The large majority of the population, the Catholics, remained unrepresented, two thirds of the seats were nominated by patrons, and attempts at parliamentary reform were rejected. There was a great opportunity for the Anglo-Irish to create a united nation in a brief moment of history between 1782 and 1800, but they failed to follow the lead Grattan gave in such ringing terms in 1782:

I found Ireland on her knees, I watched over her with a paternal solitude; I have traced her progress from injuries to arms, and from arms to liberty. Spirit of Swift! Spirit of Molyneux! Your genius has prevailed. Ireland is now a nation.

It was not to be. The influence of the French Revolution inspired the political, the revolutionary aims and activities of the United Irishmen, and, after the bloody events before, during and after the 1798 Rebellion, just as the eighteenth century ended, the Act of Union destroyed the Parliament in Dublin. Dublin began the nineteenth century no longer a capital city. What had happened in literature—apart from Swift—in the eighteenth century? The philosopher Bishop Berkeley for one, whose spirit was so much gentler than Swift's. He was not set to sway his readers like Swift exercising either that savage indignation, the *saeva indignatio* of his own epitaph, or else in milder mood asserting his method 'of reforming is by laughing, not be storming'.

No, Berkeley the philosopher was careful even to desire his reader to be upon his guard against the fallacy of words:

Let him beware that I do not impose on him by plausible empty talk, that common dangerous way of cheating men into absurdities. Let him not regard my words any otherwise than as occasions of bringing into his mind determin'd significations, so far as they fail of this they are gibberish, jargon and deserve not the name of language. I desire and warn him not to expect to find truth in my book or anywhere but in his own mind. Whatever I see myself 'tis impossible I can paint it in words.

Berkeley wrote easily and fluently, at times catching an Irish idiom. He regarded himself as Irish. Younger than Swift, he had not been unsettled by civil war, as Swift had; nor by the shock of emerging from Irish poverty into English wealth, as Swift had. In his *Philosophical Commentaries* he wrote:

There are men who say there are insensible extensions, there are others who say the wall is not white, the fire is not hot, etc. We Irish men cannot attain to these truths.

The mathematicians think there are insensible lines; about these they harangue, these cut in a point, at all angles these are divisible *ad infinitum*. We Irish men can conceive no such lines.

The mathematicians talk of what they call a point, this they say is not altogether nothing nor is it downright something, now we Irish men are apt to think something and nothing are next neighbours.

Berkeley went to America to found a college, but found the English ministry obstructive at a distance. Was it this experience that made him, too, take up a position like that of Swift—and Molyneux before him—asking in his book *The Querist* in 1735 whether

if there was a wall of Brass a thousand cubits high, round this kingdom of Ireland, our Natives might not nevertheless live cleanly and comfortably, till the land, and reap the fruits of it.

He shared Swift's dislike of Ireland's poverty. How, he asked, can

a Gentleman who hath seen a little of the world and observed how men live elsewhere ... contentedly sit down in a cold, damp, sordid Habitation, in the midst of a bleak Country inhabited by Thieves and Beggars.

## II

Swift and Berkeley may have complained about Ireland but they stayed there, Swift in a Deanery, Berkeley in a Bishop's palace; but after all they didn't really need the London stage. Several of the most famous Anglo-Irish writers, however, did feel a need to leave. Many of those who moved out of Ireland into England were not so much concerned with the situation of the country they had left behind as with the need to further their own careers in England. Here is George Bernard Shaw's account of why he left Dublin.

My business in life could not be transacted in Dublin out of an experience confined to Ireland. London was the literary centre for the English language and for such artistic culture as the realms of the English language (in which I proposed to be king) could afford. There was no Gaelic League in those days nor any sense that Ireland had in herself the seed of culture. Every Irishman who felt that his business in life was on the higher planes of the cultural profession felt that he must have a metropolitan domicile and an international culture: that is, he felt that his first business was to get out of Ireland. I had the same feeling. For London as London, or England as England, I cared nothing.

Shaw was one in a long line of Anglo-Irish dramatists who knew their audience was in London, and they knew how to please it. There were so many among them in the seventeenth century; they included, for instance:— Nahum Tate, Thomas Southerne, and Susanna Centlivre, as well as Congreve, master of the sparkling wit of Restoration comedy. Congreve was formed by his education in Ireland, as a school boy at Kilkenny College and then as an undergraduate at Trinity College, Dublin. His family lived in Ireland, and like Swift and many others he left it when Trinity College was closed during the Revolution of 1688. It is likely that Congreve, who fled to England at the age of 18 or 19, saw the neighbouring island with a sharper sense of clarity through arriving at an age when he was mature enough to be critical, formed enough in mind and in the experience of one island to make comparisons, and ready to record what he saw so sharply in his new surroundings. The fine ladies and gentlemen in Congreve's plays are the way of the world he saw with the clarity of a stranger's viewpoint from the London coffee houses, and their financial doings were what he heard of in the Middle Temple where he studied law. His novel *Incognita*, probably written four years earlier when he was an undergraduate in Dublin, came out in 1692, by which time he seems to have been accepted as a poet in London. He was fortunate in having Dryden's friendship, for his first comedy *The Old Batchelor* was given its 'fashionable cut' by the older author; he was also helped by Thomas Southerne—another graduate of Trinity College Dublin—in the last stages of revision. The actress Anne Bracegirdle established her fame in it, and became the darling of the theatre. Congreve, who obviously loved her very deeply, wrote of her to his friend Joseph Keally in Dublin that she had performed to a miracle. The Anglo-Irish obviously enjoyed each other's company in London. Swift wrote to Stella in 1710 that he had been to see Congreve, who was almost blind with cataracts in his eyes:

besides he is never rid of the gout, yet he looks young and fresh, and is cheerful as ever. He is younger by three years or more than me, and I am twenty years younger than he. He gave me a pain in the great toe, by mentioning the gout. I find such suspicions frequently, but they go off again.

A few months later he described how he went into the city for a walk but the person he designed to dine with was not at home so he came back and called at Congreve's:

Dined with him and Eastcourt and Langhed till six, then went to Mr. Harley's. Congreve's nasty white wine has given me the heart burn.

Eastcourt was yet another Dubliner, an actor, who had been at the Smock Alley Theatre in Dublin and probably met Congreve when he was an undergraduate.

In his plays Congreve seems to have expressed a disillusioned realism: he tried to bring order out of complexity in his comedies, showing tragedy under the polished surface of life in the drawing rooms, giving us characters—Angelica and Jeremy, in *Love for Love*, Millamant and Mirabel, in *The Way of the World* —who want more than an ordinary, an orthodoxly-arranged marriage. Thus we have the brilliant scene between Millamant and Mirabel where they pretend not to be violently in love: a kind of insurance, really, an insistence upon making marriage something better than the way of the world has it. This is a case for the reality rather than the appearance of love. Here is Millamant, deeply involved putting the case for mutual respect:

MILLAMANT: ...My dear Liberty, shall I leave thee? My faithful Solitude, my darling Contemplation, must I bid you then Adieu? Ay-h adieu.—My morning Thoughts, agreeable Wakings, indolent Slumbers, all ye douceurs, ye Someils du Matin adieu—I can't do't, 'tis more than impossible—Positively Mirabell, I'll lye a Bed in a Morning as long as I please.
MIRABELL: Then I'll get up in a Morning as early as I please.
MILLAMANT: Ah! Idle Creature, get up when you will—And d'ye hear, I won't be call'd Names after I'm Marry'd; positively I won't be call'd Names.
MIRABELL: Names!
MILLAMANT: Ay as Wife, Spouse, my Dear, Joy, Jewel, Love, Sweet-heart, and the rest of that Nauseous Cant, in which Men and their Wives are so fulsomely familiar—I shall never bear that,—Good Mirabell don't let us by familiar or fond, nor kiss before Folks, like my Lady Fadler and Sir Francis: Nor go to Hide-Park together the first Sunday in a new Chariot, to provoke Eyes and Whispers; And then

never to be seen there together again; as if we were proud of one another the first Week, and asham'd of one another ever after. Let us never Visit together, not go to a Play together, but let us be very strange and well bred: Let us be as strange as if we had been marry'd a great while; and as well bred as if we were not marry'd at all.

MIRABELL: Have you any more Conditions to offer? Hitherto your Demands are pretty reasonable.

MILLAMANT: Trifles,—As Liberty to pay and receive Visits to and from whom I please; to write and receive Letters, without Interrogatories or wry Faces on your Part; to wear what I please; and chuse Conversation with regard only to my own Taste; to have no Obligation upon me to converse with Wits that I don't like, because they are your Acquaintance; or to be intimate with Fools, because they may be your Relations. Come to Dinner when I please, dine in my dressing Room when I'm out of Humour without giving a Reason. To have my Closet Inviolate; to be sole Empress of my Tea-Table, which you must never presume to approach without first asking leave. And lastly, where-ever I am, you shall always knock at the Door before you come in. These Articles subscribed, if I continue to endure you a little longer, I may by degrees dwindle into a Wife.

Congreve defended the eccentricity he saw tolerated in England. Like Swift he appreciated 'the great freedom, privilege and liberty which the common people of England enjoy'. He wanted more than farce or grotesquerie from comedy:

For my part, I am as willing to laugh as any body, and as easily diverted with an object truly ridiculous: but at the same time, I never care for seeing things that force me to entertain low thoughts of my nature. I don't know how it is with others but I confess freely to you I could never look long upon a monkey without very mortifying reflections, though I never heard anything to the contrary, why that creature is not originally of a distinct species.

Congreve creates magnificent liveliness in his characters. Here Mirabell describes Millamant approaching:

MIRABELL: Here she comes i'faith full sail, with her fan spread, and her streamers out and a shoal of fools for tenders

She does not disappoint us when she speaks:

MILLAMANT: O the Vanity of these Men! Fainall, d'ye hear him? If they did not commend us, we were not handsome! Now you must know they could not commend one, if one was not handsome. Beauty the Lover's Gift—Lord, what is a Lover, that it can give? Why one makes Lovers as fast as one pleases, and they live as long as one pleases, and they die as soon as one pleases: And then if one pleases one makes more.

But Congreve's sense both of the ridiculous and the pathetic keeps breaking out. Here is Lady Wishfort, the fifty-five year old widow, who does not want to face her age. She is talking to her maid Foible while she is at her toilet, making free use of make-up—and cherry brandy too—as she waits for a visit from a possible suitor (who is actually Mirabel's servant disguised as a suitor, in the best traditions of comedy).

LADY WISHFORT: But art thou sure Sir Rowland will not fail to come? Or will a not fail when he does come? Will he be Importunate, Foible, and push? For if he should not be Importunate—I shall never break Decorums—I shall die with Confusion, if I am forc'd to advance—Oh no, I can never advance—I shall swoon if he should expect Advances. No, I hope Sir Rowland is better bred, than to put a Lady to the necessity of breaking her Forms. I won't be too coy neither. I won't give him Despair—But a little Disdain is not amiss; a little Scorn is alluring.
FOIBLE: A little Scorn becomes your Ladyship.
LADY WISHFORT: Yes, but Tenderness becomes me best—a Sort of a Dyingness—You see that Picture has a sort of a—Ha Foible? A Swimmingness in the Eyes—Yes, I'll look so—My Niece affects it; but she wants Features. Is Sir Rowland handsome? Let my Toilet be remov'd—I'll dress above. I'll receive Sir Rowland here. Is he handsome? Don't answer me. I won't know: I'll be surpriz'd. I'll be taken by Surprise.
FOIBLE: By Storm, Madam. Sir Rowland's a brisk Man.
LADY WISHFORT: Is he! O then he'll Importune, if he's a brisk Man. I shall save Decorums if Sir Rowland importunes. I have a mortal Terror at the Apprehension of offending against Decorums. O I'm glad he's a brisk Man.

Lady Wishfort considers how she will receive him:

LADY WISHFORT: Well, and how shall I receive him? In what figure shall I give his Heart the first Impression? There is a great deal in the first Impression. Shall I sit?—No, I won't sit—I'll walk—ay I'll walk from the Door upon his Entance; and then turn full upon him—No, that will be too sudden. I'll lye—ay, I'll lye down—I'll receive him in my little Dressing-Room, there's a Couch—Yes, yes, I'll give the first Impression on a Couch—I won't lye neither, but loll and lean upon one Elbow; with one Foot a little dangling off, jogging in a thoughful way— Yes—and then as soon as he appears, start, ay, start and be surpriz'd, and rise to meet him in a pretty Disorder—Yes—O, nothing is more

alluring than a Levee from a Couch in some Confusion—It shews the
Foot to advantage, and furnishes with Blushes, and re-composing Airs
beyond Comparison. Hark! There's a Coach.

Her concern for appearances emerges in her conversation with
the supposed Sir Rowland:

LADY WISHFORT: Well, Sir Rowland, you have the way,—You are no
Novice in the Labyrinth of Love—You have the Clue—But as I am a
person, Sir Rowland, you must not attribute my yielding to any sinister
Appetite, or Indigestion of Widow-hood; nor impute my Complacency
to any Lethargy of Continence—I hope you do not think me prone to
any Iteration of Nuptials.
WAITWELL: Far be it from me—
LADY WISHFORT: If you do, I protest I must recede—or think that I
have made a Prostitution of Decorums, but in the vehemence of
Compassion, and to save the Life of a Person of so much Importance—
WAITWELL: I esteem it so—
LADY WISHFORT: Or else you wrong my Condescension—
WAITWELL: I do not, I do not—
LADY WISHFORT: Indeed you do.
WAITWELL: I do not, fair Shrine of Virtue.
LADY WISHFORT: If you think the least Scruple of Carnality was an
Ingredient—
WAITWELL: Dear Madam, no. You are all Camphire and
Frankincense, all Chastity and Odour.

Just as Congreve's *The Way of the World* had marked the supreme
achievement of Restoration comedy, the world of the witty
rakes, of libertinism and levity, so George Farquhar from
Londonderry, who followed him to London, showed the stage
a new direction. In *The Recruiting Officer* and *The Beaux Stratagem*
he moved comedy away from the topics of elegant London life
to those of the countryside, and presented his characters with
sympathy. There is an Irish quality at work here, neither wit nor
humour, but fun. After Farquhar came Richard Steele, born and
brought up in Ireland till his teens, and losing an estate in
southeast Ireland by enlisting as a private in the Coldstream
Guards; he also had this sense of fun. But he weakened it a little
by a sentimental approach.

  We can see how far comedy had moved from the days of the
Restoration wits, who despised city merchants, when we realise
that Mr. Sealand, one of Steele's characters in *The Conscious
Lovers*, is delivering a smug piece of self-praise about the
merchant class to which he belongs, calling them 'as honourable

and almost as useful as you landed folks that have always thought yourselves so much above us'.

There continued to be so many other dramatists from Ireland, among them Arthur Murphy, John O'Keefe, James Kenney, and Hugh Kelly, who became an arch priest of sentimental comedy. This was a *genre* which Oliver Goldsmith loathed; he thought it a bastard form of tragedy, and his own two plays, *The Good Natur'd Man* and *She Stoops to Conquer*, were written out of a belief in the simple need to amuse people.

*She Stoops to Conquer*, still popular, a play that even the worst amateur productions cannot injure, is a model of absurdity and anti-climax. Its comic contrivance and classical clarity make the audience aware of its ironies, the author's amusement irradiating the activities of the characters, as their mistakes build up the play's dashing momentum. It develops one of Goldsmith's own experiences. When a shy lad in Ireland he had thought a house belonging to a friend of his father's was an inn, and behaved correspondingly in it, ordering his host and his household about in no uncertain fashion.

Two years after Goldsmith's *She Stoops to Conquer* came Richard Brinsley Sheridan's *The Rivals*, with its fire-eating Irishman Sir Lucius O'Trigger, probably founded on another Irish character, Sir Callaghan O'Brallaghan, whom the Irish actor and playwright Charles Macklin had created in his *Love à la Mode*. Sheridan's father was the son of Swift's younger friend, the clergyman Thomas Sheridan who shared Swift's interest in clever trifling, nonsense verses, riddles, jokes. The clergyman's son was Swift's godson who was a most successful actor, thought by many to be the equal of the famous David Garrick. He moved to England and taught Elocution with great success as well as writing a *Dictionary of the English Language*.

So Richard Brinsley Sheridan grew up in a family with strong literary and dramatic traditions. His own life in Bath, where his father was teaching, was romantic; he fought two duels with a man who was pestering Elizabeth Ann Linley, whom Sheridan escorted to the continent, and subsequently married.

In *The Rivals* Sheridan casts a detached, amused eye on the kind of society he saw in Bath rather as Congreve had earlier portrayed the wits and libertines of London. Sheridan satirised the effect of circulating libraries and their morals on romantic girls; like Goldsmith he disliked and distrusted sentimentality and, particularly, sentimental comedy, which he ridiculed in a new prologue when *The Rivals* proved successful.

Sheridan's best known drama, *The School for Scandal*, was yet another comic exploration of the differences between appearance and reality: here mistaken identity, unexpected reversals, and the exposure of hypocrisy all work together very effectively.

The dialogue is sparkling, the total result being a play still enjoyed for its elegance and well constructed plot. Here is a passage in the play where Lady Sneerwell, Joseph Surface, Crabtree and Sir Benjamin Backbite are having a conversation:

LADY SNEERWELL: Nay, positively, we will hear it.
JOSPEH SURFACE: Yes, yes, the epigram, by all means.
SIR BENJAMIN: Plague on't, uncle! 'tis mere nonsense.
CRABTREE: No. no; 'fore gad, very clever for an extempore!
SIR BENJAMIN: But ladies, you should be acquainted with the circumstance,—you must know, that one day last week, as Lady Betty Curricle was taking the dust in Hyde Park, in a sort of duodecimo phaeton, she desired me to write some verses on her ponies: upon which, I took out my pocket-book and in one moment produced the following:
   'Sure never were seen two such beautiful ponies!
   Other horses are clowns, and these macaronies!
   Nay, to give 'em this title I'm sure isn't wrong—
   Their legs are so slim, and their tails are so long'.
CRABTREE: There, ladies—done in the smack of a whip, and on horseback too!
JOSEPH SURFACE: A very Phoebus, mounted—indeed, Sir Benjamin.
SIR BENJAMIN: O dear sir—trifles—trifles.

Mrs. Candour thinks they are so scandalous she'll forswear their company, but then joins in the general bitchery: Lady Teazle asks her

LADY TEAZLE: What's the matter, Mrs. Candour?
MRS. CANDOUR: They'll not allow our friend Miss Vermilion to be handsome.
LADY SNEERWELL: Oh, surely, she's a pretty woman.
CRABTREE: I am very glad you think so, ma'am.
MRS. CANDOUR: She has a charming fresh colour.
LADY TEAZLE: Yes, when it is fresh put on.
MRS. CANDOUR: O fie! I'll swear her colour is natural—I have seen it come and go.
LADY TEAZLE: I dare swear you have, ma'am—it goes of a night, and comes again in the morning.
MRS. CANDOUR: Ha! ha! ha! how I hate to hear you talk so! But surely, now, her sister is, or was, very handsome.

CRABTREE: Who? Mrs. Evergreen?—O Lord! she's six-and-fifty if she's an hour!

MRS. CANDOUR: Now positively you wrong her; fifty-two or fifty-three is the utmost—and I don't think she looks more.

SIR BENJAMIN: Ah! there is no judging by her looks, unless one could see her face.

LADY SNEERWELL: Well, well, if Mrs. Evergreen does take some pains to repair the ravages of time, you must allow she effects it with great ingenuity—and surely that's better than the careless manner in which the widow Ochre caulks her wrinkles.

SIR BENJAMIN: Nay, now, Lady Sneerwell, you are severe upon the widow. Come, come, it is not that she paints so ill—but, when she has finished her face, she joins it on so badly to her neck, that she looks like a mended statue, in which the connoisseur may see at once that the head's modern, though the trunk's antique!

CRABTREE: Ha! h! h! Well said, nephew.

MRS. CANDOUR: Ha! ha! ha! Well, you make me laugh, but I vow I hate you for't.

Sheridan was playwright, theatre manager—and politician. His oratory held audiences spellbound. In the House of Commons his first speech on the impeachment of Warren Hastings lasted five and a half hours and was a complete triumph, as was his second speech. He had been persuaded to speak by his friend Edmund Burke, the giant statesman whose intellectual abilities tower over his contemporaries in the latter half of the eighteenth century.

Like Swift, Burke used irony; and both of them probably were ironic because they were not fully in tune with the assumptions of the ages in which they lived. Burke wisely dreaded revolution. He saw government as a process of compromise and barter, and he put his views in superb prose, seeing very clearly, from an Irish point of view, the inevitable results of political extremism. While he exerted his energies on behalf of Ireland in Westminster his views were those not of a politician but a statesman, his largeness of vision seeing the true significance of events in America and France, his prose putting his view that the state should be reformed, but within a continuity of growth: 'not local purposes not local prejudices, ought to guide', he said, 'but the general good resulting from the general reason on the whole'.

Burke had an idealistic view of parliament. It was not, he argued, a congress of ambassadors from different and hostile interests—which interests, he said, each must maintain as an agent and advocate against other agents and advocates, 'but parliament is a *deliberate* assembly of *one* nation, with *one* interest, that of the whole'. Burke saw society as a continuity; he had an instinctive, emotional understanding of the violence that revolution brought; he held fast, as he said, to peace, 'which has in her company charity, the highest of the virtues'. He never liked

this continual talk of resistance and revolution, or the practice of making the extreme medicine of the constitution its daily bread. It renders the habit of society dangerously valetudinarian; it is taking periodical doses of mercury sublimate, and swallowing down provocatives of cantharides to our love of liberty.

He was for compromise and barter as the basis of all government; all human benefit and enjoyment. He warned that if the Westminster government became one thing and the colonists' privileges another, if the two things existed without a mutual relationship, then the cement was gone, the cohesion 'loosened and everything would hasten to decay and dissolution'. This is why he wanted to preserve the sovereign authority of the English government as a sanctuary of liberty. That was where his own genius flowered.

Burke was like the Anglo-Irish dramatists: he needed the larger opportunities offered by the London stage. And similarly, in the later part of the nineteenth century, Oscar Wilde and George Bernard Shaw made their way to London.

True, Shaw wrote a superb play about Ireland in *John Bull's Other Island*, reversing stereotypes and situations in his usual way, but both Wilde and he were not particularly Irish in their interests: they needed a larger stage, more universal subjects. What they had brought across the Irish sea from Dublin was a sense of paradox and epigram. Their skill lay in words, in quick speech, in the exaggeration of the unexpected, the reversal of the orthodox, the accepted. Words are the cheapest form of entertainment, especially in a poor country, and its cheapest export.

In giving his reasons for leaving Dublin and moving to London Shaw mentioned the Gaelic League, founded by the poet and scholar Douglas Hyde (who later became the first President of Eire in 1937). He should, however, also have mentioned the effect of Yeats and the Irish Literary Societies in Dublin and London, and later the effect of the Abbey Theatre: all the activities and ideas that comprise what is sometimes known as the Irish Literary Renaissance or the Irish revival, the great outpouring of literature which began in the eighteen-nineties. It united the two streams of culture, English and Irish, for the first time, in a deliberate way. To understand it we need to skim rapidly through the different paths of Gaelic and English literature in Ireland.

## III

Gaelic culture, rich in oral literature, goes back twelve centuries. Its poets and story-tellers were given a long training in composition and memorising. That we know anything of this literature is probably the result of Christian monks writing down this traditional pagan material. This poem, 'The Ivy Crest', a mixture of Christian and pagan elements, is referring to one of these oratories in the woods where the Irish hermits loved to live:

> In Tuaim Inbhir here I find
> No great house such as mortals build,
> A hermitage that fits my mind
> With sun and moon and starlight filled.
>
> 'Twas Gobban shaped it cunningly
> —This is a tale that lacks not proof—
> And my heart's darling in the sky,
> Christ, was the thatcher of its roof.
>
> Over my house rain never falls,
> There comes no terror of the spear;
> It is a garden without walls
> And everlasting light shines here.

The earliest manuscripts date from the sixth century, but there was a sharp break in this literary work when the Vikings plundered Ireland over several centuries. Here is a translation by Robin Flower of a MS written as he says on some stormy night in a country constantly exposed to Viking raids:

> The bitter wind is high tonight
> It lifts the white locks of the sea
> In such wild winter storm no fright
> Of savage Viking troubles me

Then in the eleventh and twelfth centuries the monks put together the old materials, the sagas and tales. Meanwhile the professional poets went on composing their complex court poetry in Irish. Religious poems were written in the tradition of Medieval Latin religious poetry and there were also some superb lyrics, mostly written by monks. Here is one by Donnchadh Mor Ó Dalaigh:

> Wrens of the lake, I love them all,
> They come to matins at my call,
> The wren whose nest lets through the rain,
> He is my goose, my cock, my crane.
>
> My little bard, my man of song
> Went on a foray all day long;
> Three midges were the poet's prey,
> He cannot eat them in a day.
>
> He caught them in his little feet,
> His brown claws closed about the meat;
> His chicks for dinner gather round,
> Sure, if it rains they'll all be drowned.
>
> The crested plover's lost her young,
> With bitter grief my heart it stung;
> Two little chicks she had—they're gone:
> The wren's round dozen still lives on!

The prose contained mythological material as in 'The wooing of Etain', a lovely mortal woman, won by Midir, an elf king. There were accounts of the war between the Tuatha de Danaan, the pre-historical Gods or magicians, and their enemies the Formorians. These are vague stories filled with primitive magic and fantasy. Fantasy, exaggeration and some comedy mark another group of stories about Finn MacCumaill and his soldiers, the Fianna.

In one of them Finn's son Oisin travels to the timeless land of youth, *Tir na nog,* with the fairy Niamh, and spends three hundred years there, which go like a day.

There were other kinds of stories, some about the tribal kings and their deeds, a mixture of history and legend, and others about the Christian Saints which are akin to those about the kings. Voyages, visions and journeys occupied the imagination of the story tellers, who incorporated much magic as well as satire in their compositions. Satire was a powerful weapon for Gaelic poets; they let fly at kings who had not been hospitable or generous to them, at scholars or clerics who fell short of their exacting standards. Here is Eamonn Ó Caiside's impromptu answer to some bitterness uttered by another poet, Matha Ó Luinin:

> A good mate's Matthew,
> But not to pass the bottle;
> Uprising or downsitting,
> God's curse in Matthew's throttle.

They parodied, they indulged themselves in savagely ironic fantasies. And they inspired fear as well as respect.

The best of the Gaelic material is contained in the Red Branch or Ulster cycle of Tales; these probably existed in oral form before the fifth century. The main story is that of the *Tain Bo Cuailnge*, the Cattle Raid at Cooley. Here we have traditional epic material. The hero of the *Tain* is Cuchulain, the greatest of the warriors of King Conor of Ulster. He reminds us of the fierce Achilles in Homer's *Iliad*. King Conor had intended to marry a girl called Deirdre and had her brought up in a secluded place. But she fell in love with Naoise, one of Conor's warriors, and ran away with him to Scotland along with his two brothers. After some years Conor sent them a message inviting them back to Ireland under the safe conduct of Fergus MacRoigh, who had been king before Conor but had abdicated in his favour. Deirdre, who is very reminiscent of Cassandra in the Greek legend, did not want to leave Scotland, for she suspected Conor of treachery, correctly as it turned out. When they returned to Ireland Fergus was invited to a feast, and in his absence Conor had Naoise and his brothers killed. He then asked Deirdre to live with him, until she committed suicide by running a chariot on to a rock. He asked her:

'What do you see that you hate most?' 'You, of course', she said, 'and Eogan mae Durthact!' 'Go and live for a year with Eogan, then', Conchobar said. Then he sent her over to Eogan. They set out the next day for the fair of Macha. She was beside Eogan in the chariot. She had sworn that two men alive in the world together would never have her. 'This is good, Deirdre', Conchobar said, 'Bewteen me and Eogan you are a sheep eying two rams'. A big block of stone was in front of her. She let her head be driven against the stone, and made a mass of fragments of it, and she was dead.

Fergus, in disgust at Conor's treachery, had fought the King in a bloody battle. He left Conor's court and went to that of King Aillil and Queen Maeve in Connaught. When Maeve wanted to recover a bull which once belonged to her but was in Conor's possession she sent her armies into Ulster under the command of Fergus to recover it. In the course of this expedition there was much fighting, and, in particular, the heroic battle between Cuchulain and his friend and foster brother Ferdia.

Often savage, the Gaelic sagas can be balanced by the lighter, more personal poetry written by the monks and scholars, full of delight in the sheer beauty of living. Here, for example, is a translation by Robin Flower of a wandering Irish scholar's very personal poem about his cat Pangur Ban:

> I and Pangur Ban my cat,
> 'Tis a like task we are at:
> Hunting mice is his delight,
> Hunting words I sit all night.

Here is the essence of the writer's craft. It leads on to the work of Swift, Goldsmith, Sheridan and Wilde and, above all, Yeats, who talked of gathering words and reached a point where words obeyed his call. There is a gentle touch of ironic self-mockery at work here, which sounds through the tradition, notably in Goldsmith. But back to the monk and his cat:

> I and Pangur Ban my cat,
> 'Tis a like task we are at:
> Hunting mice is his delight,
> Hunting words I sit all night.
>
> Better far than praise of men
> 'Tis to sit with book and pen;
> Pangur bears me no ill will,
> He too plies his simple skill.
>
> 'Tis a merry thing to see
> At our tasks how glad are we,
> When at home we sit and find
> Entertainment to our mind.
>
> Oftentimes a mouse will stray
> In the hero Pangur's way;
> Oftentimes my keen thought set
> Takes a meaning in its net ...
>
> When a mouse darts from its den
> O how glad is Pangur then!
> O what gladness do I prove
> When I solve the doubts I love!

So in peace our tasks we ply,
Pangur Ban, my cat, and I;
In our arts we find our bliss,
I have mine and he has his.

Practice every day has made
Pangur perfect in his trade;
I get wisdom day and night
Turning darkness into light.

The Irish monks had a great delight in the light and shade of their nature scenery; here is an anchorite rejoicing in his surroundings:

Over my head the woodland wall
Rises; the ousel sings to me;
Above my booklet lined for words
The woodland birds shake out their glee.

That's the blithe cukoo chanting clear
In mantle grey from bough to bough!
God keep me still! for here I write
A scripture bright in great woods now.

The Norman invasion of Ireland in 1169 brought in its train new patrons for the Irish poets, brought, too, traditions of troubadour poetry to enrich the poets' material:

Of women no more evil will I say,
The lightsome loves that help my heart to live
—The sun sees nothing sweeter on his way—
They pledge their faith and break it. I forgive,
All I forgive and scandal them no more.
I am their servant. Let the witless jeer.
Though their slain loves are numbered by the score,
I love them living and their ghosts are dear.
The cunning wits are loud in their dispraise,
And yet I know not. If their breed should fail,
What comfort were in all the world's wide ways?
A flowerless earth, a sea without a sail.
If these were gone that make earth Heaven for men,
Love them or hate, 'twere little matter then.

While the bardic poets continued to write courtly poems in Irish for the Gaelic chieftains they were also honoured and supported by the Norman feudal lords. These newcomers adopted many

Irish ways of life; they learned Gaelic. So hibernicised, indeed, did they become that in 1366 the Statutes of Kilkenny were passed to prohibit them from using the Irish language, from intermarrying with the Irish and from adopting Irish customs such as concubinage and the fostering of children. Long before Edmund Spenser's day, the English regarded the Irish bards as particularly dangerous to the English cause, and these Statutes of Kilkenny describe them as perverting the imagination by their romantic tales. Speaking up for freedom, then, could be dangerous as it still is in many countries today; the Irish Bards kept alive a sense of the past, and they taught their listeners their Gaelic cultural inheritance, their traditions; they sang the glories of their chiefs or kings in war. But by the time of the Tudor and Elizabethan English relations between the Irish, the descendants of the Norman invaders, known as the Old English, and the centralising forces in England had become much worse. There was also the religious factor, for the Reformation had had less effect in Ireland, which remained largely Catholic.

The Gaelic culture, however, was in effect broken by the beginning of the seventeenth century. Elizabeth's army and navy defeated the Irish, whose minor chieftains were often divided among themselves and lacked any cohesive sense, any political awareness of Ireland as a nation. The flight of the two great Irish earls, O'Neill and O'Donnell, to Spain in 1607 marked the end of the Gaelic aristocracy's power in Ireland. Without aristocratic patrons the audience for poetry changed. The poets met occasionally, they lived now among a pitiably poor peasantry, and, so with some notable exceptions, not much outstanding new poetry was composed in the eighteenth century. There are laments in plenty—Eileen O'Leary's lament for her husband Art O'Leary, murdered for not selling a horse to a protestant landlord, Egan O'Rahilly's 'A Grey Eye Weeping' which records the reactions of an Irishman to the new landlords who have taken his land from him. And there is the anonymous poem 'Kilcash' lamenting the decline of a noble family driven into exile.

> My grief and my affliction
> Your gates are taken away,
> Your avenue needs attention,
> Goats in the garden stray.

The courtyard's filled with water
And the great Earls where are they?
The Earls, the lady, the people
Beaten into the clay.

Yet another kind of Gaelic poetry was exemplified in Brian Merryman's grotesque satire 'The Midnight Court', a lively, highly humorous treatment of the plight of young women who lack husbands, and that of a young woman married to a very old man, as well as such matters as free-love and clerical celibacy.

The popular audience for such poetry seems to have diminished as the movement from a use of Gaelic on a large scale to a fairly general employment of English accelerated in the nineteenth century. This may partly have been due to the influence of Daniel O'Connell who led a successful political movement for Catholic emancipation. He thought people needed to use English for political purposes. The economic aftermath of the appalling mid-nineteenth famine also had its effect, for the population of Ireland dropped down, through deaths by starvation and epidemic and particularly by emigration, from about eight million before the famine to four million by the end of the nineteenth century.

An antiquarian interest in Gaelic culture had, however, appeared towards the end of the eighteenth century. Sylvester O'Halloran's *History of Ireland*, published in 1778, heralded this, for it showed something, not always very accurately, of the past of Ireland and its rich, complex culture, knowledge of which was by no means general. A keen interest in Irish music also developed. A notable festival of Irish harpers was held in Belfast in 1792. This stimulated Edward Bunting's curiosity. He began to collect old Irish music and published three volumes of it. Edward Hudson, the flautist, also collected and transcribed Irish airs, but it was his friend Thomas Moore who popularised the work of both Bunting and Hudson in his famous *Irish Melodies*. Sentimental these often are, celebrating Irish places and people in a pervasive but pleasing melancholia. They are meant to be sung and heard rather than read, for they are true lyrics, with fluent rhymes and liquid runs of vowels permeating their plangent haunting sound. 'Tis the last Rose of Summer', 'Believe me, if all those endearing young charms', 'The Minstrel Boy' and 'At the mid-hour of Night' are well known. 'Oft in the Stilly Night' is an excellent example of Moore's sense of melody. He had an insouciant sense of rhymical variety; witness this song:

The time I've lost in wooing
In watching and pursuing
The light that lies
In Woman's eyes
Has been my heart's undoing
Though Wisdom oft has sought me,
I scorn'd the lore she brought me.
My only books
Were woman's looks,
And folly's all they've taught me.

Moore created an audience in England as well as Ireland for these songs which were new both in their style and subject matter; his own pleasant personality contributed to his success story in England. Lady Morgan, born Sydney Owenson, who played the harp herself and had published *Twelve Original Hibernian Melodies*, wrote a novel in 1806 which effectively made her name and helped to develop the audience which Moore had found for Irish subject matter overseas. Her novel was *The Wild Irish Girl*, a romantic tale about a highly romantic heroine. A young Englishman goes to the West of Ireland where he discovers Glorvina, a beautiful cultivated girl who, like her creator, plays the harp and sings elegantly. She is the daughter of an old Irish chieftain living in his ruined castle amid the memories and ways of an older Gaelic civilisation. The novel is filled with antiquarian information about Gaelic traditions, on some pages the length of footnotes exceeding the length of the text.

Here, for instance, is Glorvina replying to a question from the hero about how the Irish could procure so expensive an article as saffron for dying their clothes:

'I have heard Father John say' she returned, 'that saffron, as an article of importation, would never have been at any time cheap enough for general use. And I believe formerly, as now, they communicated this bright yellow tinge with indigenous plants, with which this country abounds'. 'See', she added, springing lightly forward, and culling a plant which grew from the mountain's side—'see this little blossom, which they call here, "yellow lady's bed straw", and which you, as a botanist, will better recognise as the galicens borum; it communicates a beautiful yellow; as does the lichen juniperinus, or "cypress moss" which you brought me yesterday; and I think the reseda luteola or "yellow weed" surpasses them all'.

Lady Morgan had to learn not to be didactic, and to a certain extent she did. She gives us Ireland as if seen through the eyes of painters such as Salvator Rosa and Claude Lorraine. She developed her narrative skill, and her last novel *The O'Briens and the O'Flahertys*, a serious examination of the choices open to a young Irishman who wanted to serve his country, is a serious and thought-provoking piece of work.

Lady Morgan's lively writing is seldom discussed in histories of English literature, yet she has her place in the history of the novel. Here, however, is something different:

Ah, ha, you are flying from the fire, but there is a fire coming that none of you can fly from—the fire that burns forever, and ever and ever! This fire burns red and hot, but it will be hotter when your eyes are melting in their sockets; and your bodies will be like red hot iron, hard and burning, and never to be cooled, and never to dissolve like *my brain*, my *brain!*

This is a passage from *Women, or, Pour et Contre*, a little known novel by Charles Robert Maturin, an eccentric Dublin clergyman of Hugenot ancestry. He was fascinated by the terrible, and this passage is a vision of Hell described by a peasant woman—she is reminiscent of Scott's Meg Merrilees in *Guy Mannering*—and she is present at a piece of urban gothic, a city fire. This novel itself is in many ways a piece of innovation: it is perhaps the first novel ever to be written about an undergraduate's love affairs. It is psychological in its analysis of how de Courcy, the hero, feels about Eva, a quiet somewhat passive girl moving in Methodist circles, whom he falls for on arriving at Trinity College, Dublin. Then he is attracted by Zaira, a blue-stocking and an opera singer. The two women are very different. Eva is frightened by thunderstorms, Zaira loves them, and so on. There is even a primitive attempt at symbolism, which shows how strained and melodramatic nineteenth century novelists could be: de Courcy, torn between two women, clasps Eva to his bosom:

Eva's long light hair (of a different colour from *Zaira's*) diffused its golden luxuriance over his bosom; her white slender fingers grasped his with the fondling helplessness of infancy, and twined their waxen softness round and round them: her pure hyacinth breath trembled over his cheeks and lips. In clasping her closer to his heart, he felt something within his vest; he drew it out; it was the flower Zaira had given him the night before, and which he had placed there. *It was withered*; he flung it away.

The story has its moments. de Courcy abandons Eva, to whom he has become engaged, and follows Zaira to Paris. He goes back to Dublin, deciding that, after all, Eva is the girl for him. But a funeral cortège meets him on his return. Eva has died of a broken heart. de Courcy goes into a decline and dies. Zaira returns to discover that Eva was her lost daughter and the mysterious old woman is her mother. Strong stuff!

Like many an Anglo-Irish writer from the east Maturin found the largely Gaelic west of Ireland fascinating as a subject. He had lived in the west himself and found it strangely romantic— its poor rocky boggy land overcrowded since Cromwell had pushed people into it to make way for his soldiers on the richer farming land of the east and south. Maturin tried his hand on it in *The Wild Irish Boy* and in *The Milesian Chief,* a picture of a doomed revolt led by a young Irish patriot from an old Gaelic family, hopelessly entangled with an English girl. But Maturin found his true metier in the gothic novel, his horrific *Melmoth the Wanderer* being the supreme expression of the *genre.* Indeed it cries out for a Hitchcock-style treatment in film; its mixture of realism and the supernatural is impressive, and Maturin uses emotive descriptions of scenery in it with gusto.

His talents, like those of Lady Morgan, were romantic, and yet, for all their often sentimental intensity, they did not create literature to match the achievement of Maria Edgeworth. She was the first regional novelist. She wrote *Castle Rackrent,* published in 1800, to show English readers something of the wild way of life of the Irish squires before 1782. She had come to Ireland at the age of fifteen, and probably saw it the clearer for coming at that age. She knew it well, too, for she acted as her father's assistant, and learned the practicalities of business, of running a large estate, in a way few women of her time could achieve.

She began writing by composing stories for children—there were twenty-two of them in the Edgeworth household—and wrote many novels. Besides *Castle Rackrent,* she devoted three other tales to the land, *Ennui, The Absentee,* and *Ormond,* which is arguably her best novel. In it she tells of a young man growing up in two different environments, one that of the Anglo-Irish ascendancy, the other that of a Gaelic milieu.

Maria Edgeworth's successful exploration of Irish subject matter inspired Sir Walter Scott to write his *Waverley* novels about Scotland. Her interests were moral: she wished to promote an intelligent approach to farming and to encourage fair treatment of the tenant farmers who suffered from absentee landlords: she showed good and bad management of estates, for instance, in *The Absentee*, a novel which also explored suburban vulgarity in Dublin and the state of decline into which the city fell after its parliament had been eliminated by the act of union in 1800, itself probably caused by the fears aroused by the revolution of 1798:

> Who fears to speak of Ninety-eight?
> Who blushes at the name?
> When cowards mock the patriot's fate,
> Who hangs his head for shame?
> He's all a knave, or half a slave,
> Who slights his country thus;
> But a true man, like you, man,
> Will fill your glass with us.
>
> We drink the memory of the brave,
> The faithful and the few;
> Some lie far off beyond the wave,
> Some sleep in Ireland, too;
> All, all are gone; but still lives on
> The fame of those who died;
> All true men, like you, men,
> Remember them with pride.
>
> Some on the shores of distant lands
> Their weary hearts have laid,
> And by the stranger's heedless hands
> Their lonely graves were made;
> But though their clay be far away
> Beyond the Atlantic foam,
> In true men, like you, men,
> Their spirit's still at home.
>
> The dust of some is Irish earth,
> Among their own they rest,
> And the same land that gave them birth
> Has caught them to her breast;
> And we will pray that from their clay
> Full many a race may start
> Of true men, like you, men,
> To act as brave a part.
>
> They rose in dark and evil days
> To right their native land;
> They kindled here in a living blaze

> That nothing shall withstand.
> Alas! that might can vanquish right—
> They fell and passed away;
> But true men, like you, men,
> Are plenty here to-day.
>
> Then here's their memory—may it be
> For us a guiding light,
> To cheer our strife for liberty,
> And teach us to unite—
> Through good and ill, be Ireland's still,
> Though sad as theirs your fate,
> And true men be you, men,
> Like those of Ninety-eight.

That poem was written by a quiet don in Trinity College, Dublin, John Kells Ingram. It shows something of the numbing effect of the revolution of 1798 and the Act of Union. However, the development of cultural nationalism gave a fresh fillip to interest in the faded glories of the Gaelic past. This new cultural nationalism had developed out of the earlier romantic antiquarianism; it spread rapidly in the 1840s, mainly through *The Nation*, a weekly journal begun by Charles Gavan Duffy, John Blake Dillon and Thomas Davis in 1842 as the organ of the Young Ireland party. Davis had been influenced by the French historians Michelet and Thierry, who thought Ireland's true independence lived in her songs.

He argued that the traditions of the past could shape a new culture 'racy of the Irish soil'. Unlike Daniel O'Connell—whom the Young Ireland party at first supported and with whom they later quarrelled—Davis thought that Catholic and Protestant Ireland could be united, that literature could imbue nationalism with spiritual overtures, that it could persuade contemporary Ireland to become free to follow its own nature. And so Davis wrote prose and verse to this end in *The Nation* and urged others to write similarly.

He composed poetry—of a sort—incessantly, and the ballads published in *The Nation* were widely popular in Ireland for the same reason that Tom Moore's lyrics had been, because they were sung to traditional airs. They bridged gaps between oral and written traditions, and though most of them use crude, almost journalistic symbolism, some few, judged as song, are very effective. Although after the early death of Davis in 1845—he was only thirty-four—cultural nationalism lost its political impetus, his ideas had a vast influence on popular culture in Ireland.

There was another kind of interest at work also. Scholars were busily translating and editing the large amount of Irish manuscript material. A group of them—George Petrie, Eugene O'Curry and John O'Donovan—were employed by the Ordnance Survey, and John O'Daly and Brian O'Looney were also actively engaged in this work of discovering the Irish past. *The Dublin University Magazine*, begun nine years before *The Nation*, had sought to publish genuinely Irish literature, and both James Clarence Mangan and Sir Samuel Ferguson contributed to it in its early days. Their interest in Gaelic literature gave them a dimension lacking in most of their Anglo-Irish contemporaries, Victorian poets such as Sir Aubrey de Vere, say, or George Darley. Mangan, himself an eccentric and gentle creature, wrote profusely for various magazines and journals. He used material from the prose translations of Gaelic material made by others, but like Moore, he also transplanted into his writing in English echoes of the intricate inner rhymes and assonance, the lilting notes, inversions, and dragging cadences which mark Irish poetry. His 'Siberia', published when he joined *The Nation*, had a deep note of gloom, intensified perhaps by the first winter of the famine, while his version of 'O'Hussey's Ode to the Maguire', magnificent lamentation that it is, also conveys a clear call for revenge:

Though he were even a wolf ranging the round green woods,
Though he were even a pleasant salmon in the unchainable sea,
Though he were a wild mountain eagle, he could scarce bear, he,
This sharp sore sleet, these howling floods.
O, mournful is my soul this night for Hugh Maguire!
Darkly, as in a dream he strays! Before him and behind
Triumphs the tyrannous anger of the wounding wind,
The wounding wind, that burns as fire!
It is my bitter grief—it cuts me to the heart—
That in the country of Clan Darry this should be his fate!
O, woe is me, where is he? Wandering, houseless, desolate,
Alone, without or guide or chart!

And Mangan's 'Dark Rosaleen' also carried a touch of evocative menace. Mangan had used some of Ferguson's translations of Gaelic, and Ferguson himself found his best material in the old Irish sagas, though he also wrote about the Irish countryside with delight, showing a striking skill in creating new combinations of words, as in his vigorous 'Lament for the Death of Thomas Davis:'

> I walked through Ballinderry in the springtime,
> When the bud was on the tree,
> And I said, in every fresh-ploughed field beholding
> The sowers striding free,
> Scattering broadcast for the corn in golden plenty,
> On the quick, seed-clasping soil,
> Even such this day among the fresh-stirred hearts of Erin
> Thomas Davis, is thy toil!

Ferguson's translations get the toughness of Irish material clearly across to the reader but his poems did not become popular. They march along, impressive in their strength, encased in their complex syntax, but they lack a sensuous quality and the intensity that Mangan could impart. Ferguson's epic *Congal* is his most ambitious work, but, even allowing for Victorian restraints, 'The Vengeance of the Welshman of Tirawley', who offered their prisoners the choice of being blinded or castrated, and even more, 'Deirdre's Lament for the Sons of Usnach' are the poems that remain echoing in the reader's mind. Here are two of its stanzas:

> The lions of the hill are gone,
> And I am left alone—alone—
> Dig the grave both wide and deep,
> For I am sick and fain would sleep!
>
> Woe is me! By fraud and wrong
> Traitors false and tyrants strong—
> Fell Clan Usnach, bought and sold
> For Barach's feast and Conor's gold.
>
> Woe to Eman, roof and wall!—
> Woe to Red Branch, hearth and hall!—
> Tenfold woe and black dishonour
> To the false and foul Clan Conor!
>
> Dig the grave both wide and deep
> Sick I am, and fain would sleep!
> Dig the grave and make it ready
> Lay me on my true love's body

Gaelic material received exciting treatment from Standish O'Grady, whose translations made the legend of Cuchulain available in exotic prose. His *History of Ireland: Heroic Period* of 1878 departed from the accurate and indispensable spade work of earlier translators, leaving pedantic prose behind, and appealing effectively to the imaginative response of his readers, particularly the younger poets.

Literature in Ireland in the middle of the nineteenth century had been bedevilled by politics. After Davis died, a spirit of hate burst out in the writing of John Mitchel, who gave a sharper edge to the earlier revolutionary nationalism of Wolfe Tone. Mitchel wrote savage satire in Swiftian vein, focussing on the failure of the English bureaucrats to fathom the extent of the emergency created by the catastrophe of the famine. 'The almighty indeed', he said, 'sent the potato blight, but the English created the famine'. Here is an example of his caustic rage:

There, in the esplanade before the 'Royal Barracks', was erected the national model soup-kitchen, gaily bedizened, laurelled, and bannered, and fair to see; and in and out, and all around, sauntered parties of our supercilious second-hand 'better classes' of the castle-offices, fed in superior rations at the people's expense, and bevies of fair dames, and military officers, braided with public braid, and padded with public padding; and there, too, were the pale and piteous ranks of model-paupers, broken tradesmen, ruined farmers, destitute sempstresses, ranged at a respectful distance till the genteel persons had duly inspected the arrangements—and then marched by policemen to the place allotted them, where they were to feed on the meagre diet with chained spoons—to show the 'gentry' how pauper spirit can be broken, and pauper appetite can gulp down its bitter bread and its bitter shame and wrath together;—and all this time the genteel persons chatted and simpered as pleasantly as if the clothes they wore, and the carriages they drove in, were their own—as if 'Royal Barracks', castle, and soup-kitchen, were to last forever.

Mitchel's writings were too strong for Duffy's taste; and so Mitchel left *The Nation* to found a journal called, after Wolfe Tone's movement, *The United Irishman*. He was arrested twice, and sentenced to fourteen years' transportation. Out of this came his *Jail Journal*, a classic account of suffering told with pungent force—autobiography very unlike Oscar Wilde's 'Ballad of Reading Gaol'. Mitchel was followed to Tasmania by Smith O'Brien, who led the abortive 1848 rising, and by other young Ireland leaders. Mitchel's *Jail Journal* tells of their meetings in and escapes from Tasmania. Finally Gavan Duffy gave up his involvement in Irish politics and literature and sailed for Australia, becoming Prime Minister of Victoria in 1871. The next rising was that of the Fenians in 1867; after it came the Land Wars of the 1880s and the Parnellite period of parliamentary struggle at Westminster.

It was not till Parnell's death in 1891 that there was any lull in Irish political activity. Into this vacuum W.B. Yeats launched the literary movement which we now call the Irish Renaissance.

## IV

Yeats had grown up, like most Anglo-Irish people of his time, in an English literary tradition: indeed he never learned Gaelic. But he was introduced to its subject matter by John O'Leary, who had been involved in the 1848 rising and later, through editing the *Irish People*, a weekly Fenian journal, he was arrested in 1865—the year in which Yeats was born—and sentenced to twenty years' imprisonment. He was released after nine years on condition he stayed out of Ireland, but returned to Dublin in 1885 when this condition was waived.

By 1885 Yeats had left school and was at the School of Art in Dublin. He decided to become a poet, and O'Leary lent him books of which he had never heard before. These made him free of a culture unknown by or largely looked down upon by the Anglo-Irish. O'Leary guided him, father-like, to Irish novelists of uneven achievement such as William Carleton, the Banim brothers and to his own friend Kickham, all of whom took Ireland as their subject matter—and none of whom are usually mentioned in histories of English literature. But more significant than this, he introduced him to the stilted and often pedantic translations of the Gaelic sagas made by such pioneering scholars as Eugene O'Curry, John O'Donovan and Brian O'Looney, to the poems of Mangan and Ferguson, and to the balladry and polemics of Thomas Davis.

O'Leary did all this, fully recognising the youthful Yeats's genius. And Yeats immediately realised the potential of the legends he absorbed from the translations. Through them he realised he could break into and release what could be excitingly new subject matter for his contemporary Ireland, which had virtually forgotten its Gaelic past: the traditions, the mythology and the subject matter of Irish literature. Through the legends, too, he could avoid the history of the more immediate past, the emotive force of which could be a negative force in Ireland.

Yeats spent some of his time at an English school in Hammersmith, but had not been able to identify himself with

English myths—of victories such as those of Agincourt or Trafalgar. But when he was in the west of Ireland, staying for long periods with his mother's parents in Sligo, he could not identify with Irish Catholics' myths either—of defeats such as those of Augrim or the Battle of the Yellow Ford. But now, thanks to John O'Leary, he could go back to the remoter heroic mythological past of the Gaelic sagas and legends, and he could use this Gaelic material to shape Ireland's future national, intellectual and spiritual consciousness. He had found his subject matter—no small thing for a young poet starting out on his career—he had seized on an old and powerful mythology in the Gaelic legends. He saw himself in the tradition of his predecessors, and listed Davis, Mangan and Ferguson in his poem 'To Ireland in the Coming Times', feeling himself at the outset of his writing no less important than they had been. Indeed he intended to go far further than they had. He could show Ireland the cultural identity that it possessed but had neglected or had failed to treat with imaginative insight and dignity. It was an exciting challenge he set himself and he responded to it magnificently.

An early idea of his had been to write of Sligo in the west of Ireland where so much of his boyhood had been spent, and many of his poems refer to it—even in his old age. The best known of these is 'The Lake Isle of Innisfree' which first brought him fame:

I will arise and go now, and go to Innisfree,
And a small cabin build there, of clay and wattles made:
Nine bean-rows will I have there, a hive for the honey-bee,
And live alone in the bee-loud glade.

And I shall have some peace there, for peace comes dropping slow,
Dropping from the veils of the morning to where the cricket sings;
There the midnight's all a glimmer, and noon a purple glow,
And evening full of the linnet's wings.

I will arise and go now, for always night and day
I hear lake water lapping with low sounds by the shore;
While I stand on the roadway, or on the pavements grey,
I hear it in the deep heart's core.

Now, however, there were wider horizons for Irish imaginations to reach beyond the mere description or evocation of Irish scenery. And so Yeats hurled himself into action. He formed Irish literary Societies in the eighteen nineties, he reviewed Irish books—his first review was in enthusiastic praise of Sir Samuel Ferguson's work—he criticised, he edited, he encouraged others to share his belief that Ireland could have its own national literature—and one purged of provincialism. The rhetoric, indeed the vulgarity, of Thomas Davis and the young Irelanders had to go, and all stage Irishism, melodrama and crude symbolism—what he called the harps and pepper pots—the round towers—which had become tired literary and political clichés.

Yeats wrote his long poem *The Wanderings of Oisin*, and when it was published in 1889 it ushered in a new kind of poetry, with its style of delicate wistful beauty, with its story of the Irish Oisin and the fairy maiden Niamh visiting the three mysterious islands of the other world, staying for a hundred years in each of them, the Islands of Dancing, of Victories and of Forgetfulness, until Oisin returned—to despair of what Ireland had become. In this poem Yeats was trying to blend the pagan inheritance of the Gaelic past with the Christian traditions of modern Ireland. Indeed St. Patrick reproaches Oisin at the end of the poem.

Yeats, still influenced by the romantics, the pre-Raphaelites and some late Victorian poets, wrote a dreamy vague idealistic poetry. His plays and his prose were in this rein, and his treatment of the Gaelic legends became known as the Celtic twilight.

His love poetry written to Maud Gonne added to his fame. She refused to marry him but he went on writing her beautiful poetry such as 'He wishes for the Cloths of Heaven'.

> Had I the heaven's embroidered cloths,
> Enwrought with golden and silver light,
> The blue and the dim and the dark cloths
> Of night and light and the half-light,
> I would spread the cloths under your feet:
> But, I, being poor, have only my dreams;
> I have spread my dreams under your feet;
> Tread softly because you tread on my dreams.

He also wrote her a patriotic play *Cathleen ni Houlihan* in which she appeared in the title role. The play had an explosive effect on the audience, and Yeats wondered in old age if it had an influence on the men who launched the 1916 rising.

Then Yeats created the Abbey Theatre. This was done with the aid of Lady Gregory, herself perhaps the most effective translator of the Irish legends in her two fine books *Cuchulain of Muirthemne* and *Gods and Fighting Men*. She used a form of English modelled on the speech of country people in Galway, and called Kiltartan after an area near her big house, Coole Park. Here is an example of it, part of a series of stories about the Irish sea-god Manannan MacLir.

And it was through Manannan the wave of Tuaig, one of the three great waves of Ireland, got its name, and this is the way that happened. There was a young girl of the name of Tuag, a fosterling of Conaire the High King, was reared in Teamhair, and a great company of the daughters of the kings of Ireland were put about her to protect her, the way she would be kept for a king's asking. But Manannan sent Fer Ferdiad, of the Tuatha de Danaan, that was a pupil of his own and a Druid, in the shape of a woman of his own household, and he went where Tuag was, and sang a sleep-spell over her, and brought her away to Inver Glas. And there he laid her down while he went looking for a boat, that he might bring her away in her sleep to the land of the Ever-Living Women. But a wave of the flood-tide came over the girl, and she was drowned, and Manannan killed Fer Ferdiad in his anger.

The Abbey Theatre brought world-wide attention to the Irish legends as well as to new styles of acting, and new expressions, notably in J.M. Synge's plays and later, in Sean O'Casey's, of th Irish temperament. All of this literary activity surged forward, not always as Yeats himself would have wished, for the Abbey audiences preferred realistic comedies of cottage life to his poetic dramas on exalted, heroic themes.

Politics began to stir again. Douglas Hyde, the son of a country rector, collected folktales, and published *Beside the Fire*, his first collection of them, in 1889. His *Love Songs of Connacht* with his own fine verse translations, followed in 1893, by which time Yeats was pouring out his unrequited love poems to Maud Gonne, who seemed to him to symbolise Ireland. She was a violent revolutionary, though Yeats argued that his literary aims and ambitions of creating a national literature were just as useful to Ireland's cause as revolutionary politics. He became increasingly disillusioned with Irish politics by the end of the century. And Hyde, who had founded the Gaelic League to encourage the learning of Irish, and Irish games and dancing, wanted it to be non-political, and non-sectarian. But the League developed an inevitable impetus towards nationalism, and disliking this, Hyde finally resigned from its presidency in 1915. Yeats had earlier become disappointed in him, thinking that involvement in the politics of the Gaelic League had sapped his poetic talent. George Moore, too, was yet another disappointment.

Moore was an Irish landlord who has studied art in Paris before finding his true metier as a novelist. He described his youthful days there in his *Confessions of a Young Man:*

...our salon was a pretty resort—English cretonne of a very happy design—vine leaves, dark green and golden, broken up by many fluttering jays. The walls were stretched with this colourful cloth, and the armchairs and the couches were to match. The drawing-room was in cardinal red, hung from the middle of the ceiling and looped up to give the appearance of a tent; a faun, in terra-cotta, laughed in the red gloom, and there were Turkish couches and lamps. In another room you faced an altar, a Buddhist temple, a state of Apollo, and a bust of Shelley. The bedrooms were made unconventional with cushioned seats and rich camopies; and in picturesque corners there wre censers, great church candlesticks, and palms; then think of the smell of burning wax and you will have imagined the sentiment of our apartment in Rue de la Tour des Dames. I bought a Persian cat, and a python that made a monthly meal off guinea-pigs; Marshall, who did not care for pets, filled his room with flowers—he used to sleep beneath a tree of gardenias in full bloom.

Moore came back to Ireland to help Yeats and Lady Gregory with the nascent theatre movement. He is usually described in histories of English literature for his novel *Esther Waters* which brought Zola's techniques into the English novel, but during his return to Ireland he wrote his equally effective Turgenev-like stories of *The Untilled Field*, achieved the magnificent melodic prose line of *The Lake* with all its evocation of the natural beauty of the west of Ireland; but then, after he had left Dublin for London, came his highly sardonic account of Dublin life in *Hail and Farewell*, a masterpiece of malice, which stirred Yeats into fierce poetry and into writing his first volume of *Autobiography*, a view of his family as well as of the way he had come to Irish literature. Moore, of course, had an outrageous quality and enjoyed administering shocks. Here is an account of his quarrel with Mrs. Craigie, an American hieress with whom he seems to have fallen in love and with whom he quarrelled intently:

'I was walking in the Green Park', he said, 'and saw her in front of me. I was blind with rage and I ran up behind her and kicked her'. At first he related this story with some embarrassment, but when he grew accustomed to his invention, with relish. The scene in the Green Park was afterwards used in the sketch 'Lui et Elles' . . . where a heartless woman on whose face he detected a mocking smile, receives the assault 'nearly in the centre of the backside, a little to the right', and seems highly gratified to find that she has aroused such a display of feeling. It was inevitable, I said, part of the world's history, and I lost sight of all things but the track of my boot on the black crêpe de chine'.

One of Yeats' earliest friends, George Russell, the visionary painter and writer, known as AE, had also irritated Yeats by praising younger Irish poets, who had copied his celtic twilight manner after he himself had abandoned it. He was learning to write more directly, in a less dreamy fashion, to let his poems move away from the mists of mythology into the fires of contemporary controversy over such things as the famous row in the Abbey Theatre about Synge's *Playboy of the Western World* and Dublin's philistine reception of Sir Hugh Lane's offer of his pictures to the city. Yeats published his *Collected Works* in 1908, when he was 43; at this time he spent a lot of his time in London—as well as his summers at Coole Park, Lady Gregory's house in Galway. He had grown out of sympathy with nationalism, and, when the 1916 Rising took place, wrote a poem on it, 'Easter, 1916', which has since become a classic in its realisation of the force of martyrdom and the cult of sacrifice launched by a young Irish poet and one of the leaders of the rising, Patrick Pearse—and for its question of whether the sacrifice was, in fact, necessary.

Yeats himself had a superb recrudescence of poetic vigour in his last twenty years. This is the period when his youthful dreams came true. He married in 1917 at the age of fifty-two, had two children, lived part of the year in an ancient Norman tower he had bought in the west of Ireland. His poems reached into minds throughout the world. One of the giants of an age, he had created a universality, to which the award of the Nobel Prize for poetry paid tribute. His status as a writer—and perhaps as a youthful nationalist—led to his appointment as a Senator of the Irish Free State in 1922.

In the twenties he wrote his Tower poems, rich complex poems on civil war, poems raging at the coming of old age, poems on his friends, poems which reflect his interest in history and philosophy. In the nineteen-twenties, too, he discovered his true literary ancestors. He read Swift, he read Bishop Berkeley, he read Oliver Goldsmith, and he read Edmund Burke. He recognised these eighteenth century Anglo-Irish writers as his own people. Speaking of them in the Senate he said

We are ... no petty people. We are one of the great stocks of Europe.
We are the people of Burke; we are the people of Grattan; we are the
people of Swift, the people of Emmet, the people of Parnell. We have
created the most of the modern literature of this country. We have
created the best of its political intelligence.

His early interest in Gaelic mythology, in the old legends and
folk literature had been genuine. He had made Cuchulain and
Conor, Deirdre and Niamh part of modern Irish consciousness.
As a nationalist he had turned delightedly to this material,
avoiding the Anglo-Irish authors who had seemed to be merely
part of a garrison, an ascendancy. But he had learned how to
make the Gaelic material come alive in a modern period—
through his knowledge of the English romantic tradition, and by
developing his own kind of symbolism out of his interest in the
occult as well as his careful study of Blake and Shelley and his
awareness of what the late nineteenth century French sym-
bolists were doing. He wrote a strange book about his ideas
called *A Vision* and it provided a scaffolding for his poetry. Here
is an example of how his gloomy despair about what was
happening in the world was expressed with confidence in a
powerful rhetoric as he contemplated the possible ending of the
Christian era in a terrible reversal, a tide of anarchy and destruction overwhelming it

### The Second Coming

Turning and turning in the widening gyre
The falcon cannot hear the falconer;
Things fall apart; the centre cannot hold;
Mere anarchy is loosed upon the world,
The blood-dimmed tide is loosed, and everywhere
The ceremony of innocence is drowned;
The best lack all conviction, while the worst
Are full of passionate intensity.

Surely some revelation is at hand;
Surely the Second Coming is at hand.
The Second Coming! Hardly are those words out
When a vast image out of Spiritus Mundi
Troubles my sight: somewhere in sands of the desert
A shape with lion body and the head of a man,
A gaze blank and pitiless as the sun,
Is moving its slow thighs, while all about it
Reel shadows of the indignant desert birds.
The darkness drops again; but now I know

> That twenty centuries of stony sleep
> Were vexed to nightmare by a rocking cradle,
> And what rough beast, its hour come round at last,
> Slouches towards Bethlehem to be born?

Yeats, more than anyone, brought into fusion the Gaelic and the English elements; he took his place in the Anglo-Irish line that began with Swift, he is its flowering. He had insisted from the start upon the need for skill, for patient craftsmanship, and an exacting standard of achievement. But now that he began to read them in his middle age, the Anglo-Irish writers were a revelation to him: they provided a sanction for the way his own art was developing, and for his own public and political attitudes. They were an encouragement to write directly and out of an ease and strength that came from long practice, from endless rewriting in the search for the right words in the right oder, from long wrestling with his craft of verse:

> A line will take us hours maybe;
> Yet if it does not seem a moment's thought,
> Our stitching and unstitching has been naught.

Because he had come into his strength words did indeed obey his call.

Words. In Ireland they have come to writers out of the tension of the main cultures. There is a rich inheritance, a complex linguistic stockpile. It comes from the Gaelic, from the Latin of the monks, from the Danish of the east and south-east seaboard, from the Norman French that came in with the Normans—and the English spoken and written in Ireland which draws upon this idiosyncratic richness, with imaginative enjoyment of its resources, its range and flexibility.

The master of it is James Joyce. Just as Laurence Sterne, born in Ireland in the eighteenth century, had explored the stream of consciousness in *Tristram Shandy*, that great experimental novel that turned the novel form upside down, so Joyce, supremely, used language to convey the inner images of the mind. Building on Lewis Carroll's style of portmanteau words, employing vast learning and a devastating sense of mocking parody, he developed his use of language from the 'scrupulous meanness' of his early realistic stories of *Dubliners* through the experimental beauty of *Portrait of the Artist as a Young Man*, with all its skilled recapturing of the hell fire sermon, its moments of aesthetic beauty and of the undergraduates' bawdy talk into the vast *tour*

*de force* of the different styles of *Ulysses,* where his ear captured,
in particular, the nuances of Dublin speech. Here is a passage
from an early work, *Stephen Hero,* which shows his sense of
humour at work

Temple took off his cap and, bareheaded, he began to recite after the
fashion of a country priest, prolonging all the vowels (and) jerking out
the phrases, and dropping his voice at every pause:
—Dearly beloved Brethren: There was once a tribe of monkeys in
Barbary. And ... these monkeys were as numerous as the sands of the
sea. They lived together in the woods in polygamous ... intercourse
... and reproduced ... their species ... But, behold there came into
Barbary ... the holy missionaries, the holy men of God ... to redeem
the people of Barbary. And these holy men preached to the people ...
and then ... they went into the woods ... far away into the woods ...
to pray to God. And they lived as hermits ... in the woods ... and
praying to God. And, behold, the monkeys of Barbary who were in the
trees ... saw these holy men living as hermits ... as lonely hermits ...
praying to God. And the monkeys who, my dearly beloved brethren,
are imitative creatures ... began to imitate the actions ... of these holy
men ... and began to do likewise. And so ... they (left their wives)
separated from one another ... and went away far away, to pray to
God ... and they did as they had seen the holy men do ... and prayed
to God ... And ... they did not return ... any more ... nor try to
reproduce the species ... And so ... gradually ... these po ... or
monkeys ... grew fewer and fewer ... and fewer and fewer ... And
today ... there is no monkey in all Barbary.

Set against this the lyric beauty which graces the Dublin
seascape in *A Portrait of the Artist as a Young Man*

A day of dappled seaborne clouds.
The phrase and the day and the scene harmonised in a chord. Words.
Was it their colours? He allowed them to glow and fade, hue after hue:
sunrise gold, the russet and green of apple orchards, azure of waves,
the grey fringed fleece of clouds. No, it was not their colours: it was the
poise and balance of the period itself. Did he then love the rhythmic
rise and fall of words better than their associations of legend and
colour? Or was it that, being as weak of sight as he was shy of mind,
he drew less pleasure from the reflection of the glowing sensible world
through the prism of a language many coloured and richly storied than
from the contemplation of an inner world of individual emotions
mirrored perfectly in a lucid supple periodic prose?
...Disheartened, he raised his eyes towards the slow-drifting clouds,
dappled and seaborne. They were voyaging across the deserts of the
sky, a host of nomads on the march, voyaging high over Ireland,
westward bound. The Europe they had come from lay out there beyond

the Irish Sea. Europe of strange tongues and valleyed and woodbegirt and citadelled and of entrenched and marshalled races. He heard a confused music within him as of memories and names which he was almost conscious of but could not capture even for an instant; then the music seemed to recede, to recede, to recede, and from each receding trail of nebulous music there fell always one long-drawn calling note, piercing like a star the dusk of silence.

Then came the sharply observed Dublin of *Ulysses* and, after it, *Finnegans Wake* and in it his very personal use of language—often superbly witty—to evoke the nature of dreams.

Joyce, steeped in Irish folk memory, knew the problems for the Irish writer of handling English. There is a passage in *A Portrait of an Artist as a Young Man* that strikes to the root of it. Stephen Daedalus is having a conversation with the Dean of Studies; he has told the Dean that he is thinking about aesthetics by the light of one or two ideas of Aristotle and Aquinas. He says that if the lamp smokes or smells he will try to trim it. The Dean replies with a scholarly comment on the lamp of Epictetus, Stephen discusses the use of words in the literary tradition and that of the market place and the Dean replies:

—To return to the lamp, he said, the feeding of it is also a nice problem. You must choose the pure oil and you must be careful when you pour it in not to overflow it, not to pour in more than the funnel can hold.
—What funnel? asked Stephen.
—The funnel through which you pour the oil into your lamp.
—That? said Stephen. Is that called a funnel? Is it not a tundish?
—That, The ... the funnel.
—Is that called a tundish in Ireland? asked the dean. I never heard the word in my life.
—It is called a tundish in Lower Drumcondra, said Stephen, laughing, where they speak the best English.
—A tundish, said the dean reflectively. That is a most interesting word. I must look that word up. Upon my word I must.

The dean repeats the word yet again:

Tundish! Well now, that is interesting!

Stephen felt with a smart of objection that the man to whom he was speaking was a countryman of Ben Jonson. He thought:

—The language in which we are speaking is his before it is mine. How different are the words home, Christ, ale, master, on his lips and on mine! I cannot speak or write these words without unrest of spirit. His language, so familiar and so foreign, will always be for me an acquired speech. I have not made or accepted its words. My voice holds them at bay. My soul frets in the shadow of his language.

This passage illustrates the extremes within the English used in Ireland. The Dean is English, born into a literary, written tradition. Stephen is Irish, but from an English-speaking family. His origins were, probably, a long way back, Gaelic—if they were like those of James Joyce, his creator – and his feelings about English stem from that far-off Gaelic ancestry—and from the fact that so much of Ireland's population had—and probably still has—a largely oral approach to literature and language. That Gaelic ancestry has greatly influenced the English spoken in Ireland. An obvious example is that Gaelic has a present habitual tense, which can be translated as 'do be'. 'I do be having a drink every morning' meaning 'I am in the habit of having a drink every morning'.

When this tense is assimilated, it given an obvious enrichment to the English used in Ireland. And while there are many Gaelic constructions in use, there is more to it than merely Gaelic grammar or syntax, there is a rich use of Gaelic words which add to the vocabulary. In the history of Irish writing in English there have been many authors who have enjoyed this rich exuberant language (sometimes called Hiberno-English) and they have based their work on a careful attention to it, drawing particularly on the uninhibited speech of the less well educated who were not pushed through the sieve of formal education.

Let us return to Maria Edgeworth here, who was the first writer of stature to have given us this Irish use of English. Her novel *Castle Rackrent* is related by Thady Quirk, the steward of the Rackrent family, and a glossary and an appendix are needed to explain some of the English he uses to English readers. For instance, Thady is told that Lady Rackrent is 'all kilt and smashed'. A footnote explains that kilt does not mean killed but hurt. In Ireland, she adds drily, not only cowards but the brave die many times before their death. And she adds to this in an appendix:

Our author is not here guilty of an anti-climax. The mere English reader, from a similarity of sound between the words *kilt* and *killed*, might be induced to suppose that their meanings are similar, yet they are not by any means in Ireland synonymous terms. Thus you may hear a man exclaim, 'I'm kilt and murdered?' but he frequently means only that he has received a black eye, or a slight concussion. *I'm kilt all over* means that he is in a worse state than being simply kilt. Thus, *I'm kilt with the cold* is nothing to *I'm kilt all over* with the rheumatism.

Maria loved the exuberance and exaggeration of the English used in Ireland. Here is an extract from one of her commonplace books. She sent it to Walter Scott in 1824, and told him there were things in this record that she could have made better – but did not because she respected 'the truth of nature':

A gentleman who passed through Bridge Street in Dublin on the 12th of June last after the news of Langan the boxers defeat had reached Dublin saw a crowd of people assembled, listening to a woman who stood with one arm akimbo and with her stick in the other hand struck the ground exclaiming:

'Oh Langan! Langan! Langan! Where are you now! You're Be't! you're be't—Be't by an English buck!—Well be't so ye are and kicked—Och! that ever I should see this day!—That Paddy's land should ever see this day!—To see the shamrock trodden under *fut* (foot) by an English buck!—But the devil mend ye!—

Oh Donolly Donolly! Sweet Dan Donolly! It's you that could fight your way like a jantleman, so you could—You never was be't, but you came home with your victories to die dacent in Paddy's land. My *darlent* (darling) you was!—I'll drink your health as long as I live so I will—and who dares say I wont.

Is it not a poor thing that I should lose my whole estate upon you Langan?—Isn't it a pretty way I am in?—I lost my estate and I must give up my six horses, and my coach to the back of that and all for you! you! YOU-Y-Spalpeen-you!—But it's not for the estate, nor for the horses, nor for the coach I'm grieving, but O it's the shame!—it's the shame!—it's the shame!—Please God I might recover the estate, but I never can recover the shame! the shame! the SHAME!—

They say you fought like a man but they lie—I say you sold yourself and your country but no matter!—Some tells me you ran away to Warwig (Warwick)—Some tells me you wouldn't fight—Some tells me you are dead—Some tells me you are sick and took physic and were blistered and plaistered—and others tells me ... I don't know what to b'live—I don't know *what* to believe—I don't know what to believe!—Och that Paddy's land should ever see this day! ...

If you do come itself you must cross the say (sea)—and if you do cross the sea you must come in some sort of a ship and if you do get into a ship I'll curse that ship, and it shall never reach Paddy's land!—

Having said this the woman thumped her stick upon the flag with great emphasis—then walked off in a leisurely dignified manner—A little chimney sweeper met her—as she passed along she looked calmly at him and said 'Get out of my way my little flour merchant' and so walked on.

This delight in Irish rhetoric was also shown in the *Essay on Irish Bulls* which Maria wrote jointly with her father, notably the chapter on the Dublin shoeblack, on trial for his life after a quarrel at pitch-and-toss which ended in his stabbing another shoeblack with a knife, stamped near the hilt by the name of its maker Lamprey. Here is his account of the action:

'Why, my lard, as I was going past the Royal Exchange I meets Billy. "Billy", says I, "will you sky a copper?" "Done", says he, "Done", says I; and done and done's enough between two jantlemen. With that I ranged them fair and even with my hook-em-snivey—up they go. "Music!" says he, "Skulls!" says I; and down they come three brown mazards. "By the holy! you fles'd em" says he. "You lie", says I. With that he ups with a lump of a two year old, and lets drive at me. I outs with my bread-earner, and gives it him up to Lamprey in the bread-basket'.

Maria then explains the language to the English reader with dry ironic wit.

We find her treatment echoed in later writers. William Carleton's novels, his *Traits and Stories of the Irish Peasantry*, catch the quality of country speech in nineteenth century Ireland, with all its powerful rhetoric, the vigorous extravagance of language that could turn crime into heroism. This was what Synge did later, for his play, *The Playboy of the Western World*, shows us how Christy Mahon eventually becomes the creature of his own exuberant language. In this tragi-comedy there is a vast difference between the poetic image, the idealism, of Christy's language and the reality of life; and this is emphasised by the widow Quin's reply to him, as she insists on the realities of life:

Arn't I after seeing the love-light of the star of knowledge shining from her brow, and hearing words would put you thinking on the Holy Brigid speaking to the infant saints, and now she'll be turning again, and speaking hard words to me, like an old woman with a spavindy ass she'd have, urging it on a hill.
WIDOW QUIN: There's pretty talk for a girl you'd see itching and scratching and she with a stale stink of poteen on her from selling in the shop.

Christy, shy and dumb, blossoms into an apparent hero. He

thinks he has killed his father, and he has run away, only to be greeted with respect:

CHRISTY: It's great luck and company I've won true in the end of time—two fine women fighting for the likes of me—till I'm thinking this night wasn't I a foolish fellow not to kill my father in the years gone by.

The language expands, his description of killing his father assumes heroic proportions; next he falls in love with Pegeen, who betrays him once it is discovered that he didn't kill his father. Then, ironically, he becomes heroic in defying his opponents. The story is comic. The language develops. Violence can be condoned because of it. For instance, here is Christy's account:

CHRISTY: I first riz the loy and let fall the edge of it on the ridge of his skull, and he went down at my feet an empty sack, and never let a grunt or groan from him at all.

Later he enjoys elaborating the sardonic element in his story

CHRISTY: Then I turned around with my back to the north, and I hit a blow on the ridge of his skull, laid him stretched out, and he split to the knob of his gullet.

This is the use of Hiberno-English for comedy. It can be equally effective in tragedy. In the novel Carleton's *The Black Prophet* has a sombre use of it. Synge uses it to give tragic effect in *Riders to the Sea*. In Sean O'Casey's tragi-comedies it conveys notably the suffering which war, especially civil war, brings to women.

O'Casey used his language very flexibly. In his autobiographical writing it can vary between the extremes of poetry and the prose of good conversation. And to make one's writing sound like talk has been a test of good prose since the early days of the Royal Society which in the seventeenth century enacted a close, naked prose from its members. And how many Irish writers have captured it. The talk in Charles Lever's exuberant, early novels *Harry Lorrequer* and *Charles O'Malley* is good, but the more reflective prose of his serious, sombre novels such as *Sir Brooke Fossbrooke* and *Lord Kilgobbin*—which explored the coming downfall of the Anglo-Irish as a landowning aristocracy—is better, just as the comic conversations created by Somerville and Ross are well created in their *Irish RM* stories set in West Cork, but the unfolding of tragedy in their great novel

*The Real Charlotte* is even better. This range of speech was there in George Moore, along with a capacity to talk to his reader, such as was possessed by Oliver Gogarty, one of Dublin's better wits and an excellent minor poet. It is indeed obviously necessary in drama, and is there in the surely-handled well-made light comedies of Lennox Robinson, the no less effective satiric comedies of Denis Johnston, or the evocative comedies of Brian Friel. Brendan Behan's effervescent rhodomontade or Samuel Beckett's astringent negativity contain the same potentially explosive mixture of words.

How can one bring such a rich variety of talent into the order of history? The question of subject matter may help. For instance, there is a *genre* of writing which explores childhood, where many writers have shown their capacity to remember, to encapsulate, to communicate the joys and sorrows of childhood. And we can see a continuation of those Gaelic complexitites of rhyme and rhythm first captured in the nineteenth century by Moore, Davis, Mangan and Ferguson handled with sureness and skill in more recent times by the poet Austin Clarke; overshadowed by Yeats in his early and middle years, Clarke's music suddenly achieved remarkable power in his old age. Or we could look at the short story, so well handled by Carleton and George Moore, where the form necessarily imposes constraints, with great advantage, in the case of, say, such authors as James Stephens, Lord Dunsany, Frank O'Connor, Sean O'Faolain, Mary Lavin, and William Trevor all of whom have been able to capture a mood and yet transcend the short limit of a story's length, by their use of dialogue to extend the characters' immediate situations into prospects of their lives and the human issues these raise.

Talk, then, good talk, is a feature of Anglo-Irish writing. We remember how Swift had the proofs of his writings read out to his servants and until he was satisfied they fully understood what he had written he did not pass them for press. This emphasis, this insistence upon clarity, upon the good manners of direct speech, of clear communication is there always. The Anglo-Irish writer is aware of his audience: and so good talk can range from the intensity of Swift's ironic anger through the sheer fun of Farquhar's comedies, from the benevolence of Bishop Berkeley's idealism to the sparkle of Sheridan's speeches, from the passion of John Mitchel to the paradoxes of Shaw, from the wit of Wilde's comedies to the elegance of Elizabeth Bowen's novels, from Patrick Kavanagh's forlorn

*Tarry Flynn* to Kinsella's heroic translation of the *Tain*. And there is the superb fantasy; reaching back to the grotesque exhuberance of Brian Merryman is the equally amazing crazy invention, the learning, the Dubliners' talk of Brian O'Nolan who, as Flann O'Brien, wrote *At Swim-Two-Birds*. Talk is a constant feature of Irish life—the inheritance, perhaps, from a past where words were the cheapest form of entertainment, an essential ingredient of life. The exhilarating talk still goes on; it is what attracts tourists to the Dublin pubs or anywhere in the countryside.

There is another thing about Anglo-Irish writing that keeps coming to mind: the fact that so many of these writers have sought to capture the visual effects of that Irish countryside. Changeable, yet constant, it is there in the unexpected as well as the obvious places, in Maturin's minatures of the rain falling on the flat midland plains just as in Joyce's evocation of the snow falling on the dark waves of the Shannon, in the botanical yet atmospheric accuracy of Emily Lawless as in her novel *Hurrish* she describes the Burren, that limestone area of miraculous beauty in Clare, as in Yeats's simple description of his tower in Galway:

> An ancient bridge, and a more ancient tower
> A farmhouse that is sheltered by its wall,
> An acre of stony ground
> Where the symbolic rose can break in flower,
> Old ragged elms, old thorns innumerable,
> The sound of the rain or sound
> Of every wind that blows,
> The stilted water-hen
> Crossing stream again
> Scared by the splashing of a dozen cows ...

Everyone will have their favourite descriptions—such as George Moore's ebullient capture of the nuances of a spring day in *The Lake*, or Joyce's Dublin day of dappled seaborne clouds in *A Portrait of the Artist* or the detailed, loving description of a lake by Somerville and Ross in *The Real Charlotte* or the vignettes of the river in Michael Farrell's moving posthumous novel *Thy Tears May Cease*, or, my own particular delight, Joyce Cary's Donegal day in *A House of Children* with all its evocation of a holiday homecoming:

My memories are full of enormous skies, as bright as water, in which clouds sailed bigger than any others; fleets of monsters moving in one vast school up from the horizon and over my head, a million miles up, as it seemed to me, and then down again over the far-off mountains of Derry. They seemed to follow a curving surface of air concentric with the curve of the Atlantic which I could see bending down on either hand, a bow, which, even as a child of three or four, I knew to be the actual shape of the earth. Some grown-up, perhaps my father, had printed that upon my imagination, so that even while I was playing some childish game in the heather, red Indians or Eskimos, if I caught sight of the ocean with the tail of my eye, I would feel suddenly the roundness and independence of the world beneath me. I would feel it like a ship under my feet moving through air just like a larger stiffer cloud, and this gave me an extraordinary exhilaration.

We travelled through this enormous and magnificent scene in tranquil happiness. We were tired from running about in the heather and already growing hungry we felt the nearness of supper, and bed, with the calm faith which belongs only to children and saints devoted to the love of God and sure of the delights of communing with him. In that faith, that certainty of coming joys, we existed in a contentment so profound that it was like a lazy kind of drunkenness. I can't count how many times I enjoyed that sense, riding in a sidecar whose swaying motion would have put me to sleep if I had not been obliged to hold on; so that while my body and head and legs were all swinging together in a half dream, my hand tightly clutched some other child's body; and the memory of bathing, shouting, tea, the blue smoke of picnic fires, was mixed with the dark evening clouds shaped like flying geese, the tall water stretching up to the top of the world, the mountains sinking into darkness like whales into the ocean and over all a sky so deep that the stars, faint green sparks, seemed lost in it and the very sense of it made the heart light and proud like a bird.

With such a description echoing in the mind fresh names crowd in immediately—of the contemporary poets who, too have captured the essence of country life, the inner climate of the mind: Seamus Heaney, John Montague, Thomas Kinsella, Richard Murphy, Brendan Kennelly. And the names of contemporary novelists occur: William Trevor, James Plunkett, Brian Moore, Francis Stuart ... contemporary writers, living, most of them, in a civilised country where writers don't pay income tax. But where should a history of a literature which is still being successfully written stop? If Swift began it, with anti-colonial writing, perhaps it should stop at 1922. That was when the 26 counties of Southern Ireland became governed by their own parliament in Dublin again. Those born after that date are, surely, Irish writers, writers no longer torn between the old pulls of English and Irish culture and history; and so the history of Anglo-Irish writing may end at that point. It's an artificial name really—why not simply call them all Irish writers? Their variety is vast, their religious and political allegiances diverse, their moods varied, changeable as the Irish skies. But their achievement is fixed in print, although we might leave James Stephens, himself a great talker, the last word. 'We write', he said, 'as well as we can, but we can never write as well as we talk'.

# LOUIS MACNEICE: AN IRISH OUTSTIDER

BRENDAN KENNELLY

> I was born in Belfast between the mountain and the gantries
> To the hooting of lost sirens and the clang of trams:
> Thence to Smoky Carrick in County Antrim
> Where the bottle-neck harbour collects the mud which jams
>
> The little boats beneath the Norman castle,
> The pier shining with lumps of crystal salt;
> The Scotch Quarter was a line of residential houses
> But the Irish Quarter was a slum for the blind and halt ...
>
> I was the rector's son, born to the anglican order,
> Banned for ever from the candles of the Irish poor;
> The Chichesters knelt in marble at the end of a transept
> With ruffs about their necks, their portion sure ...

These lines from his poem 'Carrickfergus' show that Louis MacNeice felt that in Ireland he was an outsider from birth. He was 'Banned for ever from the candles of the Irish poor'. Sean O'Casey knew poverty from his earliest days in the slums of Dublin; Patrick Kavanagh knew poverty in Monaghan and later in Dublin; and Austin Clarke wrote many poems about poverty, though his view of it tends to be that of a middle-class spectator. Yet, in their different styles, and with varying degrees of imaginative intensity, these three writers were involved in Irish society in ways that Louis MacNeice somehow never quite managed, or perhaps wished, to be. He remained an outsider to that world of seething deprivation, riotous squalor and articulate resentment so intrepidly explored by O'Casey, Kavanagh, Clarke and others. And this sense of being an outsider in Ireland is, in a deeper sense, characteristic of what we may call MacNeice's spiritual life, his developed stance as a poet. All through his poetry we encounter a man who doesn't really seem to belong anywhere, except perhaps in the fertile, mysterious, consoling and challenging land of language itself, where every fresh discovery is inextricably bound up with a new mystery. Yet even there, where a poet might reasonably be expected to feel unreasonably at home, the recurring doubts and uncertainties gnaw away at his mind and imagination. MacNeice is one of the most intelligent of all Irish poets; he is also, in his work, one of the loneliest. And he has, apart from a few loyal followers among the poets of Ulster, such as Longley, Mahon, Heaney, Ormsby, Hewitt and Muldoon, as well as the distinguished critics, Terence Brown and Edna Longley, been largely ignored in Ireland, particularly in the Republic. He is still the outsider, still 'banned', not only from the 'Irish poor', but from the anthologies which help to educate the vast majority of Irish children. It is a shame, because MacNeice is an excellent poet, a skilful craftsman, a shrewd critic of both literature and society, a thinker who makes complex thoughts lucid and shapely, a considerable dramatist, a disciplined classicist, an assured translator and an attractive personality. He achieved all this while remaining a loner. Even his early education in England helped to put him firmly in this position. Here is a moving picture of the Irish boy in that state of sophisticated exile from which he never really returned.

> I went to school in Dorset, the world of parents
> Contracted into a puppet world of sons
> Far from the mill girls, the smell of porter, the salt-mines
> And the soldiers with their guns.

To some extent, every poet is an outsider, almost by definition. But it is also true to say that many poets believe they have an audience, however reserved or limited, of their own, a coherent and patient community of sympathetic listeners. This kind of audience helps to deepen and direct a poet's imaginative energy. Kavanagh said, 'I have my friends, my people'. Yeats's poetry pre-supposes a chosen, gifted, discriminating audience. Even the hermetic Austin Clarke, labouring away in the satirical solitude of a Dublin suburb, could count on a ready audience to snap up his stinging limited editions. These poets, and many others, find their audience to a considerable extent, though by no means completely, in the Irish capital, Dublin. (When I use the term 'audience', I am not referring merely to University students of literature whose reasons for reading poetry sometimes have precious little to do with love of the thing). Yeats may have scoffed at 'the daily spite of this unmannerly town'; the same town was 'malignant Dublin' to Kavanagh; and Clarke never ceased to satirise various aspects of Dublin life. But nevertheless, all three poets were *listened to* in Dublin; and all three derived a paradoxical sustenance from the city they castigated. They learned to thrive on enmity, to flourish in a climate of spontaneous envy and disparagement. But Dublin did not listen to MacNeice; it still doesn't. And MacNeice knew it. His poem 'Dublin' acknowledges the fact that Ireland's capital city will not have him 'alive or dead'. Despite this, however, or perhaps because of it, MacNeice has a certain detached affection, the casual, steady, isolated sympathy of the outsider, for the city of Yeats, Joyce, O'Casey, Clarke—the city that ignores him. The following lines are not only an eloquent description of Dublin; they are also a revelation of MacNeice's poetic position. In MacNeice's case, description is self-revelation.

> This was never my town,
> I was not born nor bred
> Nor schooled here and she will not
> Have me alive or dead
> But yet she holds my mind
> With her seedy elegance,
> With her gentle veils of rain
> And all her ghosts that walk
> And all that hide behind
> Her Georgian facades—
> The catcalls and the pain,
> The glamour of her squalor,
> The bravado of her talk.
>
> The lights jig in the river
> With a concertina movement
> And the sun comes up in the morning
> Like barley-sugar on the water
> And the mist on the Wicklow hills
> Is close, as close
> As the peasantry were to the landlord,
> As the Irish to the Anglo-Irish,
> As the killer is close one moment
> To the man he kills,
> Or as the moment itself
> Is close to the next moment.
>
> She is not an Irish town
> And she is not English,
> Historic with guns and vermin
> And the cold renown

Of a fragment of Church latin,
Of an oratorical phrase.
But O the days are soft,
Soft enough to forget
The lesson better learnt,
The bullet on the wet
Streets, the crooked deal,
The steel behind the laugh,
The Four Courts burnt.

Fort of the Dane,
Garrison of the Saxon,
Augustan capital
Of a Gaelic nation,
Appropriating all
The alien brought,
You give me time for thought
And by a juggler's trick
You poise the toppling hour—
O greyness run to flower,
Grey stone, grey water
And brick upon grey brick.

'She will not have me alive or dead'. MacNeice might have
made the same charge against many Irish poets and critics. And
yet this being ignored may have goaded MacNeice into
contemplation, into trying to see exactly what had helped to
shape him as a poet. He learned to look clearly and critically at
himself; and he achieved the hard lucidity of the loner. He
writes:

Speaking for myself, I should say that the following things, among
others, had conditioned my poetry—having been brought up in the
North of Ireland, having a father who was a clergyman; the fact that
my mother died when I was little; repression from the age of six to
nine; inferiority complex on grounds of physique and class-conscious-
ness; lack of a social life until I was grown up; late puberty; ignorance
of music (which could have been a substitute for poetry); inability to
ride horses or practise successfully most of the sports which satisfy a
sense of rhythm; an adolescent liking for the role of 'enfant terrible';
a liking (now dead) for metaphysics; marriage and divorce;
Birmingham; an indolent pleasure in gardens and wild landscapes; a
liking for animals; an interest in dress.

This reads like a somewhat quirky list of influences; in fact, the
influences are clearly perceived and accurately stated. One can

appreciate how his 'inferiority complex' due to 'class-conscious-
ness' may have driven him towards his interests in Communism
in the 1930s; one can see how his 'ignorance of music' may have
led him to try to create, often with startling success, a poetry
remarkable for its rich musicality, its rhythmical assurance and
subtlety: his confessed 'liking for metaphysics' helped him to
work towards a poetry that is often complex but clear in its
thoughts; the solitary name 'Birmingham' brings home to us the
fact that MacNeice celebrates and criticises the life of cities such
as London, Dublin and Belfast with rare eloquence and insight;
and even the final 'liking for animals' and 'interest in dress'
point towards a poetry involved with ordinary human activities
and feelings. MacNeice sees the poet as a spokesman for
ordinary people. He believes that poetry should always be in
touch with what he calls 'the spontaneous colouring of ordinary
speech'.

The clarity of MacNeice's self-knowledge, the precise
presentation of influences, the candid statements concerning his
views of language in poetry—all this suggests a poet who is
honest, unpretentious, undeceived, cultivated, perceptive,
relishing the activity and bustle of the ordinary world. And
MacNeice is a truly 'worldly' poet in this sense: he looks closely
at society, at people, at his roots, at his present situation, at the
complex, changing state of the world in which he has to live.
And he moves through that world on his own, alert, watchful,
scrupulously recording what he sees and feels. To this extent,
he is not a poet of the fascinating past, or the perplexing future;
he is neither conventional historian nor aspiring prophet; he is
much more the poet of the swirling, urgent present. Many Irish
poets are deeply concerned with the past, finding in Ireland's
turbulent history images and personalities that, when
dramatised and charged with imagination, help to shed light on
current problems. Here, as in so many other respects, MacNeice
is an outsider. He is a superb chronicler of the contemporary.
His most famous poem, *Autumn Journal*, is proof of this. It is a
brilliant, sweeping, comprehensive poem.

In a prefatory note to *Autumn Journal* in the 1966 edition of *The
Collected Poems of Louis MacNeice*, (a note not included in the first
edition of the book), the poet stresses that he is writing what he
calls a 'Journal', and adds that 'In a journal or a personal letter
a man writes what he feels at the moment; to attempt scientific
truthfulness would be, paradoxically, dishonest ... It is the
nature of this poem to be neither final nor balanced ... Poetry

in my opinion must be honest before anything else and I refuse
to be "objective" or clear-cut at the cost of honesty'.

That, briefly, is a statement of the poet of conscience refusing
to surrender to the aesthetic stylist in himself. This is the logic
of MacNeice's position as an outsider. He clings to his
individual moral honesty with an unrelenting grip even as he is
deeply aware of its artistic limitations and defects. He knows
that there are overstatements and inconsistencies in his poem;
but he leaves them there, in their earned place in the work,
because they are valid aspects of his vision of contemporary
reality. The poem was written between August 1938 and early
1939; and it is steeped in a grim awareness of the coming war.
In the midst of this awareness, MacNeice turns, significantly, to
Ireland and broods, with the peculiar intensity of the outsider
he is, on the violence and lunacy of the land of his birth. Even
though this passage was written in a way which, according to
MacNeice himself, was neither 'final nor balanced', the picture
of violence, futility, self-deception, prejudice and chronic
unemployment is as true in the eighties as when MacNeice
wrote it in the thirties. Because MacNeice honestly describes
contemporary Ireland, he is hair-raisingly pertinent half-a-
century later. It may be that if a poet has the courage to be
passionately true to the passing moment he will be true to all
time.

> Who do we like being Irish? Partly because
> It gives us a hold on the sentimental English
> As members of a world that never was,
> Baptised with fairy water;
> And partly because Ireland is small enough
> To be still thought of with a family feeling,
> And because the waves are rough
> That split her from a more commercial culture;
> And because one feels that here at least one can
> Do local work which is not at the world's mercy
> And that on this tiny stage with luck a man
> Might see the end of one particular action.
> It is self-deception of course;
> There is no immunity in this island either;
> A cart that is drawn by somebody else's horse
> And carrying goods to somebody else's market.
> The bombs in the turnip sack, the sniper from the roof,
> Griffith, Connolly, Collins, where have they brought us?
> Ourselves alone! Let the round tower stand aloof
> In a world of bursting mortar!

Let the school-children fumble their sums
In a half-dead language;
Let the censor be busy on the books; pull down the
    Georgian slums;
Let the games be played in Gaelic.
Let them grow beet-sugar; let them build
A factory in every hamlet;
Let them pigeon-hole the souls of the killed
Into sheep and goats, patriots and traitors.
And the North, where I was a boy,
Is still the North, veneered with the grime of Glasgow,
Thousands of men whom nobody will employ
Standing at the corners, coughing.

All through *Autumn Journal*, we feel the impact of MacNeice's compulsive honesty. The poem has all the excitement of a long, detailed, lively letter from a friend whose thoughts are worthy of respect and whose perceptions are unfailingly stimulating. Excessive self-consciousness in poetry frequently has a deadening effect on the poem's language because the tone tends to become portentous, laboured and self-important. But MacNeice, reaching for the vitality inherent in 'the spontaneous colouring of ordinary speech', and determined to speak to his reader as if he were writing him a spontaneous letter, creates a poetry that is natural, chatty and gripping. Themes of extraordinary importance fill the day's ordinary talk.

To-day was a beautiful day, the sky was a brilliant
Blue for the first time for weeks and weeks
But posters flapping on the railings tell the fluttered
World that Hitler speaks, that Hitler speaks
And we cannot take it in and we go to our daily
Jobs to the dull refrain of the caption 'War'
Buzzing around us as from hidden insects
And we think 'This must be wrong, it has happened before,
Just like this before, we must be dreaming;
It was long ago these flies
Buzzed like this, so why are they still bombarding
The ears if not the eyes?'
And we laugh it off and go round town in the evening
And this, we say, is on me;
Something out of the usual, a Pimm's Number One, a Picon—
But did you see
The latest?

Inevitably, this deliberate chattiness leads to weaknesses in the poem. Just as diaries, journals and personal letters are often a mixture of the trivial and the serious, the irrelevant and the significant, so *Autumn Journal* contains lines, even whole passages, which add little or nothing to the poem as a whole. But this, as already stated, was deliberate on MacNeice's part. These lines and passages, therefore, are most fairly criticised when seen in the context of a flawed, conscious design, and not as weak or slight moments of which the poet is unaware.

MacNeice's stubborn honesty helps to account for his strengths and weaknesses as a poet. He is a celebrant and critic of urban life; he has, therefore, a keen eye for the characters that abound in cities (see 'The Mixer', for example, in which he effectively compares a man to a Latin word, 'often spoken but no longer heard'); he has a profound respect for the integrity of the individual and a vehement hatred for the forces which violate that respect (see 'Prayer Before Birth'); his exploration of time concentrates, for the most part, on the present so that even his most personal poetry, his love-poetry, for example, deals with the present fleetingness, or the fleeting presence of love. Paradoxically, this concentration on the present moment seems to rid him (for the moment) of the burden of time:

> Time was away and somewhere else,
> There were two glasses and two chairs
> And two people with the one pulse
> (Somebody stopped the moving stairs):
> Time was away and somewhere else...
>
> Time was away and she was here
> And life no longer what it was,
> The bell was silent in the air
> And all the room one glow because
> Time was away and she was here.

MacNeice's love-poems are among his best. The more one reads them, the more haunting they become.

These are some of MacNeice's strong points as a poet. If one must point to a weakness in his work, one must concede, I think, that it is closely connected with his concept of the poet as spokesman. Many of MacNeice's poems have a kind of sophisticated literalness which tends to limit his work to one meaning, to deny it the musical, mysterious echoes and reverberations one finds in Blake and Yeats, for example. And since this is a direct consequence of MacNeice's determination to be 'honest', it may be more accurate to describe this 'weakness' in his work as the inevitable limitation of his strength, the necessary consequence of the flaw in his declared artistic intention.

As the years went by, MacNeice became increasingly conscious of this limitation. Accompanying his dissatisfaction with the literal utterance is a growing longing for a symbolic one. The poet is not only a spokesman; he is also an explorer. He is not only a representative voice; he is also a medium for many voices. His job is to find a style and a method that will do justice to all these functions. MacNeice, while retaining his basic view of the poet as spokesman, ('I have grouped the poet with ordinary men and opposed him to the mystic proper. I do not withdraw from this position'), becomes increasingly aware of the fact that language itself is symbolic and will not, when imaginatively handled, permit itself to be restricted to mere literalism. Writing about characters, situations and occurrences in fiction, MacNeice says that 'these, if they are recognised at all by the reader as having anything to do with his own experience (and I take "experience" here to include potential experience), will at once acquire a wider reference. They will stand for something not themselves; in other words, they will be symbols'.

In his later poetry, MacNeice moves more and more deeply into a symbolic richness and resonance. I shall give one example; it is 'Charon', a late poem. Here the literal is enriched by the mythological; the poem is rooted in concrete reality but it also suggests strange worlds, mysterious possibilities. London and the Thames mingle with Virgil and Dante. Charon, son of Erebus (Darkness) and Nyx (Night), ferries the dead across the river Styx to their final abode in Hades. Here we find MacNeice writing from a very deep level of his being; he is no longer a mere spokesman for others; he is exploring the dark underworld of his mortal self. Perhaps the irony of all this is that the poet who writes uncompromisingly of his own experience, in this symbolic way, becomes in the end a more enduring spokesman for others than the poet who consciously tries to speak on behalf of others. MacNeice's poetic self included both kinds of poet; or rather, the literalist was forced, or forced himself to become a symbolist; reluctantly, the symbolist emerged as the one capable of the more complex utterance. I am not suggesting a poetic schizophrenia in MacNeice; I am talking about a slow development. Here is the poem, 'Charon'. It presents MacNeice the outsider at his most lonely and compelling.

The conductor's hands were black with money:
Hold on to your ticket, he said, the inspector's
Mind is black with suspicion, and hold on to
That dissolving map. We moved through London,
We could see the pigeons through the glass but failed
To hear their rumours of wars, we could see
The lost dog barking but never knew
That his bark was as shrill as a cock crowing,
We just jogged on, at each request
Stop there was a crowd of aggressively vacant
Faces, we just jogged on, eternity
Gave itself airs in revolving lights
And then we came to the Thames and all
The bridges were down, the further shore
Was lost in fog, so we asked the conductor
What we should do. He said: Take the ferry
Faute de mieux. We flicked the flashlight
And there was the ferryman just as Virgil
And Dante had seen him. He looked at us coldly
And his eyes were dead and his hands on the oar
Were black with obols and varicose veins
Marbled his calves and he said to us coldly:
If you want to die you will have to pay for it.

MacNeice's *Collected Poems* comprise almost six hundred pages of skilled, musical and immensely enjoyable poetry. It may well be that his very honesty led him to become the outsider he remained to the end. One thing is certain though: he deserves a more attentive, critical readership. To read through his published poems is to encounter a voice speaking for intelligent, questing, somewhat bewildered people in our modern world that remains unquestionably wonderful and is increasingly threatened.

# BRIAN FRIEL'S *FAITH HEALER*

DECLAN KIBERD

*Faith Healer* by Brian Friel may well be the finest play to come out of Ireland since J.M. Synge's *Playboy of the Western World*. It is also, without a doubt, one of the most derivative works of art to be produced in Ireland this century—and this gives rise to a question. How can a play which is indebted so heavily to a number of previous works be nevertheless a work of profound and scintillating originality? And how can a play consisting of four separate monologues by characters who never openly confront each other be a fully *dramatic* work, in any real sense of that word?

We should first consider Friel's debts. *Faith Healer* might be called an intergeneric work where the forms of novel and drama meet, for it is a kind of dramatised novel. The idea of four contradictory monologues may have come to Friel from a reading of William Faulkner's most famous novel *The Sound and the Fury*. The method is identical, even down to the detail of having one of the monologues narrated by a witness of unstable mind, in Faulkner the lunatic Benjy, in Friel the shattered and suicidal Grace Hardy. This attempt to take an outstanding device of the modern novel, and redeploy it in the dramatic form is a characteristic modernist strategy, for modernism loves to mix genres—one thinks of Eliot's fusion of drama and poetry, Joyce's use of drama in the middle of *Ulysses*, Flann O'Brien's crazy blend of cowboy tale and Celtic lore in *At Swim-Two-Birds*. Although Faulkner's novel and Friel's play both challenge the audience to judge for itself the inconsistencies between the various monologues there is one crucial difference. The novel can be reread, the play cannot be rerun to some point of contention. To that extent, the dramatic form is even more baffling and unsettling in its effect on its audience.

Friel's other debt is even more striking. *Faith Healer* is clearly a remoulding of the legend of Deirdre of the Sorrows, a tale which has been dramatised by many leading Irish writers

from George Russell to W. B. Yeats, from J. M. Synge to James
Stephens. The idea of a well-brought-up girl, destined for a
noble calling in the north of Ireland, but spirited away to
Scotland by an attractive but feckless man, to the great dismay
of an elderly guardian—that, in a nutshell, is the plot of both
Friel's and Synge's plays. In Scotland, the lovers live well
enough for many years, supported by their manager Teddy,
who discharges the same role in *Faith Healer* as that played by
Naisi's brothers, Ainnle and Ardan, in Synge's play.
Ultimately, however, their nomadic and rootless life is felt to be
increasingly hollow and stressful. With some foreboding, they
decide to return to Ireland, but in their nervousness and appre-
hensiveness, each lover attributes the decision to the other.
Their worst fears are realised on arrival in Ireland. As Francis
Hardy says: 'there was no sense of homecoming',[1] or as Synge's
Naisi says, looking at the shabby rooms and open grave, which
the King offers by way of greeting: 'And that'll be our home in
Emain'?[2] Earlier, he gloomily remarks that 'it's little we want
with state or rich rooms or curtains, when we're used to the
ferns only, and cold streams and they making a stir'[3] —a sentence which could just as aptly describe the raw, open-air life of
Francis, Grace and Teddy camping out by the fields and streams
of Scotland.

One of the great themes of Synge's play and of the original
Gaelic legend is Deirdre's love of place. Before her final
departure from Scotland, she lists the names of all the
abandoned places with tender care. So it is with her laments for
Glen Ruadh, Glen Laid, the Woods of Cuan and so on in
Synge's play. In one of his less well-known essays on 'The
People of the Glens', Synge had remarked on the 'curiously
melodious names' to be found in Wicklow—Aughavanna,
Glenmalure, Annamoe[4] —and he built lilting lists of the names
into his Wicklow plays. Friel self-consciously builds on the
ancient Gaelic tradition in those passages where Francis and
Grace recite the Scottish place-names, as the Faith Healer says,
'just for the mesmerism, the sedation, of the incantation'.[5] This
is an ancient Gaelic device redeployed by Seamus Heaney, for
example in poems such as 'The Tollund Man':

> Something of his sad freedom
> As he rode the tumbril
> Should come to me, driving,
> Saying the names

Tollund, Grabaulle, Nebelgard,
Watching the pointing hands
Of country people,
Not knowing their tongue.[6]

What is revealing in Friel's play, however, is the fact that Grace fouls up the order of her husband's incantation. She omits his third line from the list and, at the end of her monologue, is so distraught that she cannot get beyond the opening lines:

Aberarder, Kinlochbervie,
Aberayron, Kinlochbervie,
Invergordon, Kinlochbervie...in Sutherland, in
the north of Scotland...[7]

She trails off helplessly and this linguistic failure is the sure sign of her imminent collapse.

In *Faith Healer*, as in the Deirdre legend, the lovers return to Ireland with the premonition that it will be a return to disaster and even death for the hero. And this is what happens. Only at the very end does Friel depart radically from Synge's plot. Whereas Synge's Deirdre dies soon after Naisi in the romantic medieval versions, Friel follows the more hard-edged Old Irish rendition by having her live on for a year in misery, before her eventual suicide.

Wherein, it might therefore be asked, does the originality of *Faith Healer* lie? One could answer by saying that the notion of the artist as inspired con-man is one of Friel's innermost themes and that all those debts to previous works and authors raise the whole question of the artist as con-man in our minds. So the play turns out to be about itself, since it, like its central character, veers between conmanship and brilliant innovation. The artist is like the Faith Healer, a man who never knows for certain whether he has been successful in bringing off an effect, a broker in risk who must stand before the audience nightly with no assurance that his magic will rub off on others yet again. Moreover, like the Faith Healer, the artist knows that if he gives free rein to his own self-doubts, the gift may desert him. Too anxious a self-scrutiny may kill the very gift which the analysis is supposed to illuminate. This is a truth even more obvious to the manager Teddy than it is to the healer himself. In his contrast between two performing dogs, Teddy illustrates for us the sense in which the artist has to be a con-man; one dog, sensitive and resourceful, could switch on the fire, pull the curtains and leave the master's slippers by the chair, but in front of an audience she went to pieces. The other dog hadn't the brains to learn his own name, but could perform to perfection on the bagpipes for any given audience. Teddy also cites the case of the brainless Miss Mulatto who could talk to one hundred and twenty pigeons in different languages, yet never know how she did it—she just made sounds. This leads Teddy to conclude that artists must not only have talent and ambition, but that they must also have no critical self-consciousness about their gift:

They know they have something fantastic, sure, they're not that stupid. But what it is they have, how they do it, how it works, what that sensational talent is, what it all means—believe me, they don't know and they don't care and even if they did care they haven't the brains to analyse it. [8]

So the first audience the artist must con is himself. He must still those impulses to self-doubt and self-questioning which erupt in him from time to time. 'Francis Hardy, Faith Healer, One Night Only'[9] says the tattered poster. Hardy knows that that 'one night only' suggests the touch of the charlatan, the poseur who will not stay around to face the consequences of his own claims or the critical response to his performance. At times, he sees himself possessed of an awesome gift; on other occasions, a mere trickster—but there were moments, he still insists, when the gift *did* work.

When Francis Hardy talks about his gift, he sounds remarkably like Seamus Heaney discussing his involvement with poetry. 'How did I get involved? As a young man I chanced to flirt with it and it possessed me. No, no, no, no, no,—that's rhetoric'.[10] This seems close to Heaney's quotation, that a young man dabbles in verses and finds they are his life—a remark that becomes even more interesting when Heaney himself points out that it was Patrick Kavanagh who originally made it.[11] Francis Hardy claims, more humbly, that he did it because he found that he *could* do it. Heaney's account of poetry as a gift for divination is very close indeed to Francis Hardy's view of his gift. According to Heaney, divining is a gift for being in touch with what is there, hidden but real—'a gift for mediating between the latent resource and the community that wants it current and released'.[12] The water diviner resembles the poet in his function of making contact with what lies hidden. To an artist like Friel that contact may be made with further possibilities lying hidden and dormant in previous works of literature such as the Deirdre legend; but if he becomes too self-conscious about those debts, he will never create anything original, because he will have no basis on which to build. So he must ruthlessly and mindlessly assimilate whatever resources from the past may be turned to use. Heaney compares this mindless wisdom to that of a somnambulist and sees one of the great pleasures of poetry in that somnambulist process of search and surrender, like the water diviner who moves forward with eyes closed, following only the hint and tug of the wooden stick. A process as unself-conscious as this is an exercise in high risk, but to become self-analytical would be the greatest risk of all.

The artist can seldom, if ever, be his own critic. 'A poem always has elements of accident about it, which can be made the subject of inquest afterwards', commented Heaney in a radio talk, 'but there is always a risk in conducting your own inquest. You might begin to believe in the coroner in yourself, rather than put your trust in the man in you who is capable of accident'.[13] It is precisely that ailment which afflicts the Faith Healer in his final days, as he comes to believe even more in the coroner of certainties than in the creator of risks. His first monologue is far too self-analytical for his own good as an artist:

Was it all change?—or skill?—or illusion?—or delusion? Precisely what power did I possess? Could I summon it? When and how? Was I its servant? Did it reside in my ability to invest someone with faith in me or did I evoke from him a healing faith in himself? Could my healing be effected without faith? But faith in what?—in me?—in the possibility?—faith in faith? And is the power diminishing? You're beginning to masquerade, aren't you? You're becoming a husk, aren't you? ...[14]

By Hardy's second soliloquy we realise that he is in fact speaking from the dead—a device appropriate enough for a man who is indeed his own coroner. Moreover, it is clear that he has returned to Ireland and to Donegal deliberately to seek out this death, because he can no longer bear the high-risk tensions of life as an artist, the uncertainty of a life spent hovering between mastery and humiliation, the uncertainty which is the true source of his mastery just as it is the inevitable prelude to his failure.

Hardy steps before us out of the darkness and into a ray of light at the beginning of the play, and recedes into the black at the end. This light/dark strategy is identical to that employed by Beckett in many dramas. Beckett explains it as a metaphysics of risk:

If life and death did not present themselves to us, there would be no inscrutability. If there were only darkness, all would be clear. It is because there is not only darkness but also light that our situation becomes inexplicable. Take Augustine's doctrine of grace given and grace withheld ... in the classical drama, such problems do not arise. The destiny of Racine's *Phèdre* is sealed from the beginning: she will proceed into the dark. As she goes, she herself will be illuminated. At the beginning of the play she has partial illumination and at the end she has complete illumination, but there has been no question but that she moves towards the dark. That is the play. Within this notion, clarity is possible, but for us who are neither Greek nor Jansenist there is no such clarity. The question would also be removed if we believed in the contrary—total salvation. But where we have both dark and light we also have the inexplicable. The key word in my plays is 'perhaps'.[15]

Beckett's plays are poignant satires on those still foolish enough to seek for signs and certainties—on critics—and a celebration of the random and chancy—of artists. Friel takes up where Beckett leaves off and in *Faith Healer* he depicts that lust for certainty as the last infirmity of the bourgeois mind. This is pictured most satirically in Grace's account of the fearful symmetry of her family home, with its Japanese gardens, straight avenues and ordered poplars. This haven of order she abandons for a life of risk which will lead finally to her self-destruction. Her sedate solicitor-father is merely an extreme example of that rage for order which dominates most of the characters in the play. The patients who come to Hardy's performances come in search of certainty even more than a cure. In a perverse kind of way, they come to be cured of uncertainty even more than to be cured of disease. Francis Hardy understands this well:

...by coming to me they exposed, publicly acknowledged, their desperation. And even though they told themselves they were here because of the remote possibility of a cure, they knew in their hearts they had come not to be cured but for the confirmation that they were incurable; not in hope but for the elimination of hope; for the removal of that final, impossible change—that's why they came—to seal their anguish, for the content of a finality.

And they knew that I knew. And so they defied me to endow them with hopelessness. But I couldn't do even that for them ... Because, occasionally, just occasionally, the miracle would happen.[16]

In the end, the healer felt that it would have been a kindness not to go near them, not to unsettle them with hope. Yet he knows, too, that it is the function of art to terrify and unsettle a community, to insult even more than to flatter it, to be unlike its idea of itself. The community may hate the artist for the cruel and sharp light which he throws on reality, but it knows also that his is a necessary insult, a necessary evil. The healer recalls evenings when he could sense that there were hundreds of people holding their breath in the locality, 'waiting in the half-light'. They were people poised between the certainty of darkness and the certainty of light, anxiously waiting to see what would happen to those audacious enough to attend the healer's meeting, intrepid legates on behalf of those too timid to look into the artist's face and handiwork. 'And sometimes I got the impression, too, that if we hadn't come to them, they would have sought us out'.[17] So the community assaults and finally slays the artist, whose ministry it nevertheless finds essential to its well-being.

The healer can sense the poignancy of those people's search for certainty, precisely because he can feel that yearning so deeply in himself. If safe, settled folk can feel that need, then how much more will he whose life is lived on a knife-edge of risk and somnambulist groping. At the end, the broker in risk runs out of courage and decides to cash his chips in return for a racing certainty. So, in his last days, as his con-man's courage dissolves, he lacerates himself with self-doubt and deliberately seeks out a spectacular failure that will kindly put an end to his own slender surviving hope. What he has tried and failed to do for others, he hopes now to achieve for himself—the elimination of hope. As he walks towards the drunken men in the bleak morning light, he knows that nothing will happen except his own death and finds a strange consolation in that knowledge:

And as I moved across that yard towards them and offered myself to them, then for the first time I had a simple and genuine sense of home-coming. Then for the first time there was no atrophying terror, and the maddening questions were silent.
At long last I was renouncing chance.[18]

But for the artist *that* is the only mortal sin, and Hardy must ultimately be judged as an artist, for that is the only word which his wife can find to describe her dead lover to the doctor:

'He was an artist', I said—quickly, casually—but with complete conviction—just the way he might have said it. Wasn't that curious? Because the thought had never occurred to me before. And then because I said it and the doctor wrote it down I knew it was true.[19]

The thought strikes her almost by *accident*. Unlike her husband, who turns out in the end to be just like her orderly father, she has the courage to submit herself to chance. For her the accidental betokens a higher truth, for which she will die, rather than return to the world of bourgeois certainties which drove her mother mad. In the final scenario of his career, Hardy renounced change—and, in doing so, he degraded himself from the status of artist to that of mere performer. The artist always keeps his eye remorselessly on his subject, whereas the performer is always watching his audience. The artist risks the displeasure of his audience as he maintains a congenial relationship with his subject, whereas the performer risks the betrayal of his subject as he seeks a congenial relationship with his audience.

All through his career, up until this final night, Francis Hardy has been an artist, humble in the service of that mystery which has chosen to reveal itself through him, humble even to the point of believing that the world of family happiness and personal fulfilment is well lost for art. At the outset, he was so incorruptible that he resisted all the efforts of his manager to degrade his healing artistry to the level of mere performance, and so he resisted the use of background music. He scrupulously avoided stagey or theatrical effects, as on the night when in serene silence he cured ten in the village of Llanbethian. The garish Teddy is still amazed to recall that 'there was no shouting or cheering or dancing with joy' and 'hardly a word was spoken'.[20] He admires the professionalism of a healer to whom the only final reality was his work. But, as his confidence waned, Hardy began to rely on the fake support of background music and surrendered to the view of himself as a mere performer. On his last night, the erstwhile professional declines into an amateur magician and prostitutes his art in a cheap publicity stunt. Seeing the bent finger of a Donegal farmer, he feels certain that he can cure it and so he seeks his own fate. Up to now, he has gathered the audience, great or small, around himself, but now he goes in search of the audience's approval and esteem. He seeks the certainty of public acclaim and sees the corruption of his art into a gaudy ad-man's dream. Up to now, he had wisely allowed his gift to possess him, but now he falsely tries to possess his gift. It is, of course, unnecessary to elaborate on the appropriateness of Friel's attack on art-as-mere-entertainment in what is his most complex and under-rated play.

If Friel had chosen to leave things at that, this would be a deft and subtle play about art and artistic illusion, but he extends these perceptions brilliantly to show how they apply also in life. If excessive self-scrutiny can destroy an artist, the playwright shows that it can also destroy anyone. The most moving element of the play is the strange, inconclusive but very deep relationship between Francis Hardy and his wife. It is a coupling that is full of cruelty—his cruelty to her in the momentous labour of childbirth; her vicious mockery of him when his charisma fails; their joint harshness to Teddy whom they abandon for days on end; their neglect of parents whom they have left behind in Ireland. It is a relationship which, like most deep loves, has awkward zones of emptiness and inscrutability where little is shared or understood. In a perverse way, Grace resented Hardy his moments of mastery, when he would stand (she says) 'looking past you out of his completion, out of that private power, out of that certainty that was available only to him. God, how I resented that privacy ... And then, for him, I didn't exist ... But before a performance this exclusion—no, it wasn't an exclusion, it was an evasion—this evasion was absolute: he obliterated me'.[21] It is, nevertheless, a relationship as beautiful as it is baffling, full in some respects, empty in others, but, above all, clumsy and inconsistent. When it is good it is good by accident, but when the intention to make it good is too overt, then it inevitably fails. Francis and Grace were aware of the rich potential of their love, but as often as not they are baffled when a tender impulse is misconstrued. Like the artist's attitude to his secret art, theirs is a relationship of fluctuations, which neither can hope fully to control; and Friel seems to be hinting that all good couplings must stay that way. If they become self-analytical in the attempt to remove imperfections or uncertainties, then they may also remove that element of risk which is the ultimate sign of love. To love someone is to risk hurting or even losing that person, but if such risks are not run, there can be no real relationship, no sense of something freely given despite its potential cost. In general, it seems to be true that most people only begin to analyse relationships when they start to go wrong—the glossy magazines are filled with news of famous couples splitting up just two months after they had analysed and explained their happiness to some nosey reporter. In its handling of this theme, *Faith Healer* is remarkably similar to *Philadelphia Here I Come* which showed how a young man's conscious attempt to clarify his bond with his father failed. In Friel's earlier play, the

memory which Gar O'Donnell strove to make his father share
with him just would not overlap with the old man's recollection,
but in the very effort at remembrance that goal is reached
(without Gar's fully realising it) when the youth tells the Canon
'there's an affiity between old Screwballs and me'.[22] For some
strange reason, Gar still feels the need to define and analyse that
affinity, when he should have been content enough to have
sensed it.

Both dramas make great play with the distortion of memory,
the most obvious being that nobody in *Faith Healer* can summon
the courage to describe the murder in Ballybeg, just as nobody
in *Philadelphia* could accurately recall the momentous events of
the past or face the fact that Gar is about to emigrate. Both plays
focus on the importance of names as a sign of that distorted
memory—Francis Hardy, F.H., Faith Healer, if you are a
believer in fate. To name something is to exercise a power over
it, much as Hardy intones the list of those small village
communities over which he has exercised his power. He
remembers them clearly, but not the surnames or placenames of
his own wife's origin: 'Grace Dodsworth from Scarborough—or
was it Knaresborough? I don't remember',[23] as if to suggest my
earlier point that *this* is one relationship which he can never
hope to control completely. As if to confirm this loss of control,
the healer's second soliloquy becomes stuck in a groove with the
endless repetition of Kinlochbervie, the place in Scotland where
Grace bore and lost their baby. That emotional scar is too deep
to allow him to continue the recital. If by naming something we
show our power over it, by misnaming it we may be showing
its power over us. Grace thinks at first that Hardy constantly
changed her surname in order to humiliate her, that he called
her mistress instead of wife to upset her, that he said she was
from Yorkshire or Kerry or London or Scarborough instead of
Ulster to deprive her of an identity. But he told the theatre
audience that he *honestly* couldn't remember where she came
from. Because he is a lifelong healer of audiences, one assumes
that it is part of his nature to be more honest with large
audiences than with private individuals—his distrust of phoney
background music testifies to that. The real reason why he
unknowingly represses or distorts the details of Grace's background is that he feels a deep guilt over the sufferings which he
has inflicted on her and her parents. He tries to displace or
remould an emotion, the better to cope with it; and so he never
once mentions the loss of the baby in Kinlochbervie, or his own

callous behaviour there, but simply pretends that Kinlochbervie was the place in which he happened to be when news of his mother's death arrived. By remoulding an emotion that might otherwise control him, he can begin to control it, and this is why Grace rightly calls him an *artist,* with a compulsion to adjust and refashion everything around him. She denounces him for this gift and bluntly opines that she would have been far happier if he had never had this capacity to remould twisted fingers or unsatisfactory lives. She sees that those he cured were not real to him as persons but as fictions, extensions of himself that came into being only bcause of him.

Nevertheless, by the end of her soliloquy, Grace is pleading to be reinstated as one of Hardy's fictions. Recognising that she needs Hardy in order to sustain her own illusion of being, she concedes that the distortions of the artist, however frustrating on a superficial level, are in the deepest sense necessary. By naming him 'an artist', she establishes him as such, thereby reshaping and remoulding his character from quack-doctor to master artist —she engages in the very process for which she had earlier denounced him. Implicit in this is Wittgenstein's idea that the limits of my language are the limits of my world, that a thing only begins to exist when it is named as such. Of course, we cannot be sure of all the facts in Grace's own testimony, for her sentences are fragmented and she is verging on nervous breakdown. She is quite wrong to say that in his artist's egotism Hardy saw all successful cures as fictions that worked—extensions of himself— and forgot the failures. He was, in fact, haunted by his failures with clients even more than he was haunted by his failures in life. He could breathe life into others, but not into his own child, and so he suppressed all memory of the dead child and deliberately recast his own autobiography in more flattering terms. Thus, Grace's sufferings when her father fails to recognise his returned vagabond daughter are recast in the myth as Hardy's own pain at not being recognised by his father, because this makes him feel better, more sinned against than sinning. By reshaping past events into a less accusing pattern, Hardy can save himself for his art, that art which has been the cause of sufferings in others which he must pretend to have been his own. This is yet another version of history as science fiction, of past events being remodelled in terms of a utopian future. Hence, Teddy is probably right to assert that Hardy, in his weird private way, almost certainly felt and understood the plight of the grimy stillborn infant whose tragedy he had caused but refused to witness.

Teddy's soliloquy initially promises to clarify some of the discrepancies between earlier accounts, if only because he is an apparent outsider to the relationship, an objective professional manager. 'Personally, in the privacy of your heart, you may love them or you may hate them', he says, 'but that has nothing to do with it. Your client has his job to do. You have your job to do'.[24] Moreover, Francis Hardy has already hinted at unsuspected depths in Teddy, a man who was outwardly a romantic optimist but may secretly have been more realistic about their prospects. Sure enough, at the start of his talk, he does clarify one problem, as to who exactly chose the theme music. Grace chose a song which was a hit when she married Francis, but the couple soon forgot that and blamed Teddy's twisted mind for the selection. Thus they too create those necessary fictions which allow them to survive with a modicum of self-respect.

On a more serious level, it emerges from Teddy's account that Grace has also been lying to herself about the stillborn child, pretending that it was Francis who said the prayers and raised the cross, when in fact it was Teddy who did those things. Teddy remembers the village in question as sparkling and sunny; Grace recalls it as rainy and dull. Teddy is sure that the cross is long since gone; Grace that it must still be there. In the end, it is not even safe to assume that Teddy can be trusted as an objective professional witness, for it transpires that he has been secretly in love with Grace all along. This was something which Hardy, with his second sight, *knew*; and the healer may even have sought his own death so that Grace would be free to join herself to a man of compassion who could return her love.

Although a mere manager, Teddy shows a subtle awareness of the power of illusion, of the capacity of words and names to confer a sense of reality, and of the way in which this gift seemed to pass from Hardy to his clients in those successful moments of healing. So, in the Welsh village where all ten supplicants were cured, an old farmer could say: 'Mr. Hardy, as long as men live in Glamorganshire, you'll be remembered here'. 'And whatever way he said Glamorganshire', recalls Teddy, 'it sounded like the whole world'.[25] Teddy knows, however, that that power to maintain a successful illusion is jeopardised by Hardy's self-analytical brain, his self-questioning, his mockery of himself as a mere 'performer'. Soon, Teddy sees, he will come to believe even more in his own mockery than in his own performance. He could have been a great artist but he had too many brains, analytical brains which allowed him to see that everybody else is a con-man and an illusionist too. Hardy's anger at the allegations made by Grace's father does not last, for 'I had some envy of the man who could use the word "chicanery" with such confidence'.[26] Even the recognition that professional lawyers are also illusionists, employing the paraphernalia of gowns, wigs and a secret jargon, does not save the healer from himself. Hardy, the greatest liar in the play, is also the only honest man.

The healer keeps the inaccurate newspaper report of his feats not so much for reassurance as for self-identification: 'it identified me, even though it got my name wrong'.[27] The namer of things needs someone to name him; and the distorter of names and histories yearns for someone to distort his own. Like Grace, like Beckett's clowns, he too needs someone to give him the illusion that he exists. It is brutally appropriate that, in a drama which has made such play with true and false names, Hardy in the end should not even know the names of two of the men who come to kill him, thereby continuing the assault on his identity begun in the botched newspaper report. As the men advance menacingly on him, he begins to feel that they also are fictions, illusions without physical reality, and that each man present exists only in his need for others. He senses that they need the ficiton of his death in order to satisfy their rage against a life which has so cruelly maimed their friend.

*Faith Healer* is an eloquent apology for the distortions of memory, for it argues that every man must be an artist and illusionist, that every man must recast his memories into a pattern that is gratifying enough to alllow him to live with himself. As a consummate artist, Friel implicates himself in this process, for *that* is precisely what he has done in his play to the *Deirdre* legend—remoulded it subtly in accordance with his current artistic needs. There is a theory propounded by Harold Bloom in *The Anxiety of Influence* which suggests that every major artist is a kind of Francis Hardy. Bloom's strong artist creatively misreads a work of past art in order to clear a little imaginative space for himself.[28] Like Hardy, such an artist cannot afford to be a critic seeking the absolute truth, but must follow the accidents of impulse, creatively distorting an available myth in order to express something of himself— otherwise, he will be smothered by the influences of the past. The artist thus has a vested interest in misunderstanding and distorting a received text, for if he ever fully understands his model, then he will be overwhelmed by it and become a derivative writer, much as Arnold in *The Scholar-Gipsy* failed to do more than rewrite some of the better-known lines of Keats. The strong artist imperfectly assimilates past models and is therefore not overwhelmed, but saved, by his mistake. Like Blake, he goes wrong in order to go right. So Joyce in *Ulysses* can rewrite *The Odyssey*, but in the process remould it to his modern purposes, inflating the Telemachus father/son theme, while ignoring many other crucial elements, in a model of the original which is (in Bloom's immortal Dublin phrase) 'the same, only different'. As Joyce was later to show in *Finnegans Wake*, the same can somehow manage to be the new. Not for him the gloomy elegance of Beckett who opened a novel with the line: 'The sun shone, having no alternative, upon the nothing new'.[29] For Joyce, everything changes even as it remains itself and the differences give the repetitions point and meaning. Many of the deviations from *The Odyssey* are tragicomic in implication, as Hugh Kenner has pointed out—tragic when Stephen refuses to pray for his dying mother, unlike Telemachus who was tactful and considerate; comic when it dawns on the reader that Mrs. Bloom is something less than a faithful Penelope.[30] But most of the differences are finally crucial in allowing Joyce to redefine the nature of heroism for the modern world. There is a heroic honesty in Stephen's refusal to pray to a God in whom he does not believe, and a heroic wisdom in Bloom's refusal to take revenge on Boylan, unlike Odysseus who slaughtered those who tested the purity of his wife.

So it is in *Faith Healer* where Friel's heroic myth is creatively misinterpreted so that he can redefine heroism for the modern Gaelic world. In the ancient legend, Deirdre's name meant 'troubler' or 'alarmer' and she was remembered for the prophecy at her birth that many would die because of her beauty. Grace, the modern Deirdre, is heroic not so much for the suffering which she inflicts (though she has some of the cruelty of the ancient heroine) but rather for the pain which she must endure. Similarly, Teddy is not allowed the easy 'heroic' option of instant death for the man and woman he worships, but is more realistically left behind at the end to pick up the pieces that remain, in a life of quiet desperation rather than heroic enterprise. The ultimate realism is to deny Deirdre the fake glamour of a romantic death such as she had in medieval versions, and instead to give her a lonely death in a bedsitter as a nervous wreck. In this respect, Friel returns to the oldest versions of the tale, which had Deirdre dash out her brains on a rock, the hopeless act of a woman crazed with grief, a year and a day after the execution of her lover. Perhaps most significant of all is Friel's decision to give Hardy the central role, just as Naoise was the pivotal figure in the oldest version from *The Book of Leinster*.

Underlying Joyce's depiction of Bloom as a modern Ulysses, Friel's of Hardy as a modern Naoise, is the conviction that primitive myths are *not* impositions of a culture but innate possessions of every single man, who professes to be a unique being but is in fact a copy, consciously or unconsciously emulating the lives of more original predecessors. Hence, the characteristic modern *malaise* of inauthenticity, which assails men sophisticated enough to sense the frustrations of a life lived in quotation marks. Hence, also, the supreme importance to Leopold Bloom and to us of those small differences with which history repeats itself, for they are our sole guarantee of individuality. And what applies to people is true also of authors. Friel retells an old story, borrowing characters, situations, even phrases from the tale—and to that extent, like Francis Hardy, he is a con-man. But, like Hardy's pretence that his wife was barren and could not bear a child, he also remoulds his tale and his people to some private standard of excellence of his own—and, to that extent, he is indeed an artist. It adds to the poignancy of Hardy's life that he is quite unaware that he has re-enacted the story of Deirdre and the Sons of Usna, just as it adds to the poignancy of Leopold Bloom's plight that he is never for a moment aware that in his wanderings through Dublin he reenacts the voyage of Odysseus. But that very unpretentiousness and unselfconsciousness adds not only to the poignancy but also to the final likeness. This may be Friel's and Joyce's underlying point—that heroism is more often unselfconscious of itself than not.

## FOOTNOTES

1. Brian Friel, *Faith Healer*. London: Faber (1980), p.16.
2. J. M. Synge, *Collected Plays 2*, ed. A. Saddlemyer. Oxford: Oxford University Press (1968), p.249.
3. *Ibid.*, p.247.
4. J. M. Synge, *Collected Works: Prose*, ed. Alan Price. Oxford: Oxford University Press (1966), p.216.
5. *Faith Healer*, p.11.
6. Seamus Heaney, *Wintering Out*. London: Faber (1972), p.48.
7. *Faith Healer*, p.27.
8. *Ibid.*, p.29.
9. *Ibid.*, p.11.

10. *Ibid.,* p.12.
11. Seamus Heaney, 'Digging and Divining', talk on B.B.C. Radio 3, 1975.
12. Anthony Bailey, 'A Gift for Being in Touch; Seamus Heaney Builds Houses of Truth', *Quest,* January/February 1978.
13. Seamus Heaney, 'Digging and Divining'; see also 'Feeling into Words', *Preoccupations; Selected Prose 1968-78.* London: Faber (1980), p.41-60.
14. *Faith Healer,* p.13.
15. Lawrence Graver and Raymond Federman, *Samuel Beckett; The Critical Heritage.* London: Routledge and Kegan Paul (1979), p.173.
16. *Faith Healer,* p.15.
17. *Ibid.,* p.15.
18. *Ibid.,* p.44.
19. *Ibid.,* p.22.
20. *Ibid.,* p.32.
21. *Ibid.,* p.20.
22. Brian Friel, *Philadelphia Here I Come.* London: Faber (1965), p.96.
23. *Faith Healer,* p.14.
24. *Ibid.,* p.30.
25. *Ibid.,* p.32.
26. *Ibid.,* p.41.
27. *Ibid.,* p.40.
28. Harold Bloom, *The Anxiety of Influence.* Oxford: Oxford University Press (1975).
29. Samuel Beckett, *Murphy.* London: Picador (1973), p.5.
30. Hugh Kenner, *Dublin's Joyce.* London: Faber (1956), p.212.

# SEAMUS HEANEY'S NEW VOICE IN *STATION ISLAND*

ALASDAIR MACRAE

In the opening paragraph of his lecture 'The Three Voices of Poetry', delivered in 1953, T.S. Eliot explains the meaning of his title:

The first voice is the voice of the poet talking to himself—or to nobody. The second is the voice of the poet addressing an audience, whether large or small. The third is the voice of the poet when he attempts to create a dramatic character speaking in verse; when he is saying, not what he would say in his own person, but only what he can say within the limits of one imaginary character addressing another imaginary character. The distinction between the first and second voice, between the poet speaking to himself and the poet speaking to other people, points to the problem of poetic communication; the distinction between the poetic communication; the distinction between the poet addressing other people in either his own voice or an assumed voice, and the poet inventing speech in which imaginary characters address each other, points to the problem of the difference between dramatic, quasi-dramatic, and non-dramatic verse.[1]

Later in the lecture, he declares that he does not see these voices as 'mutually exclusive'; 'for me the voices are most often found together—the first and second, I mean, in non-dramatic poetry; and together with the third in dramatic poetry'.[2]

Eliot's discussion engages with basic questions concerning a poet's relationship not just with a potential audience but also with the society of which he is a member. In Western literature such questions were first articulated by Plato in his consideration of the role of the poet in his Republic. Shelley, in *A Defence of Poetry*, which was, of course, a defence of poetry as a force for morality, offers the most celebrated formulation of Eliot's first voice:

A poet is a nightingale, who sits in darkness and sings to cheer its own solitude with sweet sounds; his auditors are as men entranced by the

122

melody of an unseen musician, who feel that they are moved and softened, yet know not whence or why.[3]

Yet Shelley did not consider the poet as cocooned from his society nor did he see poetry as a private, impotent indulgence. He himself wrote poems of solid political commitment and he propounded the highest claims for the influence of poetry:

Poets are the hierophants of an unapprehended inspiration; the mirrors of the gigantic shadows which futurity casts upon the present; the words which express what they understand not; the trumpets which sing to battle and feel not what they inspire; the influence which is moved out, but moves. Poets are the unacknowledged legislators of the world.[4]

Certainly, over the past two centuries, the relation of a poet to his society has become a vexed problem. In earlier bardic societies and societies where the poet was a member of the court, his position was established by tradition and he wrote in a manner appropriate to that position; in modern European societies no such position exists. The problem for the modern poet is not lessened if he belongs to a smaller country: the pressures of loyalty, expectation and censure are stronger in a smaller community where there is no escape afforded in the anonymity of a cosmopolitan metropolis.

It is unnecessary here to rehearse the bickerings and bitternesses of Irish intellectual life or to call a roll of the literary wild geese who have fled the island of their birth on every tide. In Seamus Heaney's case, since the publication of his first book, *Death of a Naturalist,* in 1966, he has had constant and contradictory advice and admonishments from critics eager that he should write of Ireland in accordance with their views of the situation. In an introductory note to his fourth collection, *North,* in 1975, Heaney wrote:

During the last few years there has been considerable expectation that poets from Northern Ireland should 'say' something about the 'situation', but in the end they will only be worth listening to if they are saying something about and to themselves.[5]

By and large, in the first five collections, he seemed to work according to his own counsel and ranged himself with Shelley's nightingales who sing in Eliot's first voice. Looking back through these earlier volumes, the reader finds few examples of poems in Eliot's second and third voices. It is particularly rare for Heaney to address an audience directly; possibly the only case is in *An Open Letter* (Field Day, Derry, 1983). Instances of dramatic poems, poems delivered through devised voices, would include: 'For the Commander of the "Eliza" ' in *Death of a Naturalist;* 'Requiem for the Croppies', 'Undine', 'The Wife's Tale', and 'Mother' in *Door into the Dark;* 'A Northern Hoard' (possibly) and 'Shore Woman' in *Wintering Out;* 'Antaeus', 'The Digging Skeleton' (after Baudelaire), 'Bog Queen' and 'Freedman' in *North;* and 'Ugolino' (translated from Dante) in *Field Work.* These do not constitute a large proportion of his work and it could be argued, therefore, that neither Heaney's interest nor his talent lie in the dramatic mode. On the other hand, it could be suggested that his attempt to re-enact imaginatively the lives of the bog people, mainly in *North*, demonstrates an eagerness to construct characters. In *Field Work*, however, which followed *North* there are no poems using a dramatic persona, with the doubtful exception of 'Ugolino', Dante's creation.

Thus, with this view of Heaney as a rather undramatic poet firmly in our minds, we look at his new work with considerable surprise. In Britain, his two new books, *Station Island* and *Sweeney Astray*, have been published simultaneously. (*Sweeney Astray*, a translation from the medieval Irish *Buile Suibhne*, was first published in Ireland in 1983 by Field Day). The remainder of this essay will focus on *Station Island* but some comments are called for on *Sweeney Astray* even if only by way of introduction to the new collection.

What attracted Heaney to Sweeney? In the introduction to his translation, he suggests that the primary connection was 'topographical': the seventh century Sweeney had inhabited the area close to where Heaney spent the first thirty years of his life. He offers, however, some further reflections on the story of Sweeney and its relevance to contemporary readers, particularly in Ireland. After emphasising that Sweeney was an historically based character, he further explores the figure and situation of the poem:

The literary imagination which fastened upon him as an image was clearly in the grip of a tension between the newly dominant Christian ethos and the older, recalcitrant Celtic temperament. The opening sections which recount the collision between the peremptory ecclesiastic and the sacred king, and the closing pages of uneasy reconciliation set in St. Moling's monastery, are the most explicit treatment of this recurrent theme. This alone makes the work a significant one, but it does not exhaust its significance. For example, insofar as Sweeney is also a figure of the artist, displaced, guilty, assuaging himself by his utterance, it is possible to read the work as an aspect of the quarrel between free creative imagination and the constraints of religious, political and domestic obligation. It is equally possible, in a more opportunistic spirit, to dwell upon Sweeney's easy sense of cultural affinity with both western Scotland and southern Ireland as exemplary for all men and women in contemporary Ulster, or to ponder the thought that this Irish invention may well have been a development of a British original, vestigially present in the tale of the madman called Alan (Sections 46-50).

With certain obvious adjustments, Heaney's identification with Sweeney is clear and provocative. Does he really, even if in an 'opportunistic spirit', entertain a vision of a new Goidelic federation as a solution to the problems of Northern Ireland? Of course, what is most telling in relation to this essay, is how Heaney sees Sweeney as a *poète maudit* and is able to feel with and through him. The king cursed to live as a wild bird, Sweeney as an exile in his own kingdom, the wordsmith condemned to speak only to himself—these are powerful, dramatic images.

A reading of *Sweeney Astray* as a prelimary to *Station Island* is extremely useful, possibly even necessary. *Station Island* consists of three parts: Part One (untitled); Part Two: 'Station Island'; Part Three: 'Sweeney Redivivus'. In his note to Part Three, the poet says 'The poems in this section are voiced for Sweeney . . . Many of them, of course, are imagined in contexts far removed from early medieval Ireland'. 'Voiced for Sweeney' is an odd phrase, symptomatic of some ambivalence in his conception of the persona; and this ambivalence is further exposed in the second half of his comment. Some of the poems in this section are rather opaque even when the reader has the advantage of knowing what Heaney trusts is unnecessary, 'the support system of the original story'. Most of the newspaper reviewers passed over this section as if they felt unconfident as to how to handle it, and, yet, it is so noticeably meshed and cross-referenced with the other two sections that a just consideration of the whole volume has to give due attention to these poems 'voiced for Sweeney'. For example, the note to 'The King of the Ditchbacks', the final poem of Part One, refers the reader to the author's note on Part Three and the poem has a fuller meaning when the reader is able to run together Sweeney, the tinker from the ditchbacks, and King Sweeney. The opening poem of

'Station Island' also concerns Simon Sweeney, the tinker outcast, and, making him the first familiar ghost on the island, creates a bridge across the whole collection and, more particularly, betwen the personal world of Heaney's childhood and the less personal persona of the Sweeney figure adopted by Heaney as an adult. In 'The King of the Ditchbacks', he remembers how the tinkers had contrived his camouflage:

> they dressed my head in a fishnet
> and plaited leafy twigs through meshes
>
> so my vision was a bird's
> at the heart of a thicket
>
> and I spoke as I moved
> like a voice from a shaking bush.

Simon Sweeney, whom the young Heaney had willed himself to become, speaks as a ghost to the pilgrim poet:

> I was your mystery man
> and am again this morning

Later, when Heaney writes as the bird-man in 'Sweeney Redivivus', he confesses with surprise:

> And there I was, incredible to myself,
> among people far too eager to believe me
> and my story, even if it happend to be true

To say that the disguise has become complete and successful is not accurate; the poet has become aware that the Sweeney character is an aspect of himself, an aspect that has struggled to emerge for a long time, but, up till now, had not discovered a mode of expression. The title of the sequence 'Sweeney Redivivus', contains this sense of uncovering what was there.

It may be that as the bird-man, Sweeney-Heaney has found a way to fly free from a locale that was in danger of becoming poetically restrictive, a way to enlarge his territory. 'The Cleric' concludes with Sweeney conceding victory to St. Roman but also finding recompense:

> History that planted its standards
> on his gables and spires
> ousted me to the marches
>
> of skulking and whingeing.

Or did I desert?
Give him his due, in the end

he opened my path to a kingdom
of such scope and neuter allegiance
my emptiness reigns at its whim.

Some critics are apprehensive lest Heaney should desert the quarry from which he has sculpted so many marvellous poems but, in *Station Island*, he demonstrates that his hand has not lost its cunning to continue and develop that skill. There is manifested in the volume, however, a new, acute awareness of dangers, tensions, questions in writing the kind of poems he has. In essays, lectures and interviews he has explored notions of poetic development; it would be strange if such enquiries did not enter into his poems. Two of his declared masters, Wordsworth and Yeats, present him with very different examples of how poets may or may not survive middle age. Although he wrote some wonderful dramatic poems in *Lyrical Ballads*, Wordsworth did not develop this mode and his apologetic comment on *The Prelude* that, 'it was a thing unprecedented in literary history that a man should talk so much about himself', acknowledges the narrowness, the exhaustibility, of the vein of the child's development into artistic manhood, what theorists of the novel call *Künstlerroman*. Yeats's theory of Masks and of Primary and Antithetical gyres has clear implications for his poetry, a development of dramatic poetry with voices devised appropriate to the particular Mask. Wordsworth stagnated as a poet; Yeats enjoyed amazing aggrandisement in the second half of his career.

In *Station Island*, is it significant that the title of the final poem is 'On the Road'? Interspersed in the images of travelling, exile, migration, exploration are the question and answer from St. Matthew's Gospel: 'Master, what must I do to be saved? Sell all you have and give to the poor. And follow me'. Sweeney has been reduced to the most abject poverty and, in the end, dies as a Christian (according to *Sweeney Astray*). In Heaney's case, are the question and instruction to be interpreted in religious terms or in artistic terms? If the whole collection has been read in order, the reader comes on this interpretative problem with some preparation provided by pointers in the final poems of Parts One and Two. 'The King of the Ditchbacks' ends with a masked Heaney, a rich young man

leaving everything he had
for a migrant solitude.

James Joyce, the ultimate ghost and adviser to confront Heaney on his pilgrimage, reprimands him and then directs him:

'You are raking at dead fires,

a waste of time for somebody your age.
That subject people stuff is a cod's game,
infantile, like your peasant pilgrimage.

*You lose more of yourself than you redeem*
*doing the decent thing.* Keep at a tangent.
When they make the circle wide, it's time to swim

out on your own and fill the element
with signatures on your own frequency,
echo soundings, searches, probles, allurements,

elver-gleams in the dark of the whole sea'.          [my italics]

Again, it can be seen how the collection works as a whole, with poems commenting on each other, reinforcing or challenging propositions offered in individual poems and creating a sense of debate or dramatic dialogue.

If a change in the ground of his poetry is being intimated, Heaney is keenly aware of the difficulties involved in such a manoeuvre. He reconstructs in 'Chekhov on Sakhalin' the experience of the Russian writer travelling to the convict island of Sakhalin off the Pacific coast in 1890 and examines whether Chekhov found release in his venture. Himself the grandson of a serf, Chekhov is confused between images of freedom and images of bondage. The ringing sound of his smashed cognac glass blurs into the rattle of the convicts' chains; he, a free observer, is burdened with his very freedom when confronted with the sufferings in the prison island. The luxury of the cognac, the luxury as a writer, 'To try for the right tone—not tract, not thesis—/And walk away from floggings', these luxuries cannot be afforded by his conscience. Against the therapeutic ambition of writing the inherited ailment may prove too tenacious:

He who had thought to squeeze
His slave's blood out and waken the free man
Shadowed a convict guide through Sakhalin.

Something of the dilemma presented through the figure of Chekhov is reproduced in Heaney's own person in the following poem, 'Sandstone Keepsake', where as a casual stroller on a beach in the Irish Republic he faces across to the Detention Camp at Magilligan in Northern Ireland. The poem opens casually with a typically scrupulous description of a stone picked up on the beach. Equally casually, it seems, the perimeter lights of the camp across the water come on. A literary memory in the form of a question is suggested by the wet reddishness of the stone: 'A stone from Phlegethon,/bloodied on the bed of hell's hot river?' and Heaney muses on the story in Dante of Guy de Montfort consigned to suffer in the Phlegethon for his murder of Prince Henry of England in 1270. The poem has shifted from the casual to a serious tone. Although Heaney apologises for his extravagant allusion, 'but not really ... Anyhow', the simple stone has become a venerated heart and we remember that the Phlegethon is a river of boiling blood in Dante's *Inferno* where those who committed acts of violence against their neighbours are condemned to suffer. In the final two stanzas, the casual tone appears to be restored with a pun on 'free state' and the poet identified as, 'a silhouette not worth bothering about,/out for the evening in scarf and waders'. There is, however, an excessiveness in his final description of himself as, 'one of the venerators', which sends ripples back across the poem to Prince Henry's heart, 'long venerated' and alerts the reader to a quiet irony exerted by Heaney against his position as a passive observer in his 'free state of image and allusion'.

In 'Away from it All', he speaks of how quotations come to the mind 'like rehearsed alibis' and he quotes from Czeslaw Milosz, the exiled Polish writer:

> I was stretched between contemplation
> of a motionless point
> and the command to participate
> actively in history

The questions raised in some of the poems in Part One regarding the poet's relation to events and an audience provide an introduction to the concerns of the middle part of the collection, the sequence called 'Station Island'. One of the most dramatic encounters in the sequence occurs in the second half of section VIII where Heaney is confronted by his cousin, Colum McCartney, for whom he had written an elegy in *Field Work*,

'The Strand at Lough Beg'. The elegy uses some of the features of a traditional pastoral elegy; Heaney imagines that, after his cousin has been the victim of a random sectarian murder, he leads him to the shore of their native Lough Beg where he cleans his wounds with moss and dew before laying him out. Colum now appears to Seamus Heaney and accuses him of having failed to fulfil his obligations of kinship and of having romanticised his death in the elegy:

> 'You confused evasion and artistic tact. The
> Protestant who shot me through the head I accuse
> directly, but indirectly, you who now atone perhaps
> upon this bed for the way you whitewashed ugliness and
> drew the lovely blinds of the *Purgatorio* and
> saccharined my death with morning dew'.

Of course, self-rebuke is not new to Heaney. 'An Afterwards' in *Field Work* sees all poets condemned by his wife to the ninth circle of hell for backbiting. She makes some allowance for him:

> 'You weren't the worst. You aspired to a kind,
> Indifferent, faults-on-both-sides tact'

Earlier, in 'Punishment' in *North*, Heaney accuses himself of being 'the artful voyeur ... who would connive in civilised outrage'. It could be argued that he is being poetically indulgent not just with death but also with his guilt, that the measured, rhymed metres, albeit in the month of his cousin, ensure that guilt is rendered palatable. It is at this point that the scheme of the poem (and beyond the central poem, the scheme of the collection) may help to rescue the poet from such an accusation.

The conception of 'Station Island' is based on the traditions of the pilgrimage to Station Island (or St. Patrick's Pilgrimage) in Lough Derg, County Donegal. Heaney, who went on the pilgrimage three times as a schoolboy, explains the nature of the penitential ritual in his note to the poem. As a result of the communal religious atmosphere, the fasting, the lack of sleep, the repetitions of prayers, confessions, renunciations, circuits of the 'beds', it is highly probably that pilgrims will enter a strange usually unvisited zone of awareness where hallucination is indistinguishable from actuality. Heaney exploits this foundation as MacDiarmid used a different foundation in his long, free-ranging poem *A Drunk Man Looks at a Thistle*. It allows him to range beyond his personal history and have imaginary

conversations with any figures who have impressed themselves
in his consciousness although he rations himself to those who
can reasonably be connected with the purpose of his pilgrimage.
He is intent on establishing where he has come to in the middle
of his life and to sift the emotional and spiritual and artistic
accretions to ascertain what should be jettisoned.

The process of self-examination is conducted in a serious
manner but his interlocutors are not chosen for any glibly
reverential attitude. The sequence opens with Simon Sweeney,
'an old Sabbath-breaker', whose first words are ' "Damn all you
know" ' and whose parting shout of advice is, ' "Stay clear of
all processions!" ' At the far end of the vigil, James Joyce turns
on Heaney irascibly:

> 'You are fasted now, light-headed, dangerous.
> Take off from here. And don't be so earnest,
>
> Let others wear the sackcloth and the ashes.
> Let go, let fly, forget.
> You've listened long enough. Now strike your note'.

William Carleton, the author of 'The Lough Derg Pilgrim', a
caustic story about the pilgrimage, and a convert from
Catholicism, is appalled to learn that the poet is on his way to
the island and explodes: ' "O holy Jesus Christ, does nothing
change?" ' Patrick Kavanagh makes a brief appearance and
announces that in his time, ' "the odd one came here on the
hunt for women" '. In section VII, a shopkeeper relates how he
was killed in the middle of the night by "shites thinking they
were the be-all and the end-all" '; when, after hearing the
man's account, Heaney embarrassedly blurts:

> 'Forgive the way I have lived indifferent—
> forgive my timid circumspect involvement'

the shopkeeper interrupts:
>                 'Forgive
> my eye', he said, 'all that's above my head'.

Some reviewers have complained that Heaney himself sounds
sometimes ponderous, sometimes unsure of himself, sometimes
taking more than what they see as a fair share of the
conversation. None of these behaviours seems particularly
surprising if the oddity of the situation is borne in mind. If

Heaney had presented himself as confident, balanced, sure of his stance, the emotional and spiritual core of the sequence would have been uninteresting and dramatically unviable: it is Heaney's pilgrimage, embarked on precisely because of an unsureness about his stance.

Not all the sections of the sequence consist of conversations with characters. Some are communings with aspects of his self, areas of memory, vulnerable points in his psyche. In his comments, quoted earlier, on the origins of the poem, *Buile Siubhne*, he sees the seventh century Sweeney as marking the breaking-point or overlap between the old Celtic and the new Christian dispensations. These dispensations are not tidily limited to religious doctrines but include hierarchies of power and obedience, ownership of land, concepts of social order and justice, attitudes to the natural world. In his earlier volumes, Heaney has shown a special interest in old orders giving way to new; people, implements, trades, language becoming redundant. In the twentieth century, organised Christianity in many part of Europe has been atrophied by secular thought and, in Ireland, the authority of the Catholic Church has certainly slackened. Language is often slower to change than ideologies and secular ideas are presented and discussed in a diction with a strong religious flavour. In *Station Island* it is difficult to gauge how vexed Heaney is by religious scruples; what is evident is that the language of the collection has powerful residual elements of a faith that seems open to serious challenge. Having chosen the device of the penitential vigil, it would be impossible to avoid all language associated with such religious exercises and, anyway:

> When you are tired or terrified your voice slips
> back into its old first place and makes the sound your
> shades make there

As this quotation from 'The Loaning' makes clear, Heaney is aware of a residual strain in his language and the poem is partly an exploration of this strain in his mind:

> And I knew
> I was in the limbo of lost words.
>
> They had flown there from raftered sheds and crossroads,
> from the shelter of gable ends and turned-up carts

> . . .
> Then I knew why from the beginning
> the loaning breathed on me

The word 'loaning' itself is probably in a limbo for most English
speakers. He coaxes a number of words out of their customary
limbo, words such as: 'japped', 'mirled', 'slub', 'flensed',
'welted', 'tines', 'soft-deckled' and 'scrabs'. The sequence of
'Station Island' is much concerned with what he calls in section
III, 'habit's afterlife', but Heaney has memories and ghosts
which do not allow him to luxuriate in such a condition. When
he tries to impress on Carleton how similar their backgrounds
have been, the novelist butts in impatiently:

> 'I know, I know, I know, I know', he said,
> 'but you have to try to make sense of what comes'

Even where the figure who appears seems, as in section IV, to
represent the traditional dedication to the faith, this illusion is
quickly dispelled. Heaney has set the scene carefully: he is in
the penitential position, about to say the words 'I renounce the
world, the flesh and the devil'; he is aware of photographs of,
newly ordained faces', he hears ' "Father" pronounced with a
fawning relish', the young priest, his school friend, is
immaculate, 'glossy as a blackbird'. The missionary priest had
trained obediently, 'doomed to the decent thing'. When he tells
his story, however, it is a confession of failure and disenchant-
ment, his faith broken by the life in the jungle. Heaney acuses
him of having, in his student days, protected the people's
spurious religiosity and helped them to ignore the facts around
them:

> 'You gave too much relief, you raised a siege
> the world had laid against their kitchen grottoes
> hung with holy pictures and crucifixes'

In retaliation, the priest demands to know what the poet is
doing at Lough Derg:

> 'But all this you were clear of you walked into over
> again. And the god has, as they say, withdrawn.
>
> What are you doing, going through these motions?'

The section ends on a muted note but the final word 'visiting' has a chiding sharpness because it connects Heaney with the empty 'Visiting neighbours' of which he had accused the young priest. The priest's earlier self-defence, 'I at least was young and unaware/that what I thought was chosen was convention', operates against Heaney as he presents himself in the poem because he may not yet be able to distinguish between what he thinks is his choice and what is merely his tradition, spiritually and artistically.

Likewise the joys and fulfilments experienced in 'Station Island' owe little to religious enlightenment or divine intervention. Section XI opens with an image Heaney had tried out before in his group of prose poems, *Stations* (Ulsterman Publications, Belfast, 1975): a child's kaleidoscope was plunged into muddy water and emerged brilliant but spoiled. A monk confessor urges him:

> re-envisage
> the zenith and glimpsed jewels of any gift
> mistakenly abased.

Is Heaney thinking of his gifts as a poet and that he has misused them? He is instructed by the monk to 'read poems as prayers' and, as a penance, to translate something by Juan de la Cruz. The piece he translates develops his own opening image and contrasts the pure, eternal and hidden fountain with the dark night in which we live. There is no comment offered on the Spanish poem and again Heaney has resorted to a voice not necessarily indentifiable with himself. Furthermore, the translated poem, as is common with Juan de la Cruz, proffers images which are free of doctrine and can be interpreted in a non-religious way. The other instance of pleasure in the sequence occurs in section VI and seems categorically unreligious. He remembers the slow arrival of sexual satisfaction and while he plays back the tape of his memory he resists the penitential demands of the island: 'I shut my ears to the bell'. The 'beds of Saint Patrick's Purgatory' are overlaid in his mind with idyllic images of Horace's Sabine farm. In contrast to the 'breathed-on grille of the confessional' was the revelation of the body of his loved one and 'I inhaled the land of kindness'.

As Heaney returns to the mainland, sensing 'an alien comfort as I stepped on ground', he meets Joyce and, in answer to what the reader as well as the poet has in his mind to ask, he pronounces:

'Your obligation
is not discharged by any common rite.
What you do must be done on your own

so get back in harness. The main thing is to write
for the joy of it. Cultivate a work-lust
that imagines its haven like your hands at night

dreaming the sun in the sunspot of a breast'.

If Heaney accepts the advice, and, of course, it is he who, in a
sense has offered it, has the penitential vigil been a waste of
time? A 'work-lust' implies poetry and sexuality, not religious
observance, and 'haven' sounds dangerously like a secularised
heaven.

The scheme of the sequence allows Heaney to investigate
from different angles questions of concern to him. Although,
because the ground plan of the poem is founded on a religious
ritual, the terms of the investigation are religious, the poem is
not narrowly or even primarily religious. Because he has found
a device in which so many voices can be accommodated,
Heaney is freed from attempts to pin him down to one consistent, stable stance. He begins the sequence with questions; he
does not conclude with solutions. The Sweeney poems which
follow the sequence may be seen to act out Joyce's instruction
but to insist that they do is to curtail the freedom Heaney hopes
to find.

'Station Island' has dark, troubled areas and if the sequence
stood on its own there would be a chilly quality undispelled at
the end. Powerful images remain sour in the reader's mind:

A cold draught blew under the kneeling boards.
I thought of walking round
and round a space utterly empty,
utterly a source, like the idea of sound;
like an absence stationed in the swamp-fed air
above a ring of walked-down grass and rushes
where we once found the bad carcass and scrags of hair
of our dog that had disappeared weeks before.

These final stanzas of section III anticipate and answer his
cousin's accusation in section VIII. The sequence, however,
does not stand on its own but is encountered after some
wonderful, warm lyrics in Part One.

In 'The Birthplace' Heaney describes a visit to the house of

Thomas Hardy. The poem switches about in time, reconstructing Hardy from his furnishings, remembering reading Hardy thirty years before, and recalling the day of the visit and a sexual episode intricately connected with Hardy and his house. Through the shifts from descriptive to private to meditative runs an attempt to re-enact in Hardy's birthplace what Hardy stood for in Heaney's mind. In the end he has a success, in that,

> I heard
> roosters and dogs, the very same
> as if he had written them

We are reminded of Coleridge's memorable comments on Shakespeare's persuasive power, where the reader becomes a co-creator with the poet: 'If I should not speak it, I feel that I should be thinking it; the voice only is the poet's, the words are my own'.[6] Heaney has that power to draw the reader by the justness of his language into a collaborative activity where the reader's recognition is so total that he feels that he must have written the poem himself. In the poems of childhood awareness and poems commemorating objects with introjective acuteness Heaney has few contemporary peers. That ability to partake in himself of the character of an object or a creature or a place, to animate withour distortion, to perceive without imposition, is a rare artistic tact. 'A Kite for Michael and Christopher' has:

> But now it was far up like a small black lark
> and now it dragged as if the bellied string
> were a wet rope hauled upon
> to lift a shoal.

Such animations are not unrelated to a dramatic skill although the voice remains the voice of Heaney. In 'Making Strange' there is a problem of voice, Heaney finds himself standing between a sophisticated incomer:

> with his travelled intelligence
> and tawny containment,
> his speech like the twang of a bowstring

and

> another, unshorn and bewildered
> in the tubs of his wellingtons

The difficulty of communication between the two and what they

represent is solved when 'a cunning middle voice' advises him
to ' "be adept and dialect" '. In the end:

> I found myself driving the stranger
>
> through my own country, adept
> at dialect, reciting my price
> in all that I knew, that began to make strange
>
> at that same recitation.

Whether there are three persons and the voice in the poem or
only Heaney in different guises and the voice, is not a necessary
question to answer. What is significant is that 'the cunning
middle voice' advocates not a choice between the adept and the
dialect but a combination of them:

> call me sweetbriar after the rain
> or snowberries cooled in the fog.
> But love the cut of this travelled one
> and call me also the cornfield of Boaz.

Heaney's voice has achieved a wider range to 'Go beyond what
is reliable'. It is noteworthy how many of the poems in Part One
are composite, constructed of several units which allow him to
alter his focus and perspective. Looking across the whole
collection, we see that each Part is differently organised and,
when examined in more detail, the Parts are seen to comment
on and complement each other. It is not a question of which Part
is the centre or fulcrum but rather that a new dimension has
been devised by Heaney to allow him to speak in a more
dramatic voice. Although the focus of his poetry is still in his
native Northern Ireland, although the pull of emotion is still to
something behind him and much of his language manifests
'habit's afterlife', his adoption of the dramatic mode promises
a different more oblique attitude to his own background. In his
previous volumes, poems written in a foreign locality seemed
like postcards sent home to reaffirm his connection with his
familial and tribal base. Now he may be able to renegotiate his
relations with his original society and include in his poetry the
wider perspectives his travelling has given him. 'The First
Flight' concludes with what may signal his new direction:

> I was mired in attachment
> until they began to pronounce me

a feeder off battlefields

so I mastered new rungs of the air
to survey out of reach
their bonfires on hills, their hosting

and fasting, the levies from Scotland
as always, and the people of art
diverting their rhythmical chants

to fend off the onslaught of winds
I would welcome and climb
at the top of my bent

The bird-man, Sweeney Heaney, is no longer a nightingale.

## FOOTNOTES

The main collections of poetry by Seamus Heaney referred to in this essay are all published by Faber and Faber, London. They are as follows:
*Death of a Naturalist.* (1966); *Door into the Dark.* (1969); *Wintering Out.* (1972); *North.* (1975); *Field Work.* (1979); *Sweeney Astray.* (1984); *Station Island.* (1984). (In this essay *Station Island* is the whole collection; 'Station Island' is Part Two of the collection).

1. 'The Three Voices of Poetry', the eleventh annual Lecture of the National Book League, delivered in 1953. Included in *On Poetry and Poets*. London: Faber and Faber (1957), p.89.
2. *Ibid.,* p.99.
3. *Shelley's Prose,* ed. David Lee Clark. Albuquerque: University of New Mexico Press (1954), p.282.
4. *Ibid.,* p.297.
5. *Poetry Book Society Bulletin,* 85 (Summer 1975), p.1.
6. *Coleridge on Shakespeare,* edited by Terence Hawkes, Harmondsworth: Penguin Books (1969), p.161.

# PROSE FICTION IN THE IRISH LITERARY RENAISSANCE

AUGUSTINE MARTIN

The key fiction writers of the Irish Renaissance are George Moore, Forrest Reid, James Joyce, James Stephens, Seumas O'Kelly and Daniel Corkery. It may therefore seem odd to begin with the early fictions of a writer whose great reputation rests almost exclusively upon his poetry, W. B. Yeats, whose early tales and novels are virtually unknown to the majority of his readers. It may seem even more perverse to concentrate on his volume of fantastic tales, *The Secret Rose* (1897), rather than his one realistic published novel, *John Sherman*.[1] But the fact is that Yeats's experiments with symbolic narrative in the tales, especially the 'apocalyptic' tales, look forward to Joyce, Moore and the modern age. *Sherman*, for all its relevance to the personality of Yeats and the drama of his choices, looks back to the nineteenth century, to the struggle between England and Ireland in the consciousness of Lord Colambre or Henry Mortimer or in the lives of the novelists themselves, of Maria Edgeworth, Lady Morgan, Gerald Griffin or the Banim brothers. The struggle of choice is, of course, crucial to the poetry of the early Yeats, and is to be found everywhere in his early work from *The Wanderings of Oisin* to 'The Lake Isle of Inisfree', but its sentimental resolution in favour of an idyllic Sligo landscape and community is retrograde in comparison with the force and direction dramatised in Moore and Joyce through their fictional heroes, Dedalus, Rodney, Carmody, Bryden, even the narrating persona* of *Ave, Salve, Vale*. On the other hand, the romantic heroes of Yeats's tales, Robartes and Ahern, are not only precursors but exemplars for those rebellious and fugitive artist figures that have recurred in Irish fiction to the present day.

---

*Moore's Harding in 'The Way Back' is an exception, and, as John Cronin implies, an abberation.

The narrative strategies employed by Yeats in these stories were
to bear interesting fruit in the 'mythical method', whether
employed in the realist idiom of Joyce, or in the tradition of
prose fantasy which Joyce shared with Stephens, Eimar
O'Duffy and, later, Flann O'Brien—to view the phenomenon in
a purely Irish context. When T. S. Eliot coined the phrase in his
celebrated review of *Ulysses* in 1923 he wrote:

In using the myth, in manipulating a continuous parallel between
contemporaneity and antiquity, Mr. Joyce is pursuing a method which
others must pursue after him. They will not be imitators, any more than
the scientist who uses the discoveries of an Einstein pursuing his own,
independent further investigations. It is simply a way of controlling, of
ordering, of giving a shape and a significance to the immense
panorama of futility and anarchy which is contemporary history. It is
a method already adumbrated by Mr. Yeats, and of the need for which
I believe Mr. Yeats to have been the first contemporary to be conscious.
Psychology ... ethnology and *The Golden Bough* have concurred to
make possible what was impossible even a few years ago. Instead of the
narrative method, we may now use the mythical method.[2]

It is usually assumed that Eliot is referring to Yeats's poetry as
having 'adumbrated' the method. It is far more likely that Eliot
had in mind Yeats's stories: specifically a story such as 'The
Crucifixion of the Outcast' in which the death of a wandering
poet at the hands of medieval monks exactly parallels Christ's
passion, or 'The Adoration of the Magi' in which three Irish
sages journey to contemporary Paris to witness the birth of a
new savage deity from the loins of a dying Irish harlot. The case
becomes more compelling when we realise that Joyce made
these stories crucial in the development of *Stephen Hero*, his
first explicit portrayal of the Romantic artist as fictional
protagonist: there he writes that Stephen 'repeated often the
story of "The Tables of the Law" and "The Adoration of the
Magi" ',[3] choosing Robartes and Aherne as his spiritual
exemplars.

The two stories which Stephen learned by heart were not
included in *The Secret Rose* because the publisher, Bullen, took
a dislike to them, but later published them in a booklet which
the young Joyce found in a book barrow on the quays. Had they
appeared in the 1897 edition they would have clinched the
structure of a book which had been written to a remarkably
coherent historical schema, covering 'twenty centuries of stony
sleep'. It begins in pagan times with a story which records the

defeat of the Firbolgs, 'The People of the Bag', and proceeds through the centuries to Yeats's own time when Robartes and Aherne become the apostles of a new dispensation wherein the demonic energies of art and beauty overthrow and replace the Christian values. Even without the two excluded stories the book has an adequate symmetry beginning with a invocation of the 'most secret and inviolate Rose' and ending, in 'Rosa Alchemica', with Robartes and his Dionysians dancing on a mosaic of the pale face of Christ while the petals of the great rose drift downwards from the ceiling:

> Surely thine hour has come, thy great wind blows,
> Far off, most secret, and inviolate Rose?

Without exception the heroes of the book's seventeen stories are types of the visionary artist engaged in a struggle against 'darkness', in what the Dedication describes as 'the war of spiritual with natural order'. There is a bard, a saint, a gleeman, a medieval knight, a mystical lover and then Yeats's more intimate personae, Red Hanrahan, Robartes and Aherne. The historical scope of the book is impressively panoramic though shot through with the poet's curious sense of chronology and process. As I have argued elsewhere[5] it is in two senses apocalyptic. Each of the stories resolves itself in a moment of magical change or transnatural insight. Together they move towards a present which is alive with the omens of change, dissolution and renewal. The characterisations are mostly spare and typical, though the character of Hanrahan, who figures in a suite of six stories, takes on believable flesh and blood as he pursues his haunted way along the frontiers of settled society. As a work of fiction it suffers ultimately by serving a purpose external to itself, the projection of Yeats's overmastering intuitions about the state of the contemporary world and the role of the artist mage in its necessary transfiguration.

The effect of these artist heroes on the imagination of the young James Joyce was momentous, as that crucial Chapter XIII of *Stephen Hero* demonstrates. There in a 'damp and gloomy' Dublin 'Stephen had no pains to believe in the reality of their existence'.

The atmosphere of these stories was heavy with incense and omens and the figures of the monk-errants, Ahere and Robartes strode through it with great strides. Their speeches were like the enigmas of a disdainful Jesus ... anciently guilty of some arrogance of the spirit

... a mysterious ordination. Civilisation may be said indeed to be the creation of its outlaws ...

We can only speculate as to why Joyce repudiated *Stephen Hero*—apart from the fact that it was rejected by so many publishers—but the clue to his dissatisfaction with it may lie in his brother's remark that it was 'a lying autobiography and a raking satire'. It is a book of divided allegiances and uncertain emphasis, vacillating between the two great Joycean concerns, the self and the city. The same division is to be seen in *Dubliners* where the first three stories—written contemporaneously with *Stephen Hero*—are more engrossed in the self, the emergent artistic consciousness, than in the Dublin world the book had set out to mirror. The decision to liberate these two themes from each other was probably the most momentous decision Joyce made in those early years. It meant that he could now exercise his strange, objective, ventriloquial gift for recording and mediating the unself-conscious world of Dublin's lower middle classes in the bulk of *Dubliners* while creating a radical drama of the artistic consciousness in *A Portrait of the Artist as a Young Man*. It meant that, having thus separated them, he could in the fullness of time bring them together again in eloquent counterpoint within the fictive world of *Ulysses*. In his orchestration of the objective world Joyce has no serious precursor. In the protrayal of the inner, artistic sensibility his debt to Yeats is greater than anyone has acknowledged, least of all Joyce himself. The Michael Robartes who appears in the diary entry of April 6 in *A Portrait of the Artist as a Young Man* is a poor creature compared to the demonic 'monk errant' that had stalked through the twenty-third chapter of *Stephen Hero*, showing the young artist his ministry of dissent.

Having rid himself of the need for 'raking satire' Joyce was free, in *A Portrait*, to refine the terms of his 'lying auto-biography' to the unique *bildungsroman* that it became. The first sentence was now a frontal assault on traditional narrative, chronological self-revelation, circumstantial realism:

Once upon a time and a very good time it was there was a moocow coming down along the road and this moocow that was coming down along the road met a nicens little boy named baby tuckoo ...

The archetypal struggle between father and son is unceremoniously joined:

His father told him that story: his father looked at him through a glass: he had a hairy face.

Who is now telling the story? Who is looking at whom? And as the telling goes on, as the fledgling artist puts away childish things, St. Paul yields to Attic legend, and Joyce's 'mythical method' takes over as Icarus seeks progressively for his true father, his proper priesthood, his appropriate icons and ritual, and ultimately his authentic godhead:

symbols and portents, of the hawkline man whose name he bore soaring out of his captivity on osierwoven wings, of Thoth, the god of writers, writing with a reed upon a tablet and bearing on his narrow ibis head the cusped moon. [7]

Joyce's freedom to dispense with all the genial circumstances which had threatened to swamp the theme of growing creative consciousness makes *A Portrait* a watershed, a completely new achievement even in the specialised fictional work of the *kunsterroman*, the novel of artistic growth. The circumstantial world is subdued to the level of a sounding-board for the inner processes of the artist's developing consciousness, and an 'answerable style' is forged from line to line in order to monitor that inner movement. A great deal is, of course, sacrificed. Emma Clery of *Stephen Hero* is more engaging than the perfunctory and functional E.C. of *A Portrait*. And it has been argued that the great set pieces where the external world is given its chance—the Christmas Dinner and the trip to Cork—are the most vivid things in the book. But to argue thus is to forget that they are vivid for a purpose. Simon, the great earthly bungler, must be exhibited in all his strength and weakness before he is discarded in favour of Daedalus, the great sky-borne artificer. And anyway Joyce has now cleared the way for a score of such objective portraits as he turns from the self to the city in the central stories of *Dubliners*.

Though *Dubliners* has provoked two generations of 'mythical' criticism—Levin and Shattuck, Brewster Ghiselin, Nathan Halper, Bernard Benstock, Donald Torchiana and others—its main interest still resides in its more traditional strengths as fiction: its evocation of the city's atmosphere, its range of memorable characterisations, the variety of its prose style, its precision with the nuances of dialogue, its instinct for the events and objects that open vistas of private and communal experience—Lenehan's plaintive reverie over his plate of peas,

Maria's discomfiture in the cake shop, Farrington's brief glory as his repartee is applauded in Davy Byrne's, old Jack raking the cinders in the committee room, Mrs. Mooney glancing at the clock before her interview with Bob Doran, Mr. Kernan's 'farcical gravity' as he 'bars the candles ... the magic lantern business' in 'Grace'. Rather than seeking for an elaborately plotted unity underpinned by symbolic pattern and mythic archetype it is more rewarding to view the book as a tentative work in which a great fictionist begins to discover and develop his gifts and energies. The successive drafts of 'The Sisters', for instance, reveal an imagination moving from a concept of 'scrupulous meanness' to a style which in its symbolism and mystery throws shadows forward almost to *Finnegans Wake*. There is the remarkable technical leap from the routine swagger of 'After the Race' to the mastery of 'Two Gallants' where the 'mask of carnival' is so deftly drawn back from the face of Dublin by the interweave of narrative, dialogue, symbol and internal monologue. In the pub scenes of 'Counterparts', 'A Little Cloud' and 'Grace' we can already see the panorama of *Ulysses* beckoning, the sense of a large interlocking community, a shared folklore of anecdote and gossip, a rich spoken language bearing on its current the flotsam of innumerable private failures, triumphs, anxieties and consolations.

To see these 'epicleti' of *Dubliners* in this way, as stepping-stones to the broader territories of *Ulysses*, is not to deny their individual integrity as short stories, no more than Joyce denied it when he saw them as adding up to a 'chapter in the moral history of my country'. Each story is a new departure in style and technique, and each experiment brings him closer to the possibilities of the larger form. 'Ivy Day in the Committee Room' with its large cast of characters and its reliance on un-mediated dialogue is a masterpiece of impersonality. The second story of 'public life'—to use Joyce's own category—'A Mother' flounders among its proliferating *dramatis personae*, sustained chiefly by those memorable characterisations, Mrs Kearney and Hoppy Holohan. 'Grace' not only releases the towering figure of Martin Cunningham and his attendant evangelists, but it also marks Joyce's first bridgehead on the 'mythical method' which was to be his unique contribution to modern fiction. In three demotic strophes, the latrine, the sickroom and the church, the theological conscience of Dublin is stretched across the chasms of Dante's *Divine Comedy*.

It is as if Joyce had immediately realised the need for a

narrative strategy which might contain these multiplying creatures of the imaginative memory. The mythical method is born and its inventor has found a means of marching fifteen of his Dubliners into the suspended world of Leopold Bloom and Stephen Dedalus in *Ulysses*. Then, in the mild, uxorious figure of Gabriel Conroy—professor, linguist, cosmopolitan, sentimentalist and *artist manqué*—both Stephen and Bloom are foreshadowed as the volume reaches its symphonic close.

When Joyce launched his broadside against the Irish theatre movement in 1902 in *The Day of the Rabblement* it is significant that he reserved his most destructive fire-power for the fictionist George Moore, asserting that *Celibates* revealed a writer beginning to 'draw upon his literary account' and predicting that 'however frankly Mr Moore may misquote Pater and Turgenieff to defend himself, his new impulse has no kind of relation to the future of art'. There is excellent irony in the spectacle of Moore, cosmopolitan, Francophile, aesthete, the man who had delivered Naturalism to the English novel, being accused of provincialism and vulgarity by an undergraduate who has not, so far, been off the island. But it is understandable that a fledgling prose writer in Joyce's position should be alarmed and annoyed that a major Irish writer should suddenly return to Ireland and begin to fasten upon the material that the young man thought his by natural right.

The story of Moore's strange adventures with the short story form leading up to *The Untilled Field* (1903) is well known. He wrote 'model stories' in English which were then translated into Irish to help young writers in the Gaelic League movement. Then the stories were translated back into English 'much improved', to Moore's mind, 'for their bath in Irish'. The results for Moore's style were certainly salutary. The narrative style of *The Untilled Field* and *The Lake* is simpler and more supple than anything Moore had written previously, even than *Esther Waters* whose plainness of idiom is often prim and brittle. Charles Morgan calls this new style an 'idealisation of the rhythms of the speaking voice' in which Moore exchanges 'the literary approach to narrative for that of a *raconteur*'. Moore's handling of Irish dialect, which in his earlier Irish novel, *A Drama in Muslin*, had been in the worst tradition of stage-Irishry, becomes impeccable in *The Lake* and *The Untilled Field*. In short, the quality which Frank O'Connor was to single out as the characteristic virtue of the subsequent Irish short story, 'the tone of a man's voice speaking',[8] became the most salient

feature of Moore's new Irish style. Nor is it a mere passing
phase with Moore: that eloquent jarvey who narrates the story
of Julia Cahill in *The Untilled Field* finds a lively new incarnation
as Alec Trusselby of *A Storyteller's Holiday* (1918), a book whose
very title proclaims a radical shift from the Pateresque aesthete
who wrote *Celibate Lives*.

There is no doubt that Joyce read *The Untilled Field* carefully
and at a time when it could have maximum influence on the
stories that eventually appeared in *Dubliners* a decade later. In
a letter to his brother Stanislaus of November, 1904, he remarks:

I have read Moore's *The Untilled Field* in Tauchnitz. Damned stupid ...
A woman alludes to her husband in the confession as Ned. 'Ned thinks
etc.' A lady has been living for three years on the line between Bray and
Dublin. She looks up the table to see the hours of the trains ... Isn't
it rather stupid of Moore. And the punctuation! Madonna!⁹

The criticism is typical of Joyce, and valuable as a clue to his
intention and method in *Dubliners*, especially in view of the
increasing body of critics who want to read it as a minefield of
myth and symbol. Joyce, writing in his naturalistic idiom, would
never make these mistakes of fact or psychology. His shrillness
reflects his mental state at the time. Richard Ellmann records
that during the gestation of *Dubliners* Joyce was vigilant in
respect of any writer who might be 'doing the same thng as he
was'. When he heard that Seumas O'Kelly had published a
volume of short stories, *By the Stream of Kilmeen*, he sent for it
at once. He dismissed it with more good humour than he did
Moore, perhaps because he felt so much less threatened by it:

The stories I have read were about beautiful, pure faithful Connacht
girls and lithe, broad-shouldered open-faced young Connacht men ...
Maybe, begod, people like that are to be found by the stream of
Kilmeen only none of them have come under my observation.¹⁰

As it happened Joyce need not have feared; no unfavourable
comparison with Moore's book marred the modest critical
reception accorded to *Dubliners*. More recent critics take another
view: Frank O'Connor had no doubt that 'Joyce was deeply
influenced'¹¹ by *The Untilled Field*; Brendan Kennelly uses
Joyce's own phrase to declare that *Dubliners* is the second
chapter in Ireland's 'moral history' whereas 'The Untilled Field is
the first'. Eileen Kennedy, Phillip Marcus and John Cronin have
variously supported the view, instancing the panoramic view of

community shared by the writers, their use of 'epiphany', the themes of paralysis and flight, the artist, priest and clerk as hero, the role of clerical oppression in the lives of the characters.[12]

While these affinities exist they must not be allowed to obscure the radical differences, thematic and technical, between the two books. The theme of *Dubliners* is inertia: nowhere do we see the defiant individual confront the forces of established order. The only one to get out, to achieve even a limited flight, is the leering vulgarian, Ignatius Gallagher, and he carries his limitations with him. But while Moore presents a stagnant society he dramatises its inertia by means of the rebellious individual who tries to change or energise it, or otherwise finds salvation through exile—Bryden, Rodney, Carmady, Kate Kavanagh, Julia Cahill. Joyce went to Trieste to write of Dublin's earth-bound victims, Moore came home to celebrate the country's heroic exiles.

The role of the priest is significantly different in each book. Most of Moore's priests are puritanical and oppressive, enemies of human joy, of dancing, drinking, 'company-keeping'. They exercise no such tyranny over the world of *Dubliners:* Farrington is drunken and lecherous, Corley, Lenihan and Polly Mooney are sexual predators, Ignatius Gallagher is a boastful philanderer and Little Chandler wishes he were. The virginity of neither Maria nor Eveline is personally or religiously willed. The one celibate, Duffy, is an unbeliever. No priest has sought to thwart any of them in their desires. Indeed the only articulate clerical voice is that of Father Purdon in 'Grace', and he is suspiciously bland, worldly and accommodating, with his sympathy for 'our little failings' and the 'weakness of our poor fallen nature'. Apart from him the Dublin clergy cut a poor figure: Father Flynn is paralysed, Father Butler of 'An Encounter' is a harmless snob, the dead priest of 'Araby' is survived by three mouldy books and a rusted bicycle pump, Father Keon in 'Ivy Day' is mistaken for the dozen stout, Father Constantine Conroy does nothing more positive than miss the Morkans' party. It would be difficult to find two more disparate accounts of the relationship between priests and laity than those portrayed by Joyce and Moore in their short stories.

The technical implication of this difference is considerable. The typical Moore story involves a struggle between the individual and his society—usually represented by the clergy—and reaches its resolution in the hero's triumph or escape. It is by far the more romantic of the two books, depending upon a traditional sense of plot which moves dramatically towards crisis and release. Joyce, on the other hand, repudiates that old sense of plot, mediating his vision through events of minimal dramatic force. Moore's clerk, in 'The Clerk's Quest' throws over his 'well ordered and closely guarded life' and dies of hunger and exposure because his erotic nature is unmanned by the scent of perfume from a cheque. Joyce's clerks, Farrington, Chandler and Duffy, are similarly challenged and acutely disturbed, but none of them embarks on extravagant journeys or forgets to eat. They will all turn up for work the next morning. When in difficulties these Dubliners take walks, get drunk, attend sermons, beat their children, eat plates of peas or search for the corkscrew. Indeed their primary condition is neither paralysis nor flight but something that partakes a little of each, compromise. The banner of rebellion is often feebly raised but quickly lowered again: there are no Carmadies or Brydens in Joyce's world—not even an earnest Father MacTurnan.

It is, useful therefore, to see Moore's collection as enacting a crucial tension between the insubordinate individual and the forces of settled society, lay and clerical—a tension everywhere present in Synge, Yeats and Stephens and profoundly characteristic of the time. The rebellious sculptor, Rodney, figures in the first story and the last. He provides an obvious parallel to, and may have influenced, Joyce's figure of the artist especially at the end of *Portrait:* both young artists leave Ireland for almost identical reasons. The central conflict in the long story, 'Some Parishioners', is between those two marvellously drawn, and well matched, personalities—the beautiful and spirited Kate Kavanagh and that lugubrious cleric, Father Tom Maguire. Bryden chooses flight and sacrifices love rather than submit to the priest in 'Home Sickness'. In the book's most subtle and penetrating story, 'Julia Cahill's Curse' the struggle between paganism and christianity delicately underlies a human drama in which Julia Cahill brings vengeance upon the priest who had outlawed her life-affirming individuality. A similar curse accrues in its companion piece, 'A Play House in the Waste', where the same double perspective is brought to bear on the hideous fate of a girl who had violated the society's taboos. Ned Carmady in 'The Wild Goose' is obviously conceived as a national type, the traditional Irish soldier of fortune who loves his country but cannot adjust himself to its constraints. In a sequence that resembles that of Rodney, the sculptor, and of course that of Moore himself, he returns to Ireland, tries to make a career in Irish politics—marrying in the course a Catholic lady—but is defeated by restrictions of society. Father MacTurnan struggles quixotically against officials of church and state and the tide of emigration. In the last story, 'The Way Back' Carmady, Rodney and Harding—the sophisticated novelist and painter who crops up in so many Moore novels and may be a coy self-portrait—meet in London and discuss Ireland, the real heroine of the book. In an unconvincing if rather charming gesture Harding determines to return:

'I tell you that your interesting utterances about the Italian renaissance would not interest me half so much as what Paddy Durkin and Father Pat will say to me on the road'.

Moore wisely removed these first and last 'framing stories' after the first edition of *The Untilled Field:* they were not intrinsically good and the sense of unity they lent to the volume was largely spurious. Its real unity as a volume derives from its powerful, rural stories, 'Home Sickness', 'Some Parishioners', 'Julia Cahill's Curse', 'A Play-House in the Waste', 'A Letter to Rome' and 'The Exile' where the lessons of Turgenev are powerfully applied in yielding up an authentic portrait of the Ireland he had genuinely come to know.

Forrest Reid's fourth novel, and by common consent his best, *Following Darkness* appeared in 1912 and was re-written as *Peter Waring* in 1937. In contemplating this strange *bildungsroman* in its first version the reader is struck by its affinities with Yeats's stories, which certainly influenced it in theme, technique and symbol, and with the artist fictions of Moore and Joyce which appeared respectively before and after its publication. Reid was one of Yeats's first critics, publishing *W. B. Yeats: A Critical Study* in 1915 in which his enthusiasm for the 'apocalyptic tales' shows an obvious affinity with Yeats's theme and methods. The haunted young artist whose story is rehearsed in *Following Darkness* has the Yeatsian hero's taste for the Italian Renaissance and ends his mysterious life 'under the influence of strange and disreputable persons, who professed to experiment in occult sciences—spiritualism, and even magic'.[13] It is a novel of remarkable originality and strange intensity, tracing the growth of a sensitive Ulster boy first with his unsympathetic father in the idyllic countryside of County Down, then in the distasteful and cramping back streets of Belfast, his return to the countryside, a macabre attempt at suicide and ultimately his departure to the Continent. His history is edited by his friend, Owen Gill, after his mysterious death in middle age. Waring is at once original and typical of the fictional artist as a young man in which the period was so rich. We see the slow estrangement from family and faith, the dawning of romantic love and adolescent sexuality, the lure of art and of nature, the moments of heightened sensitivity, as when he lies half-naked in the grass at night:

It was well there was no-one to observe this exhibition of primitive and eternal instinct. My head was bare, the salt sharp smell of the sea seemed to have set all my nerves tingling, and I unfastened my shirt that my breast might be bare also. All the past had slipped from me, and I lived in this moment, squeezing out its ecstacy to the last drop, as I might the juice of some ripe fruit. It seemed to me that I was on the brink of finding something for which all my previous existence had been but one long preparation and search ... I imagined myself Endymion, as I lay there half naked in the moonlight. My eyes dimmed and the blood raced through my veins; it was as if the heart of the summer had suddenly opened out, like a gorgeous flower, and brought me some strange rapture.

It is remarkable that this passage appeared one year before *Sons and Lovers* and four years in advance of that remarkably similar passage of Joyce's when Stephen has his moment of ecstasy on Dollymount Strand. Even more striking is the demonic interlude recorded by Waring in his journal, where the figure of Christ, conjured in a dream, is driven out by 'a man, naked, superb, the colour of dark, greenish bronze, shot through the window as though propelled by some invisible force' who determines to send the young artist down to hell so that he might 'return again to earth, but ... be his forever'. This amalgam of Satan and Hermes derives in part from Yeats, but even more interestingly foreshadows the last chapter of *A Portrait* where Joyce's young artist adopts Hermes/Thoth as his patron and pronounces his version of the satanic *non serviam*.

*The Lake* (1905) was first conceived as a short story for *The Untilled Field* collection and in the Carra edition of 1923 both works were published in a single volume. The affinities between the novel and the short stories are in the Irish setting, the priestly theme and the authentic run of Irish speech, especially in the dialogue. But *The Lake* contains the seeds of a stylistic development that is to dominate Moore's writing from this point on, the search for a 'melodic line' to embody that sense of reverie wherein the movement of the mind between observation and memory can be dramatised in narrative. Critics describe the style by means of musical analogy, pointing out how Moore derived it from Wagner via Dujardin. The technique is not quite perfected in the first edition of *The Lake* where the authorial voice interrupts the internal reverie too arbitrarily. But in the 1921 revision of the novel, a work of remarkable texture is achieved, arguably the most perfect fiction in Moore's entire canon. Almost as striking is the portrait of the book's hero, Father Gogarty, whose obsession with a young schoolteacher and consequent flight from the country and the priesthood forms the book's plot. The narrative method allows Moore to enter the priest's thought processes and achieve a sense of sympathetic intimacy with his spiritual anxieties. In the 1921 preface Moore describes the technical challenge: 'To keep the story in the key in which it was conceived, it was necessary to recount the priest's life during the course of his walk by the shores of a lake, weaving his memories continually, without losing sight, however, of the long, winding, mere-like lake, wooded to its shores, with hills appearing and disappearing into mist and distance'.[15]

This narrative technique was, of course, to prove the ideal instrument in bringing under a rule the sprawl of biography, anecdote, memoir, gossip and self-revelation, that makes up the raw material of Moore's autobiographical masterpiece, *Hail and Farewell*.[16] Here his twelve years in Dublin when the Literary Renaissance was at its most intense, 1899-1911, are delivered to us in a style which can range easily back and forth through time and space, which can discuss its own procedures and challenge as its moves, which can record, embellish and invent so that these processes are indistinguishable in the seamless roof of the whole. The portraits of Yeats, Martyn, Russell, Plunkett, Synge, Stephens, Eglinton, Lady Gregory are portrayed with energy and penetration; the atmospheres of Dublin and the Irish countryside are evoked with an Impressionist's sense of tone and colour and the narrator's poignant love affair with 'Stella' is subtly woven through the fabric with remarkable delicacy down to that frank and unforgettable moment of defeat in the eleventh chapter of *Vale. A Story-Teller's Holiday* (1918) is Moore's last handling of Irish material and there his narrative inventiveness blends promiscuously with spoken idiom of his oral narrator, Alex Trusselby, in a skein of medieval tales in which ingenuity and self-indulgence play roughly equal roles.

James Stephens is best known for his first two novels, *The Crock of Gold* and *The Charwoman's Daughter* both of which appeared in 1912. Both are works of striking originality, and both exhibit that technical inventiveness for which the writer and his period are remarkable. *The Crock of Gold* seized upon the mythic and folk material which had been handled with such solemnity by Standish James O'Grady, Yeats and Lady Gregory and, in a spirit of gleeful mockery, made it yield up a radical vision of contemporary society. The book begins with a countryman consulting a Philosopher about the theft of a washing-board by Leprecauns and the abduction of his daughter by the god Pan, and ends wtih the awakening of the Celtic gods and heroes, Aengus Og, Cuchulain, Finn and Oisin, to liberate the world from the Urizenic forces of society, 'the doctors and lawyers . . . the sly priests . . . the professors whose mouths are gorged with sawdust, and the merchants who sell blades of grass'.[17] In the sexual awakening of the heroine, Caitilin, under the influence of Pan's pipes, Stephens registers a daring pre-Lawrentian plea for freedom; in the interpolated stories a scarifying vision of social slavery is projected against the life-affirming vision of nature and magic that forms the book's permeating atmosphere. Comedy, satire, burlesque, allegory and prophesy mingle in a prose fantasy of quite dashing originality. In his other, and in many ways superior, prose fantasy, *The Demi-Gods* (1914) Stephens again deploys a Celtic hero (in this case, Cuchulain) in a modern incarnation to animate a cosmic comedy which encompasses the Christian and Theosophist heavens, hell, and the picaresque destinies of a group of tinkers travelling the roads of Ireland in the company of three 'buck angels' recently alighted on the sphere. This irreverent treatment of the Celtic hero was to continue in the fiction of James Joyce, Eimar O'Duffy and Flann O'Brien, while the tradition of satiric fantasy begun by Stephens in these books has had its modern exponents in the works of Austin Clarke, Mervyn Wall, Bryan MacMahon and Tom McIntyre.

On the flyleaf of a presentation copy of *The Crock of Gold* Stephens wrote:

In this book there is only one character—Man—Pan is his sensual nature, Caitilin, his emotional nature, Angus Og his intellect spiritualised, the policemen his conventions and logics, the leprecauns his elemental side, the children his innocence, and the idea is not rigidly carried out, but that is how I conceived the story.

There is some such design or vision behind most of Stephen's prose fiction. From his absorption in the Prophetic Books of Blake he derived a concept of the artist as visionary and art as a Blakean 'Endeavour to Restore what the Ancients call'd the Golden Age'. He shared with Yeats and AE the intuition of an apocalypse soon to come, of a mechanical world waiting to be transformed by the creative imagination. Head, heart, loins and intellect, sundered by scientific rationalism and its dark agents in the factory and the counting house, would again be united under the aegis of the imagination—like that ancient man Albion—in a rejuvenated world.

Unlike Yeats and AE, however, Stephens was a natural story teller, a fabulist with the novelist's gifts of humour and inventiveness and his skills with plot, character, dialogue and narrative. Generations have read *The Crock of Gold* for the aphoristic knockabout of the Philosophers and their wives, for the drollery of Meehawl and the leprecauns, for the comedy of the blundering policemen, for the intense and delicate drama of Caitilin's dawning sexuality, for the sunlit ambiance of the author's celtic noonday. *The Charwoman's Daughter* can easily be mistaken for a superior example of the romantic novelette without any pressing sense of its deeper implications: the drama of class which makes Mary's betrayal of her mother and humiliation by the policeman so painful: the drama of growth wherein Mary must develop from child to woman amid the ambush of first love; the drama of Dublin—here the contrast with Joyce's *Dubliners* is instructive—with its vivid but unobtrusive counterpoint of park and back-street, high fashion and working-class squalor, villa and tenement. Most memorable, perhaps, is the small cast of characters, an ensemble that recurs uncannily through most of his subsequent fictions: the adolescent heroine, poised on the brink of womanhood, reappears as Caitilin, as Mary MacCann in *The Demi-Gods*, and as Deirdre in his retelling of that mythic story; the Charwoman with her eloquence, ferocity and possessiveness returns as the Thin Woman and Lavarcham; the Policeman is given a heroic reincarnation as Conchubar and the young clerk as Naoise.

The lover's triangle is Stephens's favourite scenario. It dominates the triadic tensions and intrigues of the short stories in *Here are Ladies* and forms the theme of that rivetting novella, 'Etched in Moonlight' where a sense of nightmare permeates an action as stark and suggestive as that of a medieval exemplum. The motif of sexual jealousy that the fable explores is one of Stephen's predominant obsessions, giving force and complication to *The Charwoman's Daughter*, *The Demi-Gods*, *In the Land of Youth*, *Deirdre* and several of the short stories and the *Irish Fairy Tales*. His second recurrent theme is money and its power over the human spirit: this theme competes for priority with love in *The Demi-Gods* where, in the linked destinies of Brien O'Brien, the Seraph Cuchulain, Billy the Music and the erring tinker, Patsy MacCann, it sets up dissonant vibrations throughout heaven, hell, earth and the seven spheres of the theosophist universe.

Perhaps the most striking feature of Stephen's development is his tireless experimentation with narrative method. The fusion of a fairy-tale plot with the realities of contemporary Dublin in *The Charwoman's Daughter* set Stephens off on a path of fictional ingenuity which involved reflexive narration, time warps, tales within tales and worlds within worlds, reincarnations and transitions between different planes of reality, which inspired Lloyd Frankenberg to coin a new critical term to describe it: 'Geometry of the Translucently Faceted Dimensions of Timescape.[17] The phenomenon is most evident in *The Demi-Gods*, *Irish Fairy Tales* (1920), *In the Land of Youth* (1924) and the macabre masterpiece 'Etched In Moonlight' which is the title story of his 1928 collection of short stories. Meanwhile, in his great short story of the Dublin slums, *Hunger* (1918), he demonstrates the strength and sophistication of narrative simplicity at work upon a tragic theme.

Seumas O'Kelly (1878-1918) published his first book of short stories and sketches, *By the Stream of Kilmeen* in 1906, drawing upon himself the derision of James Joyce, who objected to its national piety and sentimentality. Joyce's recoil from the school of Yeats had been occasioned in part by Yeats's belief in the Irish peasant and the folk imagination; and in his own adversions to that milieu in his fiction Joyce was vividly astringent—we recall Mulrennan's old man, Davin's benighted countrywoman and her 'batlike soul', the milkwoman at the tower. Moore's testimony had been similar: Carmody in 'The Way Back' says 'Let the Gael disappear ... He is doing it very nicely ... His instinct is to disappear in America'; Rodney in 'In the Clay' shrinks from 'a mean ineffectual atmosphere of nuns and rosaries'. O'Kelly, an active Irish nationalist, began almost as an apologist for the opposite view of Irish rural experience, in particular for the role of tradition and community within it. With O'Kelly begins a discernible counter-movement, especially in the short story, that includes Corkery, O'Connor, O'Faolain, McLaverty and Bryan MacMahon. In a rather shapeless sketch, 'A Land of Loneliness', from his first volume, there is a passage that uneasily invokes Moore's vision of the Irish landscape:

He looked over the deserted country with that same strained look as before, and I was struck with the thought that the old man's eyes had a great look of similarity to the country around him—that similarity which I subsequently read George Moore had also noted from one of his sketches in that singular book *The Untilled Field.* [18]

O'Kelly's old man goes on to unfold a tangled history of the region, mixing fact with legend, dislocating chronology, making a weird oral travesty of what is evidently a grand and tragic retrospect.

We do not have to read far into O'Kelly's book to sense that another 'portrait of my people' is taking shape, with a different focus and camera-angle. These derelict cottages, for instance, have not been emptied by a puritanical clergy, but 'by the black work of the evictor'. The old man's monologue becomes a broken threnody over a race and civilisation that has 'suffered' and 'borne' but which we feel will survive by drawing strength from its 'mighty memories'. In a more blatant piece, 'The Story of a Spell', about the community on the island of Cape Clear, a 'suntanned fisherman' can recite 'nearly all of Oisin's songs' in Irish, the people are 'honest and industrious ... of high intelligence, religious and conscientious, and with all the warmth of heart of the true Celt ... living testimony of the dictum of Thomas Davis that a Nation's bulwark is its language'. [19] The memory of a local saint 'Cairn' completes a picture which we are to encounter again, as, for instance, in Corkery's 'On the Heights' where the argument of generations are dissolved when the name of St. Finbarr is invoked. The reader is equally aware of Pearse weaving his national pieties among the Gaels of Connemara.

In this simplistic view of the Irish reality emigration and exile are a defeat for the individual, a loss for society. Thus Thade Furey, that Galway version of Ignatius Gallagher, returns from his successful career in journalism having 'bled his brains white' and having found the world outside 'rotten and corrupt'. Denis

Donohoe in 'Both Sides of the Pond', having failed in love and been forced to emigrate, ends up capering for a drunken audience in a Bowery tavern. Unlike Moore's feat of equilibrium in 'Home Sickness' where James Bryden's mind is a register for what is good and bad in both conditions, the early O'Kelly story tends to make a melodrama of choice.

In curbing this tendency, in probing the limitations as well as the enhancements of peasant community, O'Kelly achieves his rare distinction as a short story writer. This he manages superbly, not in his two interesting but flawed novels, *The Lady of Deerpark* (1917) and *Wet Clay* (1922), but in three short stories, 'The Building', 'The Prodigal Daughter' and his most celebrated story, 'The Weaver's Grave'.

'The Prodigal Daughter' takes the unpromising theme of a prim spinster lady, Miss Hickey, who has held aloof from her township for most of her life, who leaves it when opportunity offers, and who is drawn back, shaken and humbled by a need for its community of which she had not been aware. The power of the story lies in the skill with which O'Kelly moves the reader from a sense of his heroine's social absurdity to an inexorable sense of her painful growth towards self-recognition. The ironic parallel with the debauchee of the gospel story is subtle and pleasing, as the prodigal, trembling but outwardly unbowed, resumes her dignity within her father's house. 'The Building', on the other hand, ends with a suspended chord, a moment when O'Kelly seems to have reached a crisis in his exploration of the individual's relation with the community. The hero has exultantly built a splendid stone house for his intended. On its completion she fails to return to him. As he now scans the building the 'joy of the builder' passes and is replaced by the pull of the earth. He searches the sky with 'a final and anxious, a peasant look':

the fields, the sod, the territory of his forefathers, the inheritance of his blood. Who was he that he should put up a great building on the hill? What if he had risen for a little on his wings above the common flock?

O'Kelly's artist is an Icarus who assents to his fall, takes it humbly as a rebuke to his hubris. The final moment when he goes into the neglected cabin has been consistently seen as the just triumph of the ancestral earth and its demands over its wavering son. But the attendant sense of defeat for the human spirit is unavoidable:

All was quiet, black, terrible as chaos, inside. Martin Cosgrave hitched forward his left shoulder, went in sideways, and closed the crazy door against the pale world of moonlight outside.[20]

Within the limitations of the peasant community the house, the artefact, loses its meaning, its beauty, when the housewife fails to materialise. Art is not self-authenticating; the artist must choose conformity, madness or exile. Cosgrave's palpable 'folly' stands outside in the moonlight as its maker relapses into a sleep, which O'Kelly must also see as a type of death.

There is no modern artist figure in 'The Weaver's Grave' but the tension finds its embodiment between the generations. There the search for the old man's grave brings a dying world, where every member of the community had an art and thus an identity, into subtle collision with a new world where the living, like the impersonal crosses in the new graveyard, are initially indistinguishable. For much of the story the old men and the traditional world they represent seem to have it all their own way, but the story's superb resolution again settles for the suspended chord. Quietly the anonymous young widow has been distinguishing one of the patient young grave diggers from his twin brother, and the tale ends with a mythic leap across the grave in which the pledge of the future is symbolised. The technical sophistication of 'The Weaver's Grave', and its handling of theme and symbolic action, underlines the tragedy of O'Kelly's death a year before its publication.

Daniel Corkery (1878-1964) is one of the most controversial of modern Irish writers by virtue of his challenging excursus into social history in *The Hidden Ireland* (1925), his polemical reading of Anglo-Irish literature in his book on Synge, and for the intermittent cultural chauvinism that both mars and enlivens his collections of short stories. Critics are sharply divided as to the merit of his one novel, *The Threshold of Quiet* (1917), a book in which I cannot myself find much to praise. There is general agreement as to Corkery's great importance, and as to the distinction of his short fiction, especially his penultimate volume, *The Stormy Hills* (1929), which falls outside our period.

In the first chapter of *Synge and Anglo-Irish Literature* (1931) Corkery pronounces that religion, nationalism and the land are the definitive features of Irish consciousness. Most of his stories deal with one of other of these themes and many subsume all three. It is crucial to remember that Corkery grew up among memories of the Land War, and that he learned his Irish from

countrymen who had turned these skirmishes and confront-
ations into folk literature. Then his first book, *A Munster
Twilight*, came out in the year of the Easter Rising; his next, *The
Hounds of Banba* (1920), was an undisguised celebration of the
national struggle and the dashing young guerrillas who
ambushed army lorries or burnt out police barracks round the
Munster hills. Corkery's imagination was easily excited by the
thought of his people's struggle against Britain, and, like
Pearse, he often compared it to the struggle of the Jews down
through the centuries, a struggle which also expressed itself in
terms of land, religion and nationalism. When Corkery
surrenders his artistic conscience to this patriotic enthusiasm he
is at his most vulnerable, as in such an early story as 'Joy'.
When, on the other hand, he controls this fervour, when he
makes it answer to the demands of realism and irony within the
human situation, he can produce a masterpiece such as 'Carrig-
an-Aifrinn', from his penultimate volume, *The Stormy Hills*.

The first of these stories, 'Joy', is more romantic and
sentimental than anything in O'Kelly's juvenilia. We are asked
to share an old farmer's reveries on a festive Sunday as he
moves gratefully round his farmhouse quoting 'old poems of
the Gaelic bards, old prophecies of the Gaelic saints'. He
murmurs to his daughter that 'Rooted in the soil again ... and
there'll be Kings at Tara'.[21] As the daydream proceeds Corkery
provides a background of hurling in the field nearby with priests
moving among their people, and finally a political rally outside
his house celebrating the victories of the Land War where an
orator intones 'To the Gaelic race the riches of the air above it,
the seas around it'. The old man hears his own name mentioned
as one of those who had fought the good fight. As the crowd
disperses he confides to his children:

'The best of them beasts outside—I'd send him the road to Tara—'tis
long since I had anything to give anybody'.

There is no doubt that Corkery endorses the old man's maudlin
mood and aspiration. Even in his mature work he never
examines the implications of such cultural nostalgia for his
contemporary Ireland. Even his 'republicanism' is royalist, in
the manner of the poets of his 'Hidden Ireland' who yearned for
a Stuart king and a Catholic aristocracy. This curiously archaic
vision is vividly realised in such a late story as 'The Wager' from
*The Stormy Hills* where the narrating voice is that of a latter day

Thady Quirke, a house peasant to whom the Land War has restored something of his old Gaelic pride:

The gentry weren't broken out of the country at that time; and some of them, most of them, did what they liked with us. When they were beginning to go down the hill ... many of them had to content themselves with living in their own places, instead of Dublin and London, and as often as they grew weary of the hunting, the dancing, the cards, would have to think of new pastimes for themselves.

The scene is not radically changed from that of a dozen nine-teenth century novels—a degraded and irresponsible gentry with its cohort of servile native retainers. The incident upon which the story turns arises out of a drunken wager made by the 'Master' with a neighbouring landlord, that his horse can jump the protecting sea wall to a ledge on the opposite cliff-side. They wake the servants and put the proposition to Sean O'Brosnan, the Master's best rider. O'Brosnan is proof against all persuasions till the rival landlord declares that 'There's not a Brosnan in Kilvreeda would jump it, no, nor in Muckross!' The narrator pauses here to explain why this taunt decided O'Brosnan to make the jump. Ancestral pride had been outraged, 'the ancient Brosnans' who from 'time immemorial' had been laid in Muckross Abbey had been insulted. In the moonlight, watched by drunken gentry and their servants, O'Brosnan makes the leap, loses the horse, and in the last sentence 'strode through us all, gentle and simple, as if we were so much dust on the road'.

The story was written while Corkery was maturing his critique of what he called 'the shameful literary tradition of the Prout, Maginn, Lever, Lover school of writers' in his *Synge* book which appeared two years later in 1931. There he attacked 'This Colonial literature' which was 'written to explain the quaintness of the humankind of this land, especially the native humankind, to another that was not quaint, that was standard, normal'.[22] In 'The Wager' he is redressing the balance and the story suffers from a tone of special pleading that would be intolerable were it not refracted through the persona of that peasant narrator, and through the time lapse that separates the action and its telling. It remains a story of great power, and its power is inseparable from that passionate love of Irish tradtion which animates so much of Corkery's vision.

This word 'tradition' must serve to cover what Corkery means by his formulation of Land, Religion and Nationality. In the stories every protagonist—revolutionary, horseman, landlord, peasant, rural historian—finds himself judged in the light of this tradition, even if, like the Master, he is culpably ignorant of it. In 'The Ploughing of Leaca na Naomh', the first story in *A Munster Twilight*, the narrator goes into the mountains to write the history 'of an old Gaelic family that once were lords of them'. The role gives him the advantage of mediating between the raw experience of the story he discovers and the reader. The shadow of Turgenev hangs over these tales in which some version of the great Russian's 'Sportsman' travels into remote Irish regions and filters through his consciousness some vivid feature of the place's life and values: Moore's social reformer in 'Julia Cahill's Curse', O'Connor's tourist in 'The Bridal Night' and here Corkery's social historian are obvious examples.

Here the narrator comes upon a farming family living under the shadow of some painful memory, and gradually reveals its secret. The farmer, Considine, had become obsessed with the idea of ploughing the 'Leaca' a saucer of land which was the burial place of the Irish saints. To this end he had incited a half-witted labourer, Liam Ruadh, to plough it with two great stallions who dragged the simpleton to his death across the cliff-side. The unnecessarily explicit ending where the narrator gives up his historical quest but remains haunted by the thought that Liam Ruadh 'might have been the last of an immemorial line, no scion of which ... would have ploughed the Leaca of the Saints' does not seriously impair the story's impact. The secret of its success is the dual force at work within it: the natural ambition of Considine to bring all his land under the plough—a husbandman's quality that Corkery and O'Kelly admire—and the spiritual profanation in disturbing ancestral pieties. The Master had sinned against these pieties when he mocked the Brosnan ancestors lying in Muckross Abbey. The young guerilla in 'On the Heights' in *The Hounds of Banba* vindicates them when he has a fierce and ludicrous argument with an old man shouting unseen at him from a bedroom in a mountain cottage:

' 'Tis no decent person would be travelling the hills this nights', I was answered, and there was suspicion and challenge in the tones.
There's a more decent person on your floor this night', I answered back ... than ever walked this hungry land since St. Finbarr left it, travelling to the east.
'Left it and blessed it', the voice answered me in triumph. [23]

Land, therefore, is a complex affair in Corkery. It can beget meanness and cruelty in those who till it, as in a story like 'Vanity', while even poorer land like that on the 'Heights', can have its own riches in the blessing of a local saint. Corkery's is, in a sense, a Christian version of Yeats's image of a country irradiated with pagan, spiritual forces. But because Corkery is working within the idiom of realist fiction he must face the clash between any idealised conception of the land and the greed, envy and ambition which it engenders in its possessors. The story of the Leaca had already shown his awareness of these tensions. 'Carrig an Airfrinn' is, however, his great exploration of the theme, and probably his finest story. There the two forces are seen at work in the consciousness of old Hodnett who, in his ambition, had sold his poor farm at Carrig-an-Aifrinn, 'The Mass Rock' where his ancestors had celebrated Mass in penal times. Hodnett is vividly realised both in his mystical regret for the old farm and his ferocious determination to succeed in his new holding.'

for what I was saying to myself was: 'I'll break it! I'll break it! And I was saying that because if I didn't break it I was sport for the world. Like a bully at a fair I was, going about my own land the first day I walked it!

The old man's victory over his unbroken farm is bought at immense human cost to himself and his family, and Corkery flinches from none of the brutal realities of the struggle. Indeed one of his finest touches is the irony that the sacred land of Carrig-an-Aifrinn which in his guilty nostalgia the old man sees still 'thronged with angels' has been blasted and cleared for a modern highway. Within a work of satisfactory realism Corkery has managed to balance the demands of a spiritual tradition and those necessary for a sensible attitude to the present. He achieves an imaginative equilibrium similar to that created by O'Kelly in 'The Weaver's Grave'.

It is a commonplace of Irish literary history to say that the mood of our writers changed after the Civil War and the founding of the new State in 1922 from heroism to disillusion, from romanticism to irony. Yeats's assertion that 'A terrible beauty is born' is echoed in the stories of Corkery, in a number of spirited ballads by Stephens, Russell, Ledwidge and Lady Gregory. Eimar O'Duffy tried to register a more complex sense of the period in a shapeless and floundering novel, *The Wasted Island*. In 1917 the young Austin Clarke was writing heroic epics that give no hint of the astringent satirist who, in the late

Twenties and Thirties, was to turn epic and history to telling account in his satirical reaction to the fledgling democracy. The seeds were already set for the new literature born out of the disappointed idealism of the Rising and the Troubles and the challenge of political independence. There is perhaps an excusable symmetry to be discerned in that at least the short story came formally of age with O'Flaherty's *Spring Sowing* (1924) twenty one years exactly after the first sod was broken in Moore's *Untilled Field*.

## NOTES

1.  W. B. Yeats, *John Sherman and Dhoya*, London 1891.
2.  'Ulysses, Order and Myth', *The Dial*, November 1923, p.48.
3.  *Stephen Hero*, ed., Theodore Spencer. London: Four Square (1966), Ch.XXIII.
4.  *The Secret Rose*, London 1897. In his Note to *Mythologies* (1925) Yeats explains that 'The Tables of the Law' and 'The Adoration of the Magi' were intended as part of *The Secret Rose* but that 'the publisher, A. H. Bullen, took a distaste to them and asked me to leave them out, and then after the book was published liked them and put them into a little volume by themselves'.
5.  'Apocalyptic Structures in Yeats's *Secret Rose*', *Studies*, Spring, 1975.
6.  *A Portrait of the Artist as a Young Man* ed. Chester G. Anderson. New York: Viking Critical Library (1968), Chapter I, p.7.
7.  *Ibid.*, Chapter V, p.225.
8.  *The Lonely Voice* by Frank O'Connor. London: Macmillan (1963), p.29.
9.  *Selected Letters of James Joyce*, ed. R. Ellmann. London: Faber (1975), p.44.
10. *Ibid.*, pp.133-34.
11. *The Lonely Voice*, p.29.
12. See 'Moore's *Untilled Field* and Joyce's *Dubliners*' by Eileen Kennedy, *Eire Ireland* Vol. 3, 1970; 'George Moore's Dublin Epiphanies and Joyce' by Phillip Marcus, *The James Joyce Quarterly*, Vol. 3, 1970; 'George Moore's Lonely Voices' by Brendan Kennelly, *George Moore's Mind and Art*, ed. Graham Owens. Edinburgh: Oliver and Boyd (1968); 'George Moore: *The Untilled Field*' by John Cronin, *The Irish Short Story* eds. Patrick Rafroidi and Terence Brown. Gerrards Cross: Colin Smythe Ltd (1979).
13. *Following Darkness*, London (1912), p.4.
14. *Ibid.*, pp.78-79.
15. *The Lake*, London 1921, Preface.
16. *Hail and Farewell*, reissued with Introduction and Notes by Richard Cave. Gerrards Cross: Colin Smythe Ltd (1976).
17. *James Stephens, a Selection*, ed.L.Frankenberg.London: Macmillan (1962), p.25.
18. *A Land of Loneliness and Other Stories*, ed. E. Grennan. Dublin: Gill (1969).
19. Seumas O'Kelly *By the Stream of Kilmeen*, Dublin (1906), p.40.
20. Seumas O'Kelly *Waysiders*. Dublin: Talbot (1924), p.203.
21. Daniel Corkery *The Munster Twilight*. Cork: Mercier (1967), p.84.
22. Daniel Corkery *Synge & Anglo-Irish Literature*, Cork: Mercier (1966), pp.7-8.
23. Daniel Corkery *The Hound of Banba*. Dublin: Talbot & London: Fisher Unwin (1920), pp.24-25.

# THE UNPARTITIONED INTELLECT

JOHN MONTAGUE

Yeats died in 1939, Joyce in 1941, a double blow to modern and Irish literature. In Tyrone I heard of neither event but we did gather around the green baize of our old Philco radio to hear de Valera's reply to Winston Churchill after the war: the vindication of that neutrality which made the South of Ireland seem so strange to a little Ulster boy like myself. Despite their Coronation jugs my aunts were moved by memories of their youth, Sinn Fein and Cumman na mBan. Simple, stirring patriotism, a bony repudiation of Churchill's stammering rhetoric.

Wakes and weddings, I noticed, would be interrupted by intense discussion of the doings of this dark man; the Economic War, the giving back of the ports. Finally I saw him standing some rainy evening on College Green droning on majestically about the Irish language, and the price of bread. It was the election of 1956, and I described it in a piece for *Threshold* only to have my best phrase, comparing that lonely black coated and hatted figure to a 'sacerdotal heron', censored. (The second time I was censored was by the Northern B.B.C., but I mention this only as a minor testimony to the tensions that beset all sides in our history-divided province).

So around de Valera a nexus of associations began to form, as a symbol of dark intransigence, of fiery austerity. Investigating the South of Ireland also meant exploring his mind, of which it was partly the creation. No wonder Sean O'Faolain did two studies of this much-beloved despot, who aroused both hatred and total respect. The writers of the 1930s in Ireland were obsessed by him while acknowledging his power, like that portrait of him in Liam O'Flaherty's *Shame the Devil*.

The postwar South I discovered was a limbo land, which made even the North seem lively. The tosspit and the concrete dancehall were the main distractions through the countryside. It was a land that was over 90 per cent Catholic, with a hundred thousand domestic servants, with late marriages, if ever, and half the population overseas. I take these grim details from Terence Brown's splendid study, *Ireland: A Social and Cultural History, 1922-1979*, and it was natural that the writers should withdraw. O'Faolain's story 'A Broken World' is a post-Joycean vision of the bleakness of that little state and I remember many a spat between him and Frank O'Connor and the advocates of our priest-ridden, censored land. All hail to their bravery, but it did them much harm; if you spend too much energy on a negative cause, you will absorb some of it: Tsarist Stalin helped to make Solzhenitsin into an old-fashioned Russian prophet, the scourge of the revolution, a magnificent bore. 'You become', I partly agree with AE, 'what you contemplate'.

So the South seemed to me to be a procession of sad and broken poets and complaining novelists. Why should I not go and see the patriarch of all this misery, the great apostle of gloom himself? After all, we had a common destiny, being both New York born, and then pitchforked by history back into rural Ireland. Winter, gathering darkness over Aras an Uachtaráin, the old Vice Regal lodge. I have come for tea and tea it is; not a scent or glint of a whiskey bottle in sight. I try a little Ulster Irish; he is clearly under the impression that I am speaking a foreign language. I turn to Irish literature and, to my astonishment, he seems only to know Pearse. *Buile Suibhne* he has never heard of, or my ears lost his low tones. Or *Aisling Mac Conglinne*. He accepts graciously that they are the two masterpieces of medieval Irish literature but seems to have expected me to bring copies. They are out of print for years, since the foundation of the state.

Desperately I speak of the home areas I know best, Tyrone and Fermanagh, lost green fields. He does not know that the Foyle is also the Strule, where Omagh stands. He has never head of Knockmany Hill and little of Clogher. He gave a speech once, where? Carrickmore, and remembered Pat MacCartan. Had I known it, the MacGarrity side of my family would have helped but it was his *distance* that puzzled me. I tried a joke about us both being born in New York. I said he had changed my life by his victory in the 1932 election because I came home in 1933. He seemed to take these as serious statements, not bantering homage. He had no feeling for his birthplace, he said. What would he have become there? Cardinal or Chief of police?

Twilight falling, his wife whispering in and out of the room, where was I, beyond intruding on a great ghost? There was a strange atmosphere in the room, strange but familiar. Was I in the presence of a parish priest? No, the aura was more powerful: and he was married. Was this, as his enemies declared, the great ogre, an Ayatollah of Ireland? No, he seemed distant, but kindly. An odour of chalk, of simple severity, of unassailable certainties—was I with the Dean of Studies?

Which brings us back to James Joyce. His is a Dublin-centred Ireland, dominated by the high drama of Parnell and his fall. De Valera's Clare is only distantly represented in the Gaelic ideals of Stephen's friend Davin, later parodied in the Citizen. But, although his world is pre-Independence, there is no doubt in his, or his characters', minds that Dublin is the capital of Ireland, of all-Ireland, because the concept of Great Britain and Ireland allowed for that, a position more definite than that of Edinburgh and Scotland now. Parnell, in any case, did not recognise such barriers between Irishmen, the Protestant patriot being an example of the open sensibility I wish to praise.

Because Parnell looks back to Thomas Davis and beyond that to the United Irishman old Dedalus and his Catholic cronies can recognise him as their uncrowned King, a Protestant *ard-Ri* of a largely Catholic people. Was there not a song: 'We'll crown de Valera king of Ireland?' What Ireland? The even more stagnant and narrowing one from which Beckett fled, the ingrown toenail known as Saorstat na hEireann? The minds of Joyce's characters are not as partitioned.

So it is fascinating to place Joyce beside de Valera, another lean and obsessive man—I almost said Manichee—who believed that he was chosen 'to forge the uncreated conscience of his race': political this time, of course. There is much evidence in *Finnegans Wake* that Joyce was intrigued by him, and rightly, because, since Parnell, no politician was as sure that he understood the psyche of the Irish people, because it was his own. But the larger vision of Avondale was gone, and we are right to think of Ireland, after Parnell, as suffering a split in sensibility which the simplified dream of the boy from Bruree ignores.

The ironies are many and painful. The massive ritual of Roman Catholicism, the most universal aspect of Ireland, forms a large part of the vision of James Jouce. But his is not a peasant faith for a peasant people; his Jesuits' training has placed him superciliously above the boots of the Christian Brothers whom he sees marching along the Bull Wall. Although he is our Dante forging in imagined and angry exile the uncreated conscience of his race he spurns the part of it from which de Valera derives his strength: 'I fear him. I fear his red rimmed horny eyes'.

So Joyce's view of his race is also exclusive. What race, indeed? Protestantism, either Northern or Southern, is not part of his vision, but neither is the dispossessed world of Corkery's Irish-speaking peasant. The first great voice of the Irish-Catholic consciousness in English, Joyce's achievement is based upon a repudiation of most of the ideals by which his countrymen lived. There is the fundamental difference between these two bony, implacable men: Joyce's proud definition in *A Portrait* of the nets he must fly by in the *persona* of Stephen is almost a definition of the Ireland de Valera was sustained by, sought to bring into political existence.

Together they can be seen as our long-delayed Dante, and his attendant Savonarola. De Valera did not initiate censorship, but he did not haul the books from the burning. A lean friar, at least, can one see him chortling over the last chapter of *Ulysses,* in pillow talk with Sinead? He did not flee nets, he welcomed their embrace, cultivating their intensities of narrowness. Contemplating the contradictory visions of these two great Irishmen, what ideals can we offer for our country? Some critics, influenced by Corkery, would have us believe that Irish literature escaped the Renaissance. But James Joyce did not, and if Joyce is not Irish, where are we? 'All too Irish', he said himself, meaning Southern Irish Catholic, the only kind he really knew, but his Catholicism was more that of Rabelais than of Brother Rice. The negative Catholicism we practice is far from that of Italy and France, as far perhaps as Ian Paisley from Geneva and Calvin's theology. Contemplating two forms of bigotry, the benighted Ireland over which de Valera ruled, whose list of banned books extended that of Rome and rivalled Russia, and the Orange vision of Ulster as the last stand of the True Blues, who in his right mind would chose either? Both de Valera and Paisley seem to me examples of the partitioned intellect, the result of that split in sensibility the country suffered after the fall of Parnell. Let us propose a greater vision, a creative synthesis, to try to warm them together again, in some life-enhancing embrace.

At the end of my *Selected Poems* (1982) you will find a sign, a device, the same as on the cover of *The Rough Field*, in its third edition. In both cases it was chosen by the designer as a symbol central to my work. But I am willing to accept it as an emblem to sport on my shield, not for battle but for courteous exchange, if you please, despite my ferocious Republican background.

It is the seal of the United Irishman, a harp of course, that ancient instrument the provenance of which I have often disputed with my friend the composer, Sean O Riada. This harp is swathed in a motto: *It is new strung and shall be heard.* My purpose is that we should realise its various tones. I would link it remotely with the Harp of Aeolus, the murmuring breath of romanticism, but more immediately to the events in my own country. Richness and narrowness, the world and our province: we must have both. Or rather we must have them all, remembering what Seamus Deane has brilliantly diagnosed as 'the central fact of Irish tradition—that it is always an attempt to describe what we have yet to build'.

So I would like to introduce a new element into the discussion of Anglo-Irish literature, a more inclusive term. It could descend into an intellectual parlour game, some sort of Celtic scrabble, but it might also be of use as a touchstone, at the very least a description of a certain kind of mind, an ideal inclusiveness towards which we might all aspire, a passionate welcoming, a fertile balance.

The unpartitioned intellect is a sensibility which is prepared to entertain, to be sympathetic to, all the traditions of which our country can be said to be composed. I am thinking in terms of archaeology, history and religion. But why not football as well? To be able to switch from watching the Irish doing battle against the English at Twickenham to speculating who might finally defeat Kerry in the All-Ireland should be a natural pleasure, or pastime.

All-Ireland: that is our clue. A Kerryman from Dingle or Tralee has no doubt of what that means; neither had Daniel Corkery. But for Corkery hurling was our national game, just as Irish was our language. This is narrowing, nearly racist nonsense. The *camán* or *stiotar* is not much wielded in Dublin, let alone Belfast, and indeed the G.A.A. has been accused of being a divisive force in our country. I can endorse this because at school in Armagh we spoke of something called foreign games, yet we played soccer as a relief from the serious business of Gaelic football, at which we were All-Ireland champions.

And then there is our long involvement in British affairs. A butcher in Amiens can tell my daughter that her country got beaten last night, meaning the North of Ireland in the World Cup against France. Yet when I enter the great cathedral at Amiens, I see a memorial to 600,000 soldiers from Great Britain *and Ireland* who died nearby on the Somme; British regiments or not, they died for something, and the Irish are commemorated by that extraordinary monument, the Tower of Belfast on the Somme.

So let us declare an end to all narrowness, in our thoughts at least. The unpartitioned sensibility should be able to accept, listen to, at least, the many voices, agreeable and disturbing, which haunt our land. 'The isle is full of noises' but they should be made to blend, as a symphony contains its dissonances, a symphony in the modern post-Beethoven sense, from Mahler to Shostakovitch, structures of healing.

An Ulsterman, ironically, can approach this ideal, an escaped Ulster Catholic or some form of Protestant Jacobin. An Ulster Catholic has suffered from the narrowness of that Northern statelet, and can recognise its mirror image in the South, however much more he feels at home. Liberal though the attitude towards the Protestants has been in the Free State, the peculiar equation of religion, race, and language was dangerously close to *kulturkampf*, doctrinaire, loveless, and life-denying.

So, adapting the motto of the Royal Irish, let us 'Clear the Way' to celebrate Armistice Day as well as Ivy Day. Should we not praise peace? Let us think in terms of an Ireland which runs all the way from the flints at Larne and the Boyne mounds to the harsh covenanting of Ian Paisley and the soothering vagueness of any Southern politician. Its children lie buried on the Somme as well as Kilmainham. Men choose as their place and times allow, and Ledwidge mourning the execution of the leaders of the 1916 uprising, while wearing the British army uniform in which he was to die, is a fitting symbol of the contradictory imperatives of our country. A man may make the wrong choice and still belong, if generosity can prevail. 'It is new strung and shall be heard'.

# LANGUAGE AND IDENTITY IN THE SHORTER FICTION OF ELIZABETH BOWEN

A. C. PARTRIDGE

In fiction, small things may be considered not as important as big ones, not because in themselves they lack merit, but because they are supposed to have cost the author less pains to bring forth. This may be a reason why the short story in English is so neglected a genre in criticism. But the scaling down of its status should not diminish the artistry of the short story's finest performers. The subject of this paper, Elizabeth Bowen, who retained her maiden name as an author, wrote six volumes of short stories, two of them her first publications, but established her literary reputation largely on her seven novels. She acquired great expertise in handling the shorter compass of fiction, and justifies critical admiration for the economy of her methods.

It is acknowledged that the short story, as an art form, has certain obvious limitations. It permits only minimal incident, and any plot attempted ought to be of the slenderest kind. This usually means that the writer can make little play with causality or clever arrangement. The problem is how to gain the reader's interest in a story which lacks complication, the very essence of plot. In a short story any temptation to plot development has to be stoutly resisted, bearing in mind that, in fiction, it is not the episode, but the connection between episodes, that helps to create the illusion of life.

As to character, no more than a sketch should be hinted at in a short story, the average length of which editors consider to be about three thousand words. In such space, and time, personality must needs lack fulfilment. To overcome this difficulty Miss Bowen often writes stories three times the acceptable magazine length. But the only technical advantage of the long short story over the shorter one is greater elbow room. There is a danger here, however, because the moment plot compression is relaxed, the taut economy of means suffers.

Editors of magazines tend to look askance at the longer product.

Experiments with the long short story, introduced by the American-born author, Henry James, were revolutionary in his time, because he decided to abandon the direct approach, and spoke of the 'beautiful circuit and subterfuge of thought' and feeling in fiction. James despised improvisation, of the kind that makes the tales of *The Arabian Nights* feasible. For him, the primary function of literary fiction, long or short, was the *'ex post facto* dissection of an aspect of life', this merit being well demonstrated in his long story 'The Middle Years'. This method implies that much of the attendant circumstances is left to be inferred. Imaginative reality occupies a greater space than feelings and ideas in James's writing. Any theme for a long short story needs to be pre-digested; an author has to determine how best a theme can be made to express itself. Anyone who has read Elizabeth Bowen's 'Ivy Gripped the Steps' (1945) will appreciate her debt to the Jamesian technique.

James spent most of his working time in the south-eastern counties of England; and this was an area that Elizabeth Bowen got to know equally well; it brought the sophisticated society of London and Paris within easy reach. Yet, despite cosmopolitanism, consciously or unconsciously, each writer expressed characteristics of the country of origin. In her descriptive style, Bowen has a fine sense of place; but the stories with an English background usually have no specific location.

Elizabeth Bowen was the only child of a Dublin barrister, whose family home was Bowen's Court in County Cork, where his Anglo-Irish forebears had lived for three centuries. The name 'Bowen' is, however, of Welsh origin. Elizabeth re-lived her early years at this country seat and at Herbert Place, Dublin, in her book *Seven Winters* (1943) which she published when the English Ascendancy tradition had long been in decline. In this book she was just to her Anglo-Irish inheritance, as well as critical of its philistinism and other social consequences. But her innate aristocracy of mind was not easy to reconcile with the emerging Gaelic conception of democracy. It was not from her Irish mother's choice that she was educated entirely at schools in England. She married the English educator, Alan Cameron, in 1923, the year in which *Encounters*, her first volume of short stories, saw the light.

Miss Bowen gave little thought to writing within an Irish context until nearly thirty years had passed. Her husband's work took them to important educational centres, Nottingham, Oxford and London, where literary friendships were made with John Bayley, Iris Murdoch, David Cecil, Virginia Woolf and T. S. Eliot. Yet her unfinished autobiography, *Pictures and Conversations*, makes it obvious that she remained conscious of her Irish origins. In this posthumously published account of her early life is to be found prose of a finer insight, grace and clarity than appeared anywhere else in her work. The following is an instance:

Becoming a writer knocked a good deal of nonsense out of my system ... As a novelist, I cannot occupy myself with 'characters', or at any rate central ones, who lack panache, in one or another sense, who would be incapable of a major action or a major passion, or who have not at least a touch of the ambiguity, the ultimate unaccountability, the enlarging mistiness of personages 'in history'. History, as more austerely I now know it, is not romantic. But I am ...

If you began in Ireland, Ireland remains the norm: like it or not ... My most endemic pride in my own country was, for some years, founded on a mistake: my failing to have a nice ear for vowel sounds, and the Anglo-Irish slurred hurried way of speaking, made me take the words 'Ireland' and 'island' to be synonymous.

The integrity of Miss Bowen's style comes from judicious pruning as well as evocation; its impressionism may have sprung from her original intention to become a painter. If her fiction tends to be Jamesian, this is without loss to her artistic individuality. She defends undoubted limitations of the early short stories by the need for compression, which made her give precedence to vision over feeling. These stories are the very antithesis of Liam O'Flaherty's fomulaic oral practice. The experience they offer is, however, as authentic as his, for the reason that she admitted few events or situations of which she had not had personal knowledge. A Jane Austenish preference for observed social attitudes does not deflect her from emulating the French and Russian believers in universality.

Despite a sensitive feeling for landscape and 'places', Miss Bowen disclaims any affinity with the regional novelists. Supporting her delighted reactions to place, she argues that topography gives verisimilitude to fiction; she holds that a writer must have at command 'a recognisable world, geographically consistent'. Miss Bowen had no wish to escape from her 'Irishness' as a liberation of her subjective spirit. But subjective she is in her representation of serious or frivolous female characters. Although a fairly regular church-goer, Miss Bowen often portrays luckless women without the solace of religion; they are wont to appear in situations that are frustrating, atrophying or unheroic. Stories set in Ireland are usually about Dublin and its environs, but her vision focuses on a different stratum of society from that of Joyce.

To read Elizabeth Bowen's 'Notes on Novel Writing', in John Lehmann's *Orion II* (1945) is to appreciate the acute rationalisation that went into her art of writing. The arguments are always relevant to her own difficulties, and can do with recapitulation. For instance:

Great novelists write without pre-assumption. They write from outside their nationality, class and sex. To write thus should be the ambition of any novelist who wishes to state poetic truth.

The direction of such truth, she goes on to say, 'is the moral angle of the novel'. What is meant by 'poetic truth' is not altogether explicit, but becomes apparent in a lecture delivered in America on 'the poetic element in fiction':

We who tell stories are making our demands on the imagery of the poetic language; we are trying to fuse our words not only in their meanings but, as Shelley said they can be fused, also in their sounds. Our idea of style must have muscularity and strength, but it should also be capable of being luminous and transparent.

Very relevant to the short story in this suggestive Wittgenstein tractate are the sections on 'Dialogue', 'Angle' and 'Advance'. But the limited scope of this genre did not validate all her principles.

Most stories in *Encounters* and its immediate successors are mere sketches, with no plot and little development of character. A few are more attractive in describing unusual behaviour, or the relationships between people and their environment. The most effective came later, however, when Chekov had stimulated the taste for pessimism. The dominant Bowen flair is for pure comedy, as in 'Unwelcome Idea', or comic irony, as in 'Hand in Glove', which appeared in *The Second Ghost Book* (1952). As a rule short stories avoid being anecdotal; that is to say, they do not build up to a central incident or climax, to which all other elements are subordinated. An air of pleasing inconsequentiality surrounds Miss Bowen's delineation of children, of which 'The Tommy Crans' is an admirable illustration:

'How old are you, Herbert?'

'Oh, I'm nine'.

'Do you play brigands?'

'I could', said Herbert.

'Oh, I don't; I'd hate to. But I know some boys who do. Did you have many presents? Uncle Ponto brought me a train: it's more suitable for a boy, really. I could give it to you, perhaps'.

'How many uncles—?' began Herbert.

'Ten pretence and none really. I'm adopted, because mummy and daddy have no children. I think that's better fun, don't you?'

'Yes', replied Herbert, after consideration; 'anybody could be born'.

All the time, Nancy had not ceased to look at him seriously and impersonally. They were both tired already by this afternoon of boisterous grown-up society; they would have liked to be quiet, and though she was loved by ten magic uncles and wore a pearl locket, and he was fat, with spectacles, and felt deformed a little from everybody's knowing about his father, they felt at east in each other's company.


'Joining Charles' (1929) is a splendid example of Miss Bowen's subjective technique for handling personal relationships. The story depicts the morning of Mrs. Charles's departure to rejoin her husband in France, and offers reasons for her obvious reluctance to do so. Charles Ray, sent by the bank to Lyon because of his business ability, has left Louise, his young wife, with his family for some three months, while he finds a suitable apartment for her to live in. A complex situation emerges, as the play of minds unfolds. Charles does not appear bodily, but the reader is allowed to know him by report, and it seems there are conflicting views as to his character. The first, presented by his widowed mother and sisters, shows that they idolise him, and not merely because he continues to support them.

It is taken for granted in the Ray domestic circle that Louise will in due course produce an offspring. Not even Charles seems aware, however, that the marriage has failed through incompatibility. Louise, repelled by the mother's self-assured sentimentality, nevertheless responds to her affection, but cannot bring herself to confess to the doting parent that she has lost all love for her husband. Inner conflict is the reason for her subdued nature and quietness. Polyphemus, a one-eyed cat, is the only creature in the household with whom Louise appears to have an affinity; but he is as dominating in his expectations as the fatuous sisters-in-law. Her aloofness is the reason why Louise is always referred to in narrative, as 'Mrs. Charles', and not by her Christian name. The mild antagonism of her nature is emphasised by a tendentious chice of adjectives, adverbs and other parts of speech:

Polyphemus continued to melt round the room, staring *malignly* at nothing
Leaning for a moment out of the window she breathed in *critically* the morning air
The expression of her feet in those new brogues was quite unfamiliar: the feet of a 'nice little woman' (the ironical 'tag' of the Ray family)
Her hair *infected* by this feeling of strangeness that flowed to her extremities lay in a different line against her head
She began to be carried away by this fulness, this intimacy and *queer seclusion* of family life
Thin little flames *twisted* and *spat* through the kindling

Anticipating the reception she will receive from her husband, Louise offers an emotive account of his brusque materialism, vulgar masculinity and want of finer feelings towards her. About the single state of his sisters, Charles is said to have 'a wholesome contempt for virginity'. This characterisation is in decided contrast with the family portrait—a son 'generous, sensitive, gallant and shrewd ... a knightly person, transcending modern convention'.

Elizabeth Bowen spares neither irony nor satire in presenting such thumbnail sketches; the two younger sisters are described as 'heavy, with the faces of Flemish Madonnas'. Charles, despite, his grandness, is disparaged by his wife as 'rotten all through'. He was actually responsible for the loss of Polyphemus's eye. The generation gap is emphasised in several ways. Though Louise is undoubtedly small, 'little' for her is less a term of endearment than the sign of an inexperienced generation. Louise is considered modern in her attachment to inanimate things, rather than persons; her constant chilliness is ascribed by her mother-in-law to insufficient clothing. Appropriately, therefore, when she leaves the family that has coddled her, she bequeathes to Doris her copy of Trollope's *Framley Parsonage*.

In 'The Cat Jumps' (1934) the *raison d'etre* of the story is tension and atmosphere, in a situation which dispels illusions about the ascendancy of mind over matter. The Wright family has just acquired Rose Hill, a property with terraced garden and meadows down to the river Thames. The house had been the scene of a brutal murder, and was consequently unoccupied for two years. In making this place their home, the Wrights believe themselves immune from reflections of a morbid kind. They are 'pious agnostics, earnest for social reform', readers of Freud and Krafft-Ebbing, and enjoy 'frank discussions'. Amusingly, Bowen describes such minds as 'disinfected'. The tone of her writing is thus ironical, and reveals a taste for macabre humour.

Rose Hill, being not far from London, is an ideal place for week-end house parties, where 'enlightened' friends can disport themselves in an uninhibited way. But a stuffy aroma hangs about the place, of cigarette smoke and cheap French scent spilt upon the carpets; this was not dispelled on the replacing of the floor-boards.

When the first guests arrived the weather was exceptionally warm, and 'liberated' friends relaxed on the lawns, even clothed in their pyjamas. On the second day, however, a severe rainstorm compelled the closing of windows, and the finding of entertainment within doors. This proved a disaster, perhaps because Muriel, an 'unrealised' psychopath, infected the sensibilities of listeners by recounting the unsavoury details of the notorious crime; she herself locked her bedroom door and slept with the lights on.

Confined to the library, the visitors heatedly discuss *crime passionel* and *Othello,* while the Wrights' children fight and bite each other on the stairs. The party ends in confusion when, on retiring, Muriel takes it upon herself to lock all bedroom doors on the outside. A tense Mrs Wright reaches a state of hysteria, and faints when her husband enters their chamber through the bathroom, which had been the scene of the wife-murder.

There is no characterisation to speak of in this story, and a minimum of incident. Miss Bowen's enjoyment is to make game of pure rationalists, who regard themselves as superior beings. She reveals a considerable interest in extra-sensory perception and deep-seated symptoms of mental disturbance.

'Maria', from the same collection, is Miss Bowen's interpretation of a spoilt child, who find enjoyment in being offensive to those who stand *in loco parentis.* Though only fifteen, Maria's vanity is to wear a diamond bracelet to show that she is a 'rich little girl', in spite of her motherless situation. Maria's aunt, Lady Rimlade, is an empty-headed person, whose repetitive use of 'darling' is meaningless, even hypocritical. Maria, one gathers, has been sent down from school as a disruptive element. The aunt hopes to fob off her niece, as a paying guest, with Mr and Mrs Dosely at the Rectory; she and the baronet are about to embark on a vacation cruise to the

Mediterranean. Maria, who learns much by eavesdropping, is no fool; at school she had received some formal education in 'the more innocent aspect of history and *noblesse oblige'*. It is typical of Miss Bowen's methods to include this soupçon of snobbery that gives the situation a touch of class.

Mrs Dosely is a kindly person with two daughters of her own, and has been in the habit of boarding the children of Indian civil servants; she also offers meals to the young curate, Mr Hammond, who, as a keen cricketer, has care of the Rectory playing-field. To this High Churchman the presence of teenage girls, like Maria, was distasteful. With typical gaucherie, Maria embarrasses the curate by asking at table whether he is a Jesuit, and freely admits she does not know the meaning of the word. Mr Hammond decides, with regret, to find his meals elsewhere, when he discovers that the unregenerate Maria has a 'crush' on him. She follows him round the village on a borrowed bicycle, and sits in the front pew at evensong, to the curate's utter discomfiture.

The climax arrives when Maria 'romances' mendaciously in a letter to her aunt that Mr Hammond and she are engaged, and expect to marry shortly. She threatens elopement, unless her guardians consent to their union. This was probably a ploy to ensure her removal from the Rectory, because she was tired of the food and the sedate company. At the foot of the letter was subscribed: 'Your loving full-hearted little niece'.

Meantime Mr Hammond has immured himself in his rooms, counting the days that remained of Maria's vacation. It was given out that he was busy writing a book on Cardinal Newman—a hint as to his Anglo-Catholic leanings and desire for celibacy. But Maria invades his privacy by appearing at the study window. Eventually the housekeeper admits her, on the plea that an important letter has to be delivered. Maria advises the unfortunate man to leave the village immediately, for the sake of his reputation, when it is known that he has compromised himself with a school-girl.

The curate, losing temporary control, calls Maria a hell-cat and a Bolshevik; there is an unseemly brawl in which Mr Hammond recalls that he had been sacked from his prep-school for bullying. Maria not only threatens to give the supposed affair publicity in the newspapers, but produces a copy of her letter to Aunt Ena as a trump card. Bundled unceremoniously to the Rectory, she then accuses her captor of lacking a sense of humour. She was the kind of schoolgirl who 'really enjoyed being bullied'.

But Lady Rimdale had the measure of these tactics. When a telegram to Mrs Dosely arrived, it alleged that Maria's letter had been blown from her Aunt's hand overboard, when she had read only the first sentence! Maria was, however, told to join the touring party at Marseilles.

The humour of this comedy approaches farce in its improbability, but Miss Bowne's remarkable subtlety and resources of language ensure that the fable does not become ridiculous.

Sean O'Faolain, in his critical study *The Short Story* (1948), includes a searching analysis of another short story, 'Her Table Spread', in which he draws attention to Miss Bowen's pleasure in extravagant metaphor; she herself regarded this as an Irish trait, designed to 'radiate meaning'. The art, says the critic, 'makes stringent demands on the author's wit and intelligence'; but there is a danger of its becoming too clever. Here are examples of Miss Bowen's expertise that this critic may have overlooked:

The heiress, Miss Cuffe, 'was continually occupied with attempts at gravity, as though *holding down her skirts in a high wind*'

Of Mr Alban, she writes:

'He had failed to love; nobody did anything about this: partners at dinner gave him less than half their attention. He knew *some spring had dried up at the root of the world. He was fixed in the dark rain, by an indifferent shore*'.

The illustrations are sign-manuals of a self-conscious artist, whose wit chafes at the technical restrictions of her chosen form.

O'Faolain, writing with the fervour of the Irish, relives Miss Bowen's story in a way quite as romantic as the author's; he admires especially the 'rampant Celtic emotion' with which 'Her Table Spread' exhausts itself. In the art of the short story, he writes, 'suggestion is everything'; the function of technique is merely 'to create illusion'. Miss Bowen's story, O'Faolain concludes, is worthy to rank with those of Stevenson and Turgenev; its 'thrust and urge' enables the personality of the author to be defined in a unique way.

Style, then, is Elizabeth Bowen's pre-occupation. In the long short-story, where craftsmanship is even more demanding, she essays what Stevenson called the art of 'the comely phrase', which is tested upon the supersensual ear. Her personal touch is given by characteristic phrases, as well as single words.

In 'Summer Night' from *Look at All Those Roses* (1941), the tale takes place in time of war, and reflects a period when morals were slipping; less from economy, than policy, she leaves much to the reader's imagination. It concerns Emma, a superficial and impulsive Irish wife, who has become bored with her domestic situation, which comprises a retired military husband, his aunt (a permanent lodger), and two hoydenish daughters. Emma has begun an inexplicable affair with a prosperous manufacturer, married, but separated from his wife. This man, Robinson, who is a self-sufficient ladies' man, lives sixty miles from Emma's home; so an assignation is made on the pretext that she is to spend the night with some remoter friends. Emma, stockingless and wearing sandals, travels south by car through an idyllic landscape, her impetuosity and uneasy conscience indicated by her speed. On the journey, she stops at a country-town hotel to telephone her progress to both lover and husband. The former is entertaining two unforeseen guests, who have dropped in on the score of a vague invitation; Justin Cavey, a tense city man on holiday, is accompanied by his deaf sister, Queenie. His protracted, cerebral talk means that he overstays his welcome, and Robinson tries to end the colloquy by showing Queenie portraits of his absent children.

Meanwhile the scene has shifted to the home of the domesticated Major, Emma's husband. Her telephone call had created apprehension in the mind of Aunt Fran, who knows that she herself is a tolerated person. There are symbols of discord in the house, where a harp with two broken strings vibrates forebodingly when a door is slammed. Vivie, the daughter who resembles her mother, has slipped off her nightdress, chalked her body with stars and snakes, and is busy enacting a fetish-dance on her mother's bed. She is there discovered and reproved by Aunt Fran, who reminds her that the bed she is desecrating was the place of her birth. Aunt Fran is convinced that the blood of the world has been poisoned.

Inevitably, Emma arrives just when the Caveys are departing, and is observed by them parked in her darkened car at the gate. She then enters the house in a state of nervous tension, realising the naivete of her liaison. She expects her lover to fabricate a story about the breakdown of her car. Back in his hotel, Cavey pens a priggish letter to Robinson, repudiating their acquaintanceship. But the romantic Queenie, isolated in her world of silence, takes everything in her stride, and gladly recalls an innocent encounter with her lover twenty years before, in the same locality.

'Summer Night' occupies just over thirty pages, and is like a play in episodes, rather than acts; yet its art is reflective rather than dramatic. The leading figures are capable of some complexity, because the author has more elbow-room; the influence of environment on each episode is strong. Descriptive prose preponderates, but in the dialogue nothing is set down which down which does not advance the story. There is an unremitting quest for the original word or phrase. Here are appended a few of the oddities:

'I wondered who they were', said the little woman, her eyes on the cabinet, *sippeting* at her drink. [A nonce usage, as verb, of *sippet* 'a small piece of toasted bread', perhaps in erroneous relationship to *sip*. The word is appropriate to the stature of Emma, several times called 'the little woman', with ironic reference to the bravado of her escapade]. 'Hi!' she called, 'don't forget the window in here'—looking back over her shoulder into the muslin curtains that seemed to *crepitate* with dark air ['crackle'—a frequentative verb related to 'creak', used mainly during the nineteenth century, in medical or pathological senses]. *Farouche,* with her tentative little swagger and childish pleading air of delinquency [an uncommon adjective of French origin, used by Horace Walpole in the eighteenth century; it means 'wild', 'shy' or 'sullen', according to context]. They're *mackintoshy* sort of people [a pejorative use of the waterproof overcoat, with adjectival suffix -y, probably devised by Elizabeth Bowen to denote persons with bourgeois characteristics].

'Ivy Gripped the Steps', from *The Demon Lover* (1945), occupies thirty-three pages, and looks back to the Edwardian era from the vantage of the Second World War, when history was still in the balance. The prelude has a key to the jig-saw, which a long-story writer invariably creates, to arouse curiosity, and sustain the reader's interest. The epilogue is important, too, a reminder that human affairs are transient, especially to a participator in events, when he looks back on them. The body of this tale is reminiscential.

Gavin Doddington, the narrator, was a boy of eight when he first visited Mrs Lilian Nicholson at Southstone, on the Kentish coast, in 1908. His mother, Edith, had been Lilian's dearest friend, while the girls were at a finishing school in Dresden. When Gavin arrived for his school vacation, Mrs Nicholson was a comfortably-off widow, with housekeeper, in a detached house near the theatre. The drawing-room was richly endowed with period furniture, cut-glass and bric-a-brac:

'For Southstone, dividends kept their mystic origin: they were as punctual as Divine grace, as unmentioned as children still in wombs'.

Here Elizabeth Bowen is in a more expansive mood than has been her wont. She begins her story with grown-up Gavin in civvie clothes, visiting Southstone in 1944, in order to revive memories of his youth; thirty-two years had elapsed since Mrs Nicholson's death.

Lilian's love-affair with Admiral Concannon, married to an invalid wife, to whom he wishes to be loyal, may be the central feature of the plot, but it is not material to the purpose of the story, which is to find a niche for the society of a given period, seen within the greater scope of history. Says Lilian Nicholson in an inspired moment:

'I suppose there *is* one reason for learning history—one sees how long it has taken to make the world nice'.

The boy Gavin, a midland farmer's son, soon began to look upon the leisured ease of the Edwardian gentry as sheer enchantment. While this child guest was being happily entertained by the housekeeper on the beach, Mrs Nicholson was genteely philandering with the admiral, whom she met on morning walks. Her private life seemed, at first, an enigma to the sensitive boy who returned her affection. His early enchantment, however, both with her and her way of life did not easily continue into his maturity. There was, of course, the threat of the war (expressed by the admiral, who prophesied its coming and was himself, according to the postlude, killed in it) and the divergence between Mrs Nicholson's own kind but toiless existence—a squandered leisure—and the labours of Gavin's own hard-working hard-pressed father. Thus as the boy matured he came to see the transcience, the emptiness of this kind of life of often shallow social involvements. In her use of the short story form Elizabeth Bowen indicates most economically how Edwardian wealth could strangle human values.

# IN SEARCH OF THE UNKNOWN SYNGE

ANN SADDLEMYER

'...the thoughts and deeds of a lifetime are impersonal, concrete—might have been done by anyone'. With these words John Millington Synge expressed in his notebook a conviction that only one's art—and not one's life—can express what he called 'the essential or abstract beauty of the person'.[1] It was perhaps because of this dismissal of biography that Synge allowed Yeats to publish in a preface to *The Well of the Saints* as early as 1905 so many errors about his life. By 1925 Yeats had at least made one correction, and in *The Bounty of Sweden* records that the two men first met in Paris in 1896.[2] But it took him even longer to admit that he might not have immediately discovered Synge's usefulness to his dramatic movement, or not have recommended a visit to the Aran Islands the first day they met, and he chose to retain his image of Synge wandering through-out Europe 'playing his fiddle to Italian sailors' until a later Director of the Abbey Theatre, Walter Starkie, replaced him in Yeats's mind as fiddling Bohemian.

Now, thanks to three biographies, the publication of Synge's collected letters, innumerable critical studies, the salvaging of his note books, diaries, cursory jottings—even brief notes towards an autobiography[3]—we are much closer to the recorded man. Yet how much of this detail of daily life is essential to our comprehension of the author of the poems, plays, and prose works? Are we any nearer to the real Synge? Does it matter that Yeats appropriated an icon for his private pantheon, and enshrined him in the rich poetry of 'that rooted man', 'that enquiring man' 'that dying chose the living world for text', 'that slow man, that meditative man'?[4] In the rich orotund phrases of Yeats's prose descriptions is there perhaps more truth than mere facts can capture?

...he was that rare, that distinguished, that most noble thing, which of all things still of the world is nearest to being sufficient to itself, the pure artist.

181

... his whole nature was lifted up into a vision of the world, where hatred played with the grotesque, and love became an ecstatic contemplation of noble life ... He was a solitary undemonstrative man, never asking pity, nor complaining, nor seeking sympathy ... all folded up in brooding intellect, knowing nothing of new books and newspapers, reading the great masters alone.[4]

Yet, even without the contrary proofs of Synge's own correspondence and notebooks, we are uneasy before this canonisation—Yeats is creating his own Synge, for his own purposes.[5] Other memorialists cause the same disquiet: Stephen MacKenna's devotion led him to deface Synge's letters in order to preserve his 'most perfect companion'; Edward Stephens moulded his uncle into his own image of youthful rebellion and romance; the Reverend Samuel Synge recollected his younger brother through the kindly ingenuous myopia of evangelical rectitude; John Masefield recalled his fellow poet with an awe that only reluctantly admitted a touch of modernism; even the published recollections of his fiancée Molly Allgood are coloured by the deep sense of loss over a hero who died young. Yet such is the enchantment of his art that we are even more reluctant to accept Synge's dispraisers: we shrug off Joseph Holloway's condemnation of 'the evil genius of the Abbey';[6] turn a blind eye to Daniel Corkery's misgivings about his Ascendancy status;[7] and dismiss Lady Gregory's assessment of faint-heartedness and vanity as jealousy for Yeats. There is somewhat more difficulty with the image of Synge listening at key-holes, since he unwittingly convicted himself in his preface to *The Playboy*. ('When I was writing *The Shadow of the Glen*, some years ago, I got more aid than any learning could have given me, from a chink in the floor of the old Wicklow house where I was staying, that let me hear what was being said by the servant girls in the kitchen'[8]). In part because of these equivocal responses to the man, we are tempted to seek for yet a fresh projection of the 'real' Synge.

There are further contradictions still. Despite his own disclaimer concerning personal history, Synge's brief autobiographical notes reveal a careful analysis of the forces which moulded his first twenty-four years; he replied fully to his German translator's request for biographical facts at thirty-four[9]; and among his papers are directives marked 'Biographical Material only not to be printed as literary work' and 'Early Fragments, mostly rubbish, J.M.S. xii. 1908'.[10] Indeed, he destroyed very little of his juvenilia, carefully labelled the drafts of all his plays, dated many of his poems, and preserved most of his diaries, notebooks, and correspondence. If Yeats exaggerates when he comments, 'He had under charming and modest manners, in almost all things of life, a complete absorption in his own dream'.[11] Synge was aware of the significance of his genius to others, and confident of his status in world literature.

Perhaps an even more compelling reason for pursuing the unknown Synge, therefore, is the striking contradiction commented on by many who knew him personally and by all who read his letters, the extraordinary discrepancy between the public man and his published work. How could such an apparently simple, courteous, somewhat shy scholar summon up the romping playboys, seductive tramps, and Rabelaisian tinkers of his plays? Where is the poetry and passion in this close, reserved Victorian gentleman who was shocked by any impropriety and insisted on the most severe decorum in personal relationships? What of the sensuality—the sexuality—and urgency of his plays and poems? Finally, how could this silent listener whose noted sincerity and nervous fastidiousness rejected the slightest exaggeration of fact or situation create speeches of such eloquence and daring? What is the key to this elusive personality?

The most pressing argument for biographical research is, paradoxically, provided by Synge himself, in an aesthetic creed which recognised that 'the only relative unity in art is that of a whole man's life time',[12] that the greatest of poets 'used the whole of their personal life as their material',[13] and that he himself had 'made the gradual and conscious expression of his personality in literature the aim of his life'.[14] In his life, his work, and his studies, Synge cultivated 'the prepared personality', a 'many-sided or universal' art; in an additional movement to Pater's famous dictum, he defined 'the real effort of the artist' to be the translation of the symphony that is life into music and then back into art.[15] Not only therefore are we invited to probe the life in order to find the raw material for his art, but we are urged to see those experiences reflected against the greater, more important background of the natural world. For Synge's measure is always the harmony of nature's laws. If, as he claimed, 'each work of art must have been possible to only one man at one period and in one place',[16] that life must be seen in its proper perspective against a certain time and particular setting.

Thanks to the assiduousness of his biographers, the first of whom began work shortly after Synge died and the second of whom knew his uncle from childhood, the general outline of his life is well-known. The recent publication of his collected letters has helped fill in more gaps, and the years of his work with Yeats and Lady Gregory in the Abbey Theatre are fully documented. Let us begin, then, with the facts. The youngest of eight children (three of whom died in infancy), Edmund John Millington Synge was born in the Dublin suburb of Rathfarnham on 16 April 1871. His father, a barrister from a well-known Wicklow family, died in Synge's first year, and his mother, daughter of a Protestant rector from whom she inherited her evangelical zeal, was perhaps the most profound influence on Synge throughout his life. Sickly as a child, he rarely attended school, receiving most of his formal education from a private tutor during the years before he entered college, supplemented by his mother's and grandmother's strict religious training. He was, in fact, surrounded by women, for his mother lived next door to her only daughter Annie, married to solicitor Harry Stephens, and the two families did all but dine together; Annie's younger son Ned would later become Synge's biographer and most committed advocate. Beyond the close family circle Synge had few acquaintances; apart from his older brother Sam, his closest playmate was their cousin Florence Ross with whom he raised rabbits, went bird-watching, experienced the first childish flush of passion (and rejection), and with whom he would maintain a close friendship throughout his life. Keenly interested in natural history and granted absolute liberty in both wandering and reading, he first encountered Darwin's *Origin of Species* when he was about fiteen, and suffered the agony of doubt and horror of consequences besetting a sensitive child when faced with a chasm destined to separate him from the unquestioning faith of the others within a caring and concerned, overtly restrained but inwardly watchful, family group. He wisely put aside Darwin until he felt mature enough to face these implications, but the concentrated study of natural science and theology led at last to a rupture in the close harmony between himself and his mother which was all the more painful for both because of the continuing respect and regard for honesty and search for truth they shared. If anything, Mrs Synge became all the more watchful and caring for her son's welfare as she grieved for his spiritual waywardness; while in turn her son grew more sensitive still to his mother's feelings and aware of the need to walk, develop, and speculate alone.

The following year, when he was sixteen, Synge discovered a greater attraction than natural science, one which was destined to create even further crevices in the family structure—the study of music. To take up the violin might not at first seem any less innocent than Synge's dawn observations of birds, or his solitary night roamings in search of moths, butterflies, and insects. After all, his brother Sam had studied music without any interference in his steady path towards medicine and ordination, and Florence Ross was adept at a kindred occupation, water-colouring. But music encouraged Synge to turn even further inward at that most vulnerable period of youth, puberty. Sexual awakening increased an already developed hypersensitivity to intense moments of revelation: the beauty of nature and the beauty of women henceforth would evoke the same vocabulary of epiphany, moments of insight into a greater glory in which nature, sexuality, and the painful lyricism and harmonic resonance of music are inextricably mixed. [17] Put more simply, he became a romantic.

Little wonder, then, that his entrance into Trinity College, following a long family tradition, made little or no impact on him; while close by in the Royal Irish Academy of Music he studied harmony and counterpoint so assiduously that he received scholarships, and his greatest enjoyment was participation in a student orchestra. Trinity meant not collegiality but its opposite—the opportunity to continue his solitary studies and independence of thought for three more years. If he showed any interest at all in his formal studies, it was in the study of language—but not for purposes of communication; he chose Hebrew and Irish as class subjects and studied German privately (only, he assured his mother, in order to read). Some Greek and Latin he would have required for his entrance to Trinity, but he does not seem to have pursued those subjects nor, in any organised fashion aside from attending Edward Dowden's lectures on Shakespeare, the study of English literature. When he graduated in 1892 it was with a second class B.A., while he continued to study composition and the violin at the Royal Irish Academy of Music. The only mark left by his college years is the publication of his first poem, 'Glencullen', predictably a sonnet Wordsworthian in sentiment and archaic in language, extolling the beauties of one of the Wicklow glens.

In contrast, his private notebooks gradually filled with notes and drawings on Irish antiquity, his roamings through the countryside (he was a strong cyclist and sixty miles a day was customary) dedicated to private archaeological field trips. Again, while not actively encouraging these interests, Mrs Synge's temperament and custom were great enablers. She spent each summer in Wicklow, first in the small community of Greystones, later renting a farmhouse in the country. Just as she had been sufficiently interested in music to accompany her son on the piano (and criticise the badly blotted piano parts he wrote out for his own compositions), so she shared a love of the natural world and looked forward eagerly to the annual removal of household and servants each summer. Her habit of inviting women missionaries to holiday with her provided further company and interest for her, while encouraging Synge to be more sociable on his return from fishing or cycling trips in the Wicklow mountains. Rarely did he find his mother's guests sympathetic—although there were a few exceptions—but even with the most severely evangelical he developed a con-verstaional ease which marked his relationships with women throughout his life.

It appears from Mrs Synge's letters to her older sons that even at this time Synge was contemplating a career as a music teacher, and might well have been content to follow his solitary pattern of fiddling, undistinguished compositions in verse and music, long nature ramblings and even longer cycling excursions, had two things not occurred almost simultaneously. He fell in love, and encouragement of his musical studies appeared, unexpectedly, from within the family circle. The story of Synge's first love—one hesitates to call it mature—is briefly told: Cherrie Matheson, daughter of a leading member of the Plymouth Brethren, lived with her family just three doors away from Mrs Synge's house in Crosthwaite Parke, Kingstown (now Dun Laoghaire). Like Mrs Synge, her parents had been accustomed to taking their family to Greystones for the summer, and it is likely that Synge first encountered her there. Now Cherrie became a friend and sketching companion of Florence Ross and Synge saw her frequently; the summer after his first trip to Europe she was invited by Mrs Synge to spend two weeks in County Wicklow, and either then, or before, Synge found himself deeply attracted to her. The courtship, interrupted each winter by his studies abroad, was not only sedate but circumspect; Synge accompanied Cherrie to art exhibitions in Dublin (she was an accomplished water-colourist and exhibited at the Paris Salon during the 90s), wrote her long letters about his experience as a student in Germany and Paris and Italy, finally proposed marriage in 1896. Her prompt refusal notwithstanding, he pursued his courtship for two more years, even persuading his reluctant mother to speak on his behalf despite her sympathy for Cherrie's reasons. For not only was Synge an impecunious student, dependent on his mother and with little prospect of a recognisable profession, but he was even more confirmed in his rejection of formal Christianity, especially the evangelical strain represented by the Synges and the Mathesons. It did not occur to him to be less than frank about his religious position, any more than it would have occurred to him to put aside the way of life he had chosen for the more secure financial position required of a middle class husband and father.

Instead, he pursued his own natural rhythms, aided this time by the visit of an older relative from England, the only professional musician in the Synge circle. Mary Synge was a pianist, his father's cousin and a respectable God-fearing woman. She held a piano recital in Dublin shortly after Synge left Trinity, and he took charge of the publicity and practical arrangements, doubtless using his familiarity with the concerts he had himself participated in with the student orchestra. When she discovered John's own ambitions, she encouraged him to study in Germany as she had done, and persuaded Mrs Synge to approve and finance the venture. And so, in July 1893, at the age of twenty-two, Synge departed for Germany. It cannot be called leaving home, for he continued to treat his mother's home as his, with two brief exceptions, until his death; not only was he financially dependent upon her (he was shortly to receive a small legacy which allowed him independence for part of each year), but he was physically so, returning each spring to a comfortable bed, a well-appointed table, all the material comforts he suffered without on his travels. The emotional dependence on the other hand tended from this time forth to be his mother's, a reversal which Synge tacitly accepted when his brother Sam embarked on a career as medical missionary to China; John was the last child left to care for and watch over, with a special dispensation from Providence to embrace the unbeliever in her prayers.

The Germany to which Mary Synge introduced her young cousin was at first glance not far removed from the home he had just said farewell to: a guest house on an island in the Rhine run by six sisters whose rigid social conventions could cause Mrs Synge no unrest. Here Synge stayed for five months, studying German literature, taking violin lessons, playing in the local orchestral society, attending concerts, and enjoying a privileged role in the von Eicken household. But the similarity to Crosthwaite Park fell short in one significant way—the von Eicken sisters were relaxed and expansive, more expressive of their personal feelings, encouraging laughter and open discussion, whereas the Synge household enshrined reserve, quiet demeanour, gravity of expression, and silent restraint. More important, his new community included Valeska. One of the youngest of the 'cloistered maidens' (as she referred to her family), Valeska became Synge's German teacher; on a more informal basis, she became his confidante, his mentor, and his guide, old enough to be relaxed with him (she was eight years his senior), sympathetic enough to encourage openness and frankness not only about Cherrie (whom she dubbed 'the Holy One') but about his unformed hopes and dreams of a future life as an artist. Despite their relative informality, however (she nicknamed him 'Holy Moses' because of his penchant for the phrase, he called her 'Gorse' because of the colour of her hair), she was too independent to become emotionally entangled, and her letters tend to have the freedom, gaiety and decorum of a young aunt. One might consider her the European continuation of his relationship with Florence Ross.

By Christmas Synge had realised that, pleasant though his sojourn in Koblenz was, it did not provide him with the musical training he had come for and needed, and so in January 1894 he moved to Würzburg, started to study the piano, and, for the first time, lived alone. But within a few months he had concluded that he was not cut out for a musical career, and began to study languages with even greater commitment. He read a great deal of Goethe, Lessing, Schiller, Heine, Ibsen (in German translation); he took long walks in the hills; he began to write not only poetry in German, but a play. By the time he returned to Ireland (by way of the von Eickens), he had made his second renunciation; music, no more than organised religion, was unable to provide the haven for his restless soul.

After a summer in Wicklow and an autumn dedicated to courtship of Cherrie, Synge returned to the continent, not, as he had originally intended, to study languages at a German university, but rather to Paris. Again entry to Europe was by way of the von Eicken household, where he stayed for two months studying German and French before proceeding to Paris with introductions provided by 'the cloistered maidens'. Once in Paris in January 1895, his life soon took on the pattern it was to have for the next seven years: formal lectures at the Sorbonne and the Ecole Pratique des Haute-Etudes; outings with students with whom he exchanged language lessons; frequent 'at homes' and more casual entertainments with the friends he quickly developed; long walks in the countryside; regular visits to art exhibitions and museums. Intent now on a career in literature, he sent awkward efforts at journalism to Irish newspapers, occasionally even publishing them; more and more, however, his diaries and notebooks record more serious compositions, and it is during these years he wrote the series of impressions later drawn together as 'Vita Vecchia' and 'Etude Morbide'. From these essays and from the copies he made of various stylists, including Oscar Wilde, Flaubert, Pater, Huysmans, Borrow, Pierre Loti, it is clear that he was once again following a pattern of study that he had begun as a youth and would continue to follow, in an eclectic gathering of writers in which he might recognise mood or temperament sympathetic to his own, without encroaching on his carefully maintained independence. One writer in particular seemed to have had a more direct influence, for after spending the summer as usual in Wicklow, he commissioned his brother Sam, embarking for China, to enquire about work as an interpreter on liners to the Far East; his reading of Lafcadio Hearn was perhaps made more accessible by the knowledge that Hearn was his brother-in-law's cousin and hence almost a member of the family.

However, perhaps because of his renewed involvement in art history, encouraged by his friendship with Cherrie, he decided instead to visit Italy. Once again he began with a study of the language, this time privately in Dublin; then, early in 1896, he made his way to Rome after a brief stay in Paris brushing up his French, re-establishing his territory, visiting the theatre. For two months he attended courses in Italian literature at the Collegio Romano, studied the Italian language with his landlord, and made friends among the art students. Journalistic attempts led to an increased awareness of political situations, and he kept a private journal recording the unrest over the failure of the Italian invasion of Abyssinia. From Rome he travelled northward to Florence, again making friends among the international community, two of whom, a Polish student of sculpture and an

English art historian and theosophist, would remain lifelong friends. Once again in the company of women he found freedom to debate serious issues and the release of laughter.

By now Synge was twenty-five years old and his relationship with Cherrie was soon to end; he returned the following winter to Paris having espoused the cause of Socialism, much to the dismay of his mother. Political awareness, however, did not lead to decisive action: he enrolled at the Sorbonne for courses in Italian and French literature, read not only socialist works but Thomas à Kempis, and met not only Stephen MacKenna, but William Butler Yeats. Through Yeats he met Maud Gonne and became involved in the establishment of the Association Irlandaise; whether because of this new involvement in Irish politics, or out of his discovery of Socialism, he joined a debating society and religiously entered in his diary each occasion on which he spoke.

Predictably, Synge's flirtation with Maud Gonne's extreme political views did not last long, and within months he had resigned from the Association Irlandaise; predictably also, however, he did not cease attending the meetings, and remained friendly with its founders. Socialism too began to pall and he found himself drawn into lengthy discussions with Stephen MacKenna on literature, art, and spiritualism. When he returned to Dublin his new friends drew him into their own gatherings, ranging from the Contemporary Club (which he attended with Yeats and Maud Gonne, and where he may well have met John Butler Yeats for the first time) to the Theosophical Society (which he attended with that angelic anarchist, AE). After a summer in Wicklow, he delayed returning to Paris, awaiting an operation on swollen glands in his neck. Ironically, the first manifestation of the Hodgkin's disease which would eventually kill him occurred the same year he found at last the community he had been seeking. When he returned to Paris early in 1898 it was by way of London and a visit to Yeats; while there he met yet another art student, an American named Margaret Hardon ('la robe verte' in his diary) who soon replaced Cherrie in his affections.

Although this infatuation, too, was destined to disappointment, Synge's world broadened further still: in May 1898 he made his first visit to Aran (eighteen months after his introduction to Yeats), and on his way back visited Coole. Whether Yeats and Lady Gregory, while encouraging him to write *The Aran Islands*, recognised Synge's promise is doubtful, but Synge entered on his next visit to Paris with sufficient self-confidence to create a permanent address which he would keep for the next five years. He also began to publish in literary journals, first an experience on Inishmaan, then a review of Maeterlinck's essays. He studied Breton and visited Brittany; continued to haunt museums and galleries; maintained his friendships; perhaps began what was to become his first completed play, *When the Moon Has Set*. It is likely that he arranged to return to Dublin in time (May 1899) to see the Irish Literary Theatre production of Yeats's *The Countess Cathleen* and Edward Martyn's *The Heather Field* before once again joining his mother in Wicklow. Certainly by the time he paid his second visit to Aran that autumn, he was an accepted member of the Dublin literary circle.

For the next three years his life followed the same routine: the winter months in his little room in Paris; the summer in Wicklow with his mother and her friends; the autumn on Aran with side trips to Coole and participation in Dublin's artistic activities. Once *The Aran Islands* was completed he began work on two verse plays—neither of which he completed—, revised *When the Moon Has Set*, wrote book reviews, literary articles, continued hs study of languages by enrolling in a course in Old Irish at the Sorbonne. Life was at last coming together into a coherent whole. By 1902 he had completed *Riders to the Sea* and *The Shadow of the Glen*, drafted *The Tinker's Wedding*, and become a regular visitor at the rehearsals of Willie Fay's Theatre company in Camden Street. And, finally, in 1903, as James Joyce planned his own journey to Paris, Synge returned there for the last time.[18] Henceforth his destiny belonged in Dublin. He was thirty-one years old and, to use a Yeatsian term, he was at last a 'solid' man.

It is hardly necessary to trace the last six years of Synge's life, so entwined are they with the history of the Abbey Theatre and the Irish dramatic movement. Private Synge became public playwright; life and work were at last one. Nor is it necessary to trace the story of his final love affair with the actress Molly Allgood ('Maire O'Neill'). That too is now public knowledge, as is the desolate ending to the story—an early death, his last great play unfinished, his marriage to Molly forever postponed. 'Death should be a poor untidy thing, though it's a queen that dies' (*Deirdre of the Sorrows*).

Apart from his works, Synge is best known as the perpetrator, through *The Playboy of the Western World*, of one of the finest theatre riots in the twentieth century, an occasion Yeats was to recall throughout his life with great satisfaction. Was there an organised nationalist claque on opening night, awaiting the opportunity at last to strike back at what they considered an Ascendancy-run, dictatorial, insulting usurpation of the Irish *National* Theatre? Perhaps, but I doubt it. I am more inclined to believe that the cause of the unrest for that first audience is rooted in our same disquiet over the contrast between private man and playwright: we are drawn into one world which is with great care isolated from any outside reality yet which has its own established rules and standards, has in fact such apparent solidity that we mistake it for realism. Then, once our customary safeguards—emotional, civil, religious—are down, Synge shocks us into a further reality, and we are aware that we have encouraged him to lead us on. We have been tricked, as with Synge's life, into believing in one world, only to discover that we must incorporate another, opposite, world.

In order to hoist us on our own petard, Synge carefully creates a series of oscillating rhythms throughout *The Playboy of the Western World*, reflected in the stage business and echoed in the dialogue, until we are stretched, as the characters are on stage, between two polarities, that which he referred to in his comments on the play as the Romantic and the Rabelaisian. ('the romantic note and a Rabelasian note are working to a climax through a great play of the play, and ... the Rabelasian note, the "gross" note if you will, *must* have its climax no matter who may be shocked', he wrote to John Quinn in defence of his method.[19]) The romantic element charms us into a sweet sense of freedom, music, the glory of art and nature; the Rabelaisian shocks us into laughter, awareness, objectivity, the *solar plexus* of humanity. And, in the careful, tightly-woven structuring of the play, Synge leads us from one polarity to the other so skilfully that we do not realise the entire spectrum in between.

These are, of course, the images Synge uses in his early notebooks and the drafts of his autobiographical works. They are most clearly employed in one of the early drafts of *When the Moon Has Set* where the young artist-hero, himself from the Ascendancy class, uses them to persuade his cousin, a nun of an indeterminate religious order, to renounce her vows and become his wife in a union blessed by that greater church, Nature's dawn:

'The emotions which pass through us have neither end nor beginning, are a part of eternal sensations, and it is this almost cosmic element in the person which gives all personal art a share in the dignity of the world ... The world is an orchestra where every living thing plays one entry and then gives his place to another. We must be careful to play all the notes. It is for that we are created ... Every life is a symphony. It is this cosmic element in the person which gives all personal art, and all sincere life, and all passionate love a share in the dignity of the world ... If art is the expression of the abstract beauty of the person there are times when the person is the expression of the beauty that is beyond the world'.[20]

Synge's aesthetic creed has been explored elsewhere and need not be rehearsed again here, except in the broadest of outlines. For his music is not only 'the direct expression of the human personality'[21] but of the entire natural world. The artist must 'make music' out of his experiences first, that is recognise the harmonies and lyricism of life, before he can then transmute them into art. Religious art is a regret for the past; modern art must represent our 'modern feeling for the beauty and mystery of nature';[22] that is the new divine ecstasy. Great art receives the 'dignity of nature' from 'the almost cosmic element in the person' rather than from the thoughts and deeds of a lifetime;[23] it is the artist's duty, therefore, to use his own half subconscious faculties, to *tune* them, so that his work will be as harmonious a reflection of the laws of nature as possible. 'Profound insight finds the inner and essential mood of the things it treats of and hence gives us art that is absolutely distinct and inimitable'.[24] And that insight can only be developed by the artist working first on his own experiences.

It is possible to see Synge's own autobiographical draft as the first step in this self-tuning process, and for this reason I have not quoted from it during my resumé of the first thirty years of his life. When we do examine it, certain key sentences serve as his own summation of the various stages he recognises having passed through—what Yeats would call the 'grades' of a Supernatural Order (only in Synge's case that would have to be a Sup*ra*natural Order). He had, he tells us, been a 'worshipper of nature' since childhood, wishing nature to be 'untouched by man', and preferring the 'natural' to anything 'made'. As a child also he attempted to express his feelings for 'the colour of locality' though 'syllables of no meaning', which the adults dismissed as gibberish. Religion on the other hand 'remained a difficulty and occasioned terror' for many years, even after he had recovered from the temporary dread caused by a conviction of damnation. Balanced against this personal description is a general commentary on the primitiveness of children and the pantheistic instincts of the child who betrays 'perfect traces of the savage'. From this observation Synge weaves a theory of personality as the revelation of 'evolution from before history to beyond the science of our epoch'; thus the child in his primitiveness adores nature without ever learning or wishing to admire its divinity, while 'an adult before his time' reveals the tendencies of the future. With these examples in mind, we can then comprehend more clearly his belief that 'the emotions which pass through us have neither end nor beginning—are a part of the sequence of existence'.

Such Darwinian interpretations of the personality could however cause 'horrible misery' when applied directly to oneself; because of the ill health he suffered as a child, he determined never to marry for fear of bringing forth unhealthy, suffering children. Fortunately by the time he reached puberty this phase had passed and he could praise his study of natural science for training him in 'a singular acquaintance with the essences of the world'. 'The forces which rid me of theological mysticism reinforced my innate feeling for the profound mysteries of life'. But by renouncing Christianity, he 'laid a chasm between my present and my past and between myself and my kindred and friends. Till I was twenty-three I never met or at least knew a man or woman who shared my opinions'. And he concludes his personal history by describing a 'perhaps too powerful, too nearly a physical intoxication' created by musical excitement, coinciding as it did with sexual awakening, and, having relinquished the 'Kingdom of God', 'a real interest in the kingdom of Ireland'.[25]

Thus the stages of Synge's awakening of the personality, his preparation as he himself observed it. Because the auto-biography ends with his decision to become a professional musician, while at the same intimating that the choice was miscalculated for his 'hypersensitive organisation', it is most probable that it was begun during his early years in Paris, when he was striving to make sense of his life and ambitions. By then 'the world of magical beauty' he dreamed of could not be provided by music. By the same token, I would suggest that his conscientious study of art and art history was an effort to place his love of music in a broader perspective and to relate his new devotion, literature, to a fuller spectrum of creativity. The great gap in our understanding of Synge's artistic and emotional development, then, occurs during those Paris years, from 1895 when he left the von Eickens to 1903 when he said farewell to the continent and allied himself firmly with the Irish dramatic movement.

What do we have on record for those important years? A few of his letters to friends—mainly women confidantes such as Valeska von Eicken; Thérèse Beydon, with whom he exchanged language lessons, and her mother; Albert Cugnier, a young civil servant whom he met through the von Eickens, and *his* mother; Mrs Synge's quotations from his letters and conversation in her diaries;[26] a recently published memoir by Stephen MacKenna which confirms Synge's detailed and technical knowledge of the visual arts and the austerity of his Paris life;[27] a few memories by W. B. Yeats; his own daily diary records of visits to the Louvre, his extraordinary sweeping reading habits, appointments with friends; *Vita Vecchia*, a series of impressionistic poems and prose pieces apparently relating his torment over Cherrie's rejection but more reminiscent of Dante Gabriel Rossetti than Dante; *Etude Morbide*, which he later described as a 'morbid thing about a mad fiddler in Paris which I hate' and which explores in a more sensually evocative—but certainly morbid—manner some of his sexual urges and fears for emotional and mental stability of the same time. Many pages are torn out of his diaries and notebooks, but some puzzling scraps remain among his papers—included with his exercises in various literary styles and copies of the poems in prose of Oscar Wilde and others, is a poem in French which appears to be celebrating homosexual love; various phrases of a more cynical turn jotted down at random; but overshadowing all this, annotations affirming his gradually developing aesthetic, especially comments on what is 'healthy' and 'wholesome' art as opposed to what is 'decadent' and 'Satanic'. We have also the assurance of John Butler Yeats, Jack Yeats, John Masefield and MacKenna that during those years and later he continued to strive for his own particular truth, disdaining all ethical and moral weakness as 'unhealthy', celebrating the joy and richness of life which 'plays all the stops'.

It is comforting to find some continuities, even if they are later recollections, in incidents and quotations that were sufficiently striking to be recalled many years later. MacKenna, for example, wrote about 1912,

Synge had an immense belief in taking the thing that came 'whatever came your way to absorb it, to know what was in you, and to get your true thought'. He was very anxious for impressions to sink in before they had become blurred by other later impressions. I once asked him to go for a walk with me and on his demurring reminded him that he had enjoyed this walk a few days previously. [He explained that] he wished to make his impressions of the previous day more his own and that the aspect of the place might be different to-day and would hinder him. [28]

W. B. Yeats never tired of quoting what Synge once said to him in Paris, 'We should unite stoicism, asceticism and ecstasy. Two of them have often come together, but the three never'. [29] No matter that Yeats applied this to Lionel Johnson also; it has the smack of Synge. Was it then or later that Synge defined for Yeats 'Style comes from the shock of new material'? [30] And at any time this serious student of French Literature might have delightedly described to Yeats 'an old French comedy about a man who having given away his last possession, his wooden leg — said "Now I am ready to enjoy life" ' [31]

But once again we are depending upon memorialists looking back through the years of Synge's maturity; even MacKenna, his closest male friend during the Paris years, is afflicted with the lamentable hero-worship of the dead. Will we ever come any closer to divining what happened to Synge during that period to give him the substance of the mature playwright? Did he, for example, continue to study music? experience more satisfying love affairs? go to the theatre more regularly than his diaries suggest? What provoked him towards Socialism and what turned him away from it? At what point did his life and work turn from what he himself defined as the first stage of dramatic art, childishly reproducing 'external experience' only with neither form nor philosophy, through the 'lyrical interval' to maturity, 'dealing with the deeper truth of general life in a perfect form and with mature philosophy'? [32] Certainly by the time he completed _Riders to the Sea_ and _The Shadow of the Glen_ he had reached that third stage. Until we are able to reconstruct this missing chapter in the life of John Millington Synge, the clue to this enigmatic, very private person whose self-confidence so astonished those who knew him, and whose craftsmanship resulted in such dazzlingly complete works of art, continues to elude us. We do not yet, alas, have all the notes.

## NOTES

1. 'Autobiography', constructed by Alan Price, ed. J. M. Synge: _Prose_. Gerrards Cross: Colin Smythe (1983), p.3. A slightly different wording can

be found in his first completed play *When the Moon Has Set*, J. M. Synge, *Plays Book One*, ed. Ann Saddlemyer. Gerrards Cross: Colin Smythe (1983), p.174n3.

2.  Yeats's Introduction is reprinted in *Plays, Book One*, pp.63-68; cf. *Dramatis Personae*. New York: Macmillan (1961), p.194. Yeats originally stated that they met in 1898, and in his autobiography admitted, 'I made many visits to Paris, and I cannot be certain always in which visit some event took place' *Memoirs*, ed. Denis Donoghue. London: Macmillan (1971), p.105.

3.  cf. Maurice Bourgeois, *John Millington Synge and the Irish Theatre*. London: Constable (1913); David H. Greene and Edward M. Stephens, *J. M. Synge 1871-1909*. New York: Macmillan (1959) and Andrew Carpenter, ed. *My Uncle John: Edward Stephen's Life of J. M. Synge*. London: Oxford University Press (1974) both of which are based on Stephens' monumental typescript 'Life' of his uncle; Ann Saddlemyer, ed. *Theatre Business: The Correspondence of the First Abbey Theatre Directors William Butler Yeats, Lady Gregory and J. M. Synge*. Gerrards Cross: Colin Smythe (1982). *The Collected Letters of John Millington Synge*, 2 vols. Oxford: Clarendon Press (1983, 1984); much of Synge's unpublished material was incorporated in the *Collected Works*, ed. Robin Skelton, Alan Price and Ann Saddlemyer. London: Oxford University Press (1962-68) repr. Colin Smythe (1983).

4.  'The Municipal Gallery Revisited', 'In Memory of Major Robert Gregory', 'Coole Park, 1929'.

5.  'J. M. Synge and the Ireland of his Time' (14 September 1910), *Essays and Introductions*. London: Macmillan (1961), p.323; Preface to J. M. Synge, *Poems and Translations* (4 April 1909), J. M. Synge, *Poems*, ed. Robin Skelton. Gerrards Cross: Colin Smythe (1983), pp.xxxiii, xxxv.

6.  Holloway's deep dislike of Synge's work—even though he grudgingly liked the man—is evident throughout the 221 volumes of his diary as a playgoer; cf. *Joseph Holloway's Abbey Theatre*, ed. Robert Hogan and Michael J. O'Neill. Carbondale and Edwardsville: Southern Illinois University Press (1967).

7.  Daniel Corkery, *Synge and Anglo-Irish Literature*. Dublin and Cork: Cork University Press (1931); a more recent study of Synge and 'the hidden Ireland' is Declan Kiberd's *Synge and the Irish Language*. London: Macmillan (1979), while Weldon Thornton in *J. M. Synge and the Western Mind*. Gerrards Cross: Colin Smythe (1979) provides a thorough study of Synge's experiences in the Aran Islands.

8.  *Plays, Book Two*, p.53.

9.  Letters to Dr. Max Meyerfeld, 1 and 12 September 1905, *Collected Letters*, I, pp.126-29.

10. See *The Synge Manuscripts in the Library of Trinity College Dublin*. Dublin: Dolmen (1971), pp.37 and 38.

11. Yeats, 'Journal', *Memoirs*, p.206.

12. See Ann Saddlemyer, 'A Share in the Dignity of the World', *The World of William Butler Yeats*, ed. Robin Skelton and Ann Saddlemyer. Seattle: University of Washington Press (1967), pp.207-19 for a summary of Synge's aesthetic theories.

13. Preface to *Poems and Translations*, Synge, *Poems*, ed. Robin Skelton. Gerrards Cross: Colin Smythe (1983), p.xxxvi.

14. An unpublished preface written in 1907, quoted in the introduction to *Poems*, ed. Robin Skelton, p.xiii.

15. See 'Autobiography', *Prose*, ed. Alan Price, p.3 and *When the Moon Has Set*,

*Plays Book One,* ed. Ann Saddlemyer, pp.174, 176.

16.  *Prose,* p.349.
17.  There is ample evidence throughout his prose works and even in his correspondence of this vocabulary; the words 'extraordinary', 'singular', 'brilliant', 'undreamable', 'exquisite', 'peculiarly', 'curious', 'distinction', etc., recur throughout; cf. Ann Saddlemyer, 'Art, Nature, and "The Prepared Personality" ', in *Sunshire and the Moon's Delight: A Centenary Tribute to John Millington Synge,* ed. Suheil Badi Bushrui. Gerrards Cross: Colin Smythe (1972), pp.107-120, and 'Synge and the Doors of Perception', *Place, Personality and the Irish Writer,* ed. Andrew Carpenter. Gerrards Cross: Colin Smythe (1977) pp.97-120.
18.  See Ann Saddlemyer, 'James Joyce and the Irish Dramatic Movement', *James Joyce: An International Perspective,* ed. Suheil Badi Bushrui and Bernard Benstock. Gerrards Cross: Colin Smythe (1982), pp.190-212.
19.  Letter to John Quinn, 5 September 1907, *Collected Letters,* vol. II, p.47.
20.  *Plays, Book One,* pp.174 and 176.
21.  *Ibid.,* p.176.
22.  *Prose,* p.351.
23.  'Autobiography', *Prose,* pp.3, 13.
24.  *Prose,* p.349. In his notebooks Synge quotes a passage from *Without Dogma* by Henryk Sienkiewicz: 'The human being finds a resting-place only where he is in harmony with his surroundings; and is reminded that his soul and the soul of nature are of the same organisation'. Father William E. Hart, to whom I am indebted for this identification, conjectures that Synge may have been introduced to Sienkiewicz's work by his Polish friend Maria Antoinette Zdanowska, a student of sculpture whom he first met in Florence in 1896 ('Synge and Sienciwcz', a paper presented at IASAIL conference, University of Graz, July 1984).
25.  All quotations are taken from the 'Autobiography' as reconstructed from Synge's manuscripts by Alan Price, *Prose,* pp.3-15. However, this is a composite of three different drafts, none of them dated; it does seem clear though that his autobiography was written before *When the Moon Has Set,* and perhaps revised as late as 1907.
26.  Mrs Synge's diaries are in the Manuscript Division of Trinity College Dublin Library; many of the passages relating to Synge are quoted in E. M. Stephen's unpublished 'Life'.
27.  Nicholas Grene and Ann Saddlemyer, 'Stephen MacKenna on Synge: A Lost Memoir', *Irish University Review* XII, 2 (Autumn 1982), pp.141-151.
28.  *MacKenna,* p.119.
29.  W. B. Yeats, *Autobiographies.* London: Macmillan (1955), pp.346 and 509.
30.  *Memoirs,* p.105.
31.  Letter to Olivia Shakespear, 1 August 1936, *The Letters of W. B. Yeats,* ed. Allan Wade. London: Rupert Hart-Davis (1954), p.860.
32.  *Prose,* p.350.

# FIVE FIERCE LADIES

FRANK TUOHY

I want to draw your attention to some recurrent themes in the Anglo-Irish novel. In order to do this I have chosen five writers who have several obvious characteristics in common: they were all women, they were all members of the Protestant Ascendancy, each was connected with a 'Big House'. All this might seem to some a guarantee of 'irrelevance' or perhaps of amateurishness. But this is not the case. There isn't much justice about the dissemination of literary talent, much less social justice, and my chosen five all seem to me to be excellent writers. Reading and rereading them has reinforced my loyalty to the pleasure principle as a factor in critical judgment. This is important for someone of my generation in English Studies. We were schooled in Dr. Leavis's Great Tradition to expect that novels in order to be worthy should be dull, and he included several in his approved list that I would not willingly reopen.

The five fierce ladies of my title are Maria Edgeworth (1767-1849), Edith Somerville (1858-1949) and Martin Ross (1862-1915), Elizabeth Bowen (1899-1973) and Molly Keane (born 1904). Though their lives cover over two hundred years these writers share certain resemblances of temperament. I would not claim for them that 'ancient cold, explosive detonating impartiality'[1] that Yeats talks of somewhere as being typical of the Irish Mind, they surely possess as he did the ability to 'cast a cold eye'—and this is not just the cold eye of social superiority: it falls equally on their coevals and themselves.

According to a useful and necessary distinction made by Professor Heinz Kosok, we should define Anglo-Irish literature by its subject matter rather than its authorship. I cannot, however, quite avoid using 'Anglo-Irish' in a sociological sense, to refer to those of English extraction. Edith Somerville, Violet Martin ('Martin Ross') and Elizabeth Bowen were all descended from soldiers who established themselves after Cromwell's conquest. They would have referred to themselves as 'Irish'—

for it was the peculiarity of these expatriates not only to take over the land of Ireland, but also to pre-empt even the opposition to the central government, in such persons as Robert Emmet, Charles Stewart Parnell, Erskine Childers, Con Markiewicz and many others. In addition, in the persons of Sir Samuel Ferguson, Lady Gregory, Yeats and Synge, they moved in to dominate the literary scene. That my five ladies belong to this caste need not imply that they extol its virtues. As novelists they seldom speak well of their characters. Indeed, half the fun would disappear if they did.

I have found a number of themes that appear and reappear in these novels. The first is that of the Big House—that imposing residence, usually dating from the eighteenth century, with some inexpensive landscaping from the time of the Great Famine of the mid-nineteenth century. Here the 'extended family' is assembled. In this context the native Irish are grooms, indoor servants, openers of gates—also, more importantly, lawyers, always known as attorneys.

It follows then that the second theme is snobbery, and the unbridgeable chasm established to separate themselves from the Catholic majority. Among themselves, there were infinite gradations, for those so much cognisant of the blood-lines of horses easily extended their knowledge to people. The snob's anti-self is the satirist: he strives for the invitation to the grand party that will be the target of his satire. Lady Clonbrony's disastrous soiree in *The Absentee* is in the line of similar functions described by Thackeray, Proust and Waugh.

The remaining themes involve deprivation. Not surprisingly, since comedy outlines the boundary between appearance and reality, the contrast between the pretensions of the landowner and the deficiencies of his personal life offers a major source of interest. The primary deficiency of course is that of money. Penury is as much the burden of *Castle Rackrent* (1800) as it is of *Good Behaviour* (1981). Many of these financial crises would have been due to the passion for sport, that pre-eminent reason for the tenacity of the Ascendancy class throughout the Troubles and the Second World War until today. This passion included shooting, fishing for trout and salmon, but centred on hunting and racing. Molly Keane remembered hunting as a child:

The very young may be sick with cowardice about a fence but they are more afraid not to jump it than to jump it ... It was not soft falls in water or bog that they dreaded, but that shameful, hurting falling off and the moments before you fell, their agony seeming to endure with interminable uncertainty before you went with a sort of sob and the ground hit you from behind, strangely like a house falling on you, not you falling on a house.[2]

Nevertheless she goes on: 'I really disapproved of people who didn't ride. It was the only thing that counted'. Horses, in fact, contributed much in bringing the two nations together.

If the passion for sport and financial problems together make one theme, they might be connected by some psychologists with the last on my list, that of inadequate men and masculine women. Molly Keane, publishing most recently, stresses this aspect of her fictional world. Its roots, however, go a long way back. When William Trevor, in his latest novel *Fools of Fortune*, presents Aunt Fitzeustace 'of a strong muscular appearance and with a notable jaw, given to wearing tie-pins and tweed-hats', he might be describing Edith Somerville herself.

## II

Maria Edgeworth was the eldest daughter of Richard Edgeworth of Edgeworthstown, who married four times and produced twenty-two children. Not unnaturally he developed an interest in education, and became a disciple of Jean Jacques Rousseau. P.H. Newby in his study of Maria Edgeworth[3] tells us that her father's dictum was 'No tears! No tasks! Nothing upon compulsion!' Maria's stories to illustrate his theories showed a feeling for children hardly known previously—her method of research was, she said, 'to lie down and let them crawl all over me'.

Richard Edgeworth was not universally popular (Lord Byron called him 'the worst sort of bore—a boisterous bore') but his relationship with Maria was vital to her development as a novelist. He was a great mimic of Irish speech, and together they collected Irish bulls—those self-contradictory statements considered typical of the native population. She helped him with estate management, so that John Ruskin could later say that more could be learned from *The Absentee* than from a thousand government reports.

*Castle Rackrent* shows all these influences. Technically, it provides an early and successful example of the 'unreliable narrator': Thady Quirk tells the story of the Rackrent family in terms of grovelling flattery, while their appalling history becomes obvious, together with the fact that Thady's own son, Attorney Quirk, is bringing about their downfall.

Maria Edgeworth was often compared to Jane Austen, her exact contemporary. Jane Austen was the more accomplished writer—Maria Edgeworth's comic surnames show that she belongs to an old, broader comic tradition. But their purposes were quite different. Jane Austen wants us to *recognise* her characters, to collate them with what we already know. (This is the reason for her continued popularity in England, and the complete indifference to her work in countries where virtuous spinsters arouse no interest). Maria Edgeworth does not expect us to know about the Irish, she is out to inform and even provides interesting, extensive notes. When the horrible Sir Kit Rackrent keeps his Jewish wife a prisoner until he can get hold of her jewels, Maria Edgeworth tells us that the incident actually took pace.[4] In Ireland her aim was similar to that of her first disciple, Sir Walter Scott, who wrote of his own countrymen 'to procure sympathy for their virtues and indulgence for their foibles'. The first regional novelist, her example was followed in France by Prosper Mérimée, and acknowledged in Russia by Ivan Turgenev.

## III

Successful novel writing may have a connection with membership of a large family. Maria Edgeworth was one of twenty-two, and Edith Oenone Somerville was the eldest of eight, with six brothers and a sister. Her biographer speaks of 'her great natural powers of command and leadership ... her indomitable energy and unquenchable enthusiasm'. She was born at Castle Townsend, Skibereen, Co. Cork, and for most of her life was M.F.H. of the West Carberry Hunt, thus incurring the expenses which are said to have driven her to writing.

Edith Somerville's relationship and collaboration with her cousin Violet Martin began when she was twenty-five and lasted until the latter's death in 1915. 'It was Edith', someone said, 'who wore collars and ties but Violet who took a man's name'. E. OE. Somerville and Martin Ross became famous for *Some Experiences of an Irish R.M.*, but their literary renown will always depend on one of their earlier collaborations, *The Real Charlotte* (1894).

This is a novel of many characters, but its chief concern is with Francie Fitzgerald and Charlotte Mullen. Pretty, innocently seductive, Francie grows up amid the carefully depicted

squalors of north Dublin (not very far, one perceives, from the
Eccles Street of Molly and Leopold Bloom). She arrives in
Lismoyle to stay with her cousin Charlotte, a plain, scheming
woman with a mania for acquiring land. Both are rivals for
Roddy Lambert, the cheating land agent of the Big House—
Charlotte succeeds in murdering his first wife, but it is Francie
who finally gets him. But she is also admired by Christopher
Dysart, the heir to the estate, and Gerald Hawkins, an English
army officer. *The Real Charlotte* has the range of Trollope or
Balzac; the style, though, is temperate, unhurried, restrained.
Strong-minded woman novelists are sometimes harsh to their
pretty young female characters—I am thinking of George Eliot's
rather vindictive pursuit of Hetty Sorrel or Rosamund Vincy—
but Somerville and Ross understand poor Francie, so unlike
either of them, extremely well. In addition their understanding
extends not only to humans of whatever religion or class but
also to animals: there are some cats, pungently described, and
a marvellous cockatoo. Here are two dogs:

Sitting outside the door, they listened with trembling to the discussion
that was going on in the hall, and with the self-consciousness of dogs
were convinced that it was all about themselves.[5]

## IV

The energy, the mechanical, farcical element in Somerville and
Ross, connects them with other Anglo-Irish writers. This quality
is absent from Elizabeth Bowen's writing. Unlike the others, she
was an only child, born in 1899, heiress to a large square house,
Bowen's Court, which looked rather like Lady Gregory's Coole
Park. (Like Coole, it has been knocked down). From her writing
alone, one would not endow her with the title of 'fierce', but her
biographer, Victoria Glendenning, has given us a different
picture. Elizabeth Bowen married a dull functionary of the
B.B.C., and lived in Regent's Park, London. Childless, she ran
her social life with much ferocity, a series of lovers, much social
grandeur. At one of her dinner parties, a guest, looking for the
lavatory, went through the wrong door and found Elizabeth
Bowen's husband alone, eating his dinner off a tray.

Elizabeth Bowen chose to write of shy young virginal girls,
and her one novel set in Ireland, *The Last September*, is a typical
example. The setting is the big house, in 1920, with the British
Army still in occupation. Elizabeth Bowen is clever and funny,
in the tradition of the classic English comedy of Jane Austen—

the relationships of Lois and her friend Livvy with the officers suggest *Pride and Prejudice*, Sir Richard and Lady Naylor recall *Mansfield Park*. Other major influences are Henry James and Virginia Woolf: inquisitive or sensitive writing overloads comparatively simple circumstances. And as a satirist, she seems too often to share the values of the characters she depicts. Nevertheless, *The Last September* provides a lively illustration of the themes I have outlined—the Big House, snobbery, shortage of cash, and emotional inadequacy.

I was surprised to find that Elizabeth Bowen had written comparatively little fiction set in her native land. The short story 'Her Table Spread' stands out. One of the finest she wrote—and she excelled in the short story—it sums up a period of history; like James Joyce's 'The Dead', it is resonant with peculiarly Irish experience.

In 'Her Table Spread', the big house is a castle, situated somewhere near one of the Treaty Ports, used by the British Navy from 1922 to 1938. A destroyer has arrived in the sea lough below the castle. It has been there the previous year, the officers have called at the castle but Valeria Cuffe, the heiress to whom the castle belongs, was absent. This time, she is embarrassingly excited: she is, we are told, 'abnormal—at twenty-five, of statuesque development, still detained in childhood'.[6] This being Ireland, she has impoverished dependents, her aunt, Mrs Treye and her great friend Miss Carbin, and there is also old Mr Rossiter, an elderly relative who keeps bottles of whiskey hidden in the boathouse. In addition, there is Mr Alban, a young man invited as a possible husband for Valeria, thus ensuring the future of Mrs Treye, Miss Carbin and Mr Rossiter. 'She's got a nice character', the last tells him, 'she's a girl you could shape. She's got a nice income'. Unfortunately, we are told, Mr Alban's 'attitude to women was negative, but in particular he was not attracted to Valeria Cuffe'.

On this rainy evening, Miss Cuffe plunges around in the dark garden in her red taffeta evening dress, mistaking Mr Rossiter and Mr Alban for the naval officers who she believes have come to rescue her from her sterile existence. But the destroyer sails away without any visit; in eight pages a whole world, cut off by history, has been brought to life.

## V

History is of course a major participant in many recent Anglo-Irish novels: *Troubles*, by the late J.G. Farrell, *Fools of Fortune* by

William Trevor, *The Mangan Inheritance* by Brian Moore. It is strange to realise that is the element completely absent from the work of my last writer, Molly Keane. The only equivalent case I can think of is that of Georges Simenon, one of the most prolific writers of the first three quarters of our century, who, I have been told, never once mentions the Second World War. It shows an extraordinary detachment, indifference, or perhaps bloody-mindedness. The only reason for discussing Molly Keane's *Good Behaviour* is the best one: it is one of the best-written and most entertaining novels of recent years.

During the 1930s Molly Keane had some reputation as a writer of ten light novels under the pseudonym of M.J. Farrell, and several stage comedies, produced by John Gielgud. The early novels remind me a little of F. Scott Fitzgerald—great talent spoiled by inferior ambition. Molly Keane blames her lack of education—'You can't think how neglected we were by our parents, I mean they didn't do anything with us at all, they simply didn't bother'—and the passion for horses and hunting blotted out other considerations. V.S. Pritchett has described Molly Keane as 'not knowing history socially'. The only preoccupation is the game of manners, the instinctive desire to keep boring reality at bay.

*Good Behaviour* is a black comedy set in the 1920s and, like *Castle Rackrent*, told by an 'unreliable narrator'. In this case it is Aroon St. Charles, the large plain daughter of the house. Money, of course, is in short supply, and so is love—an eccentric governess tells Aroon that 'men by their nature have to do something to you and that it hurts'. Under the lid of 'good behaviour', the primal instincts are boiling merrily away. Mrs Keane has an unerring eye for character, especially in the case of old men: Aroon's father, furtively seking his pleasures, and her would-be lover's English father, 'Wobbly' Massingham. There is a beautifully described hunt ball, and a riotous concluding sequence in which Aroon gets blind drunk at her father's funeral. *Good Behaviour*, a novel of high technical distinction, was written some years ago and laid aside when it was refused by Mrs Keane's regular publisher.

Its subsequent success must reflect on the competence of the publishing profession. So, too, must the comparative failure of *Time After Time* (1983). Here another splendid batch of characters—big house, frustration, penury, snobbery, all are here—gets lost in prolixities which a skilled editor could easily have corrected. (There is also an unpleasantly racist portrait of a Japanese).

*Good Behaviour* made its own rules and turned its isolation into a merit. It would not be surprising if it were the last of the line of Anglo-Irish novels in the tradition which I have attempted to trace. My interest has been to indicate to you once again that the novel, like poetry, can flourish in conditions which might otherwise be unpropitious, and even in circumstances which must always be considered socially and morally reprehensible.

## NOTES

1. See F. Tuohy, *W.B. Yeats*. London: Macmillan (1976), p.218.
2. See M. J. Farrell, *The Rising Tide*. London: Virago (1984), p.viii.
3. See P. H. Newby, *Maria Edgeworth*. London: Arthur Barker Ltd. (1950), *passim*.
4. See Maria Edgeworth, *Castle Rackrent* (1800). London & Edinburgh: Thomas Nelson and Sons (1953), p.99.
5. See Somerville & Ross, *The Real Charlotte* (1894). London: Oxford University Press (1948), Ch.XII, p.109.
6. See *Collected Stories of Elizabeth Bowen*. Harmondsworth: Penguin Books (1980), p.418.

# THE NARROW GROUND: NORTHERN POETS AND THE NORTHERN IRELAND CRISIS

GEORGE WATSON

The Northern Irish problem has at least the ambiguous distinction of antiquity. Sir Walter Scott remarked of his visit to that unhappy place:

I never saw a richer country, or, to speak my mind, a finer people; the worst of them is the bitter and envenomed dislike which they have to each other. Their factions have been so long envenomed, and they have such narrow ground to do their battle in, that they are like people fighting with daggers in a hogshead.[1]

That was in 1825; and of course the origins of that 'envenomed dislike' can easily be traced further back in history. That antiquity, and the prominence of the latest stage of the violence in the newspapers of the world, mercifully frees the critic from any attempt at political or historical analysis of the problem. Besides, as the Belfast graffito succinctly puts it, 'Anyone who isn't confused here doesn't really understand what's going on'. Despite the writing on the wall, this essay will examine the imaginative sense of Northern Ireland in a small group of poets, Catholic and Protestant, born in that narrow ground, and the ways in which their work illustrates cultural predispositions which, if they do not actually feed the problem, reveal its intractability. To generalise, much too sweepingly, the argument is that the Catholic imagination, as represented by Seamus Heaney and John Montague, is too caught up in the nets of history and is addicted to the creation of racial myths and racial landscapes; and that the Protestant imagination, represented by Derek Mahon and Tom Paulin, feels excluded from history and tends to regard its own culture with a contempt and bitterness which betokens a kind of inferiority complex, a lack of cultural self-confidence.

'Politics in a work of art', remarked Stendhal, 'is like a pistol shot in the middle of a concert'. There is, inevitably, some reductivism implicit in this essay's approach and no doubt these four fine poets would rightly object to their work being considered solely in relation to the pistol shot, as it were. Further, there is the obvious danger of validating poetry on extrinsic or political grounds rather than on intrinsic aesthetic grounds. As Keats implied, the imagination may transcend considerations of good and evil—'what shocks the virtuous philosopher delights the chameleon Poet'. Nevertheless, the virtuous philosopher may riposte that 'while a poet may be exempt from moral intentions—we all prefer poetry without propaganda—he or she can never be wholly exempt from moral consequences'.[2]

It is a truism that literature and politics in Ireland have always been closely entwined and that Auden's assertion in his elegy on Yeats, that 'poetry makes nothing happen', does not have an Irish application. The long-standing symbiotic relationship between literature and politics in Ireland itself lays an extra burden, a none too willingly accepted responsibility on the shoulders of the Northern Irish poet today, who resents, sometimes explicitly, the imperious claims of the blood-sodden politics. A reader can respect the natural hesitation the poet may feel at taking on a 'big theme', his awareness of the dangers in the willed forcing of sensibility into the hot angry world of bombs and bullets. The words of Patrick Kavanagh (a major influence on Seamus Heaney) are relevant here:

Stupid poets and artists think that by taking subjects of public importance it will help their work to survive. There is nothing as dead and damned as an important thing. The things that really matter are casual, insignificant little things, things you would be ashamed to talk of publicly'.[3]

Paul Muldoon, in his witty 'Lunch with Pancho Villa', amusingly burlesques the whole notion of a made-to-order poetry of commitment:

> 'Is it really a revolution, though?'
> I reached across the wicker table
> With another $10,000 question.
> My celebrated pamphleteer,
> Co-author of such volumes
> As *Blood on the Rose,*

*The Dream and the Drums,*
and *How It Happened Here,*
Would pour some untroubled Muscatel
And settled back in his cane chair.

'Look, son. Just look around you.
People are getting themselves killed
Left, right and centre
While you do what? Write rondeaux?
There's more to living in this country
Than stars and horses, pigs and trees,
Not that you'd guess it from your poems.
Do you never listen to the news?
You want to get down to something true,
Something a little nearer home'.[4]

Certainly, the Northern Irish problem is too complex to be dealt with in glib slogans or pamphleteering propaganda, yet the burden is not to be so easily shrugged off. Events since 1968 have forced its writers, in Seamus Heaney's words, to 'hug our little destiny again'. As he remarks elsewhere:

From that moment [1968] the problem of poetry moved from being simply a matter of achieving the satisfactory verbal icon to being a search for images and symbols adequate to our predicament.[5]

It would indeed be a peculiarly thin poetry which could simply ignore the (literally) shattering events in the six counties over these last sixteen years. The work of Heaney, Montague, Mahon and Paulin is, in fact, extremely rich, and allows us to see behind the superficial headlines and journalese something of a the 'felt history'—not just what happens, but what people feel about what happens—which good literature uniquely provides.

## II

Atavism: tendency to reproduce the ancestral type in plants and animals ... *Path:* recurrence of the disease or constitutional symptoms of an ancestor after the intermission of one or more generations.
*(Oxford English Dictionary)*

The great strengths of Seamus Heaney's poetry are too well known to need rehearsal here.[6] The muscularity, the intense physicality of the language of the early poems ('lug ... squelch and slap ... festered ... slobber ... clotted ... slap and plop ... knobbed ... fungus ... cud and udder ... slugged and

thumped ... plash and gurgle ... pat and slap of small spades
on wet lumps'—all within the first six poems of *Death of a
Naturalist*) is always available to him, but is schooled by chastely
perfect lyricism in later poems, such as the beautiful 'Sunlight':

> And here is love
> like a tinsmith's scoop
> sunk past its gleam
> in the meal-bin.
>
> (*North*, p.9)

Heaney's poetry is full of this 'love' and loving detail—love for
the customs and ways, for the crafts, for the turns of speech and
the reticences of his Catholic country community. In this
respect, many of his lyrics embody, as he himself said of
Montague's poem *The Rough Field*, 'a sign made in the name of
a tradition.[7] Though the terrain of the earlier Heaney volumes
is unobtrusively but peristently politicised, the mood of the
poems is on the whole expansive, affirmative, celebratory rather
than confrontational. Cultural oppositions and tension are seen
as creative, focussed on the interplay between the liquid,
guttural vowels of Irish speech with its Gaelic origin, and the
consonants of the Elizabethan English introduced to Ulster by
the planters:

> Our guttral muse
> was bulled long ago
> by the alliterative tradition

he writes in 'Traditions', and the companion poem, 'A New
Song', also from *Wintering Out*, declares:

> But now our river tongues must rise
> From licking deep in native haunts
> To flood, with vowelling embrace,
> Demesnes staked out in consonants.

There is an ambiguity here. 'Rising' is registered by the reader,
who also notices that it is a rising to 'embrace'.

   Given the nature of Northern Ireland society, it is perhaps
surprising how few poems from this enormously sympathetic
imagination deal with 'the other side', the other tradition. In
'Docker' (an early poem from *Death of a Naturalist*) the imagery
(cap 'like a gantry's crossbeam', 'plated forehead', 'sledgehead
jaw') is obviously appropriate to the man's job, but also goes a

long way to establishing what might be thought of as a cultural stereotype in suggesting the rigidity, the dourness, the Calvinist unyieldingness of the Ulster Protestant. The comparison in the last stanza—'He sits, strong and blunt as a Celtic cross'—might, of course, be ironic. On the other hand, its inappropriateness might rather suggest an imaginative lapse on Heaney's part, an inability to achieve any innerness with this strange being who is contemplated externally, as if he were a man from Mars, and whose life remains, for the poet, a mysterious silence. When that (Protestant) silence *is* broken, in the finely affectionate 'The Other Side' (*Wintering Out*, pp.34-36), it is broken in 'fabulous, biblical dismissal, that tongue of chosen people', as the voice of the neighbour 'prophesied above our scraggy acres'. The neighbour is allowed his patriarchal dignity, but Lazarus, the Pharoah and Solomon are firmly established as alien to South Derry ('too big for our small lanes') and the poet seems to strip the neighbour of any living tradition beyond his somewhat antiseptic (and basically Scottish) religion:

> His brain was a whitewashed kitchen
> hung with texts, swept tidy
> as the body o' the kirk.

In the latest collection *Station Island*, the poet remembers a Protestant neighbour who made a toy battleship for him one Christmas long ago. Again, the tone is affectionate—Heaney is the most courteous of poets—but Eric Dawson is essentially the sum of the tools and impediments of his workshop; and communication is strictly limited by the Ulster 'rules':

> if we met again
> In an Ulster twilight we would begin
> And end whatever we might say
> In a speech all toys and carpentry,
> A doorstep courtesy to shun
> Your father's uniform and gun ...
>
> ('An Ulster Twilight')

These poems may simply reflect accurately—and in the case of 'An Ulster Twilight' reflect ruefully—the difficulties of bridging the community divide in Northern Ireland. It is, perhaps, more than a symptom of 'our predicament' that an imagination which can so possess and penetrate the corpses of the bogs tends to ignore or falter before living representatives of 'the other side'.

This is not, of course, to deny that communication and understanding must be a reciprocal process; but Heaney does share with other 'Catholic imaginations' a sense that 'tradition' is all on one side. He remarks in his lecture 'Feeling into Words':

There is an indigenous territorial numen, a tutelar of the whole island, call her Mother Ireland, Kathleen ni Houlihan, the poor old woman, the Shan Van Vocht, whatever; and her sovereignty has been temporarily usurped or infringed by a new male cult whose founding fathers were Cromwell, William of Orange and Edward Carson, and whose godhead is incarnate in a rex or caesar resident in a palace in London. What we have is the tail-end of a struggle in a province between territorial piety and imperial power.[8]

The word 'temporarily' reveals at very least a grudgingness towards the notion of alternative traditions and other territorial pieties.

As 'Feelings into Words' shows, Heaney's 'search for images and symbols adequate to our predicament' takes a deeply atavistic swerve towards historical mystification, to the hunger, that is, for a myth which will contain, order, articulate and 'explain' Irish history and Irish violence. Clearly this is related to his reading of P.V. Glob's *The Bog People* (1969); the fruits are poems such as 'The Tollund Man' (*Wintering Out*, pp.47-48), and among others in *North*, 'The Grauballe Man', 'Bog Queen', 'Punishment', 'Strange Fruit' and 'Kinship'. Glob suggests persuasively that the well-preserved bodies dating from the Iron Age found in the Danish bogs are those of victims sacrificed to some kind of territorial Goddess. Heaney finds in this suggestive metaphors which he transposes and elaborates into myth to account for the violence of Irish history, and especially of Northern Ireland. Thus the Tollund Man becomes a kind of patron saint, himself a sacrificial victim, of all the victims of the 'man-killing parishes' not only in Jutland, but nearer home, of

> The scattered, ambushed
> Flesh of labourers,
> Stockinged corpses
> Laid out in farmyards ...

The problem is that sacrificial victims presuppose some deity to whom sacrifice is made; and Heaney's reading of the Northern Irish crisis through these mythic spectacles then assumes deeply sinister overtones. Killing becomes ritualised, in the full sense

of that word—it is a religious rite. In 'Kinship' Tacitus is asked
to return and to

> Read the inhumed faces
> of casualty and victim;
> report us fairly,
> how we slaughter
> for the common good
>
> and shave the heads
> of the notorious,
> how the goddess swallows
> our love and terror.

Again and again, Heaney aestheticises the stark facts of
brutality—contemplating the 'slashed throat' of his 'Grauballe
Man', he asks rhetorically:

> Who will say 'corpse'
> to his vivid cast?
> Who will say 'body'
> to his opaque repose?

In short, a terrible beauty is born; or, as Edna Longley observes,
'the poem almost proclaims the victory of metaphor over
"actuality" '.[9] The notorious ending of 'Punishment' explicitly
rejects 'civilised outrage' as merely a superficial response to
republican punishments: the truth of the feeling is the deep
'tribal' approval of vengeance, irrational, atavistic. The embrace
of the Bog Queen, this 'indigenous territorial numen', not only
blunts Heaney's moral sensitivity to the realities of slaughter;[10]
even in more compassionate poems, such as 'Funeral Rites', the
urge to assuage the pain of 'each neighbourly murder' in an
imaginative appropriation of the ceremonies of mythic ritual
(associated with 'the great chambers of Boyne') dignify the
killing and give it a disturbing sense of affirmatory ('our slow
triumph') inevitability. As Ciaran Carson says of these poems in
*North:*

he seems to have moved ... from being a writer with the gift of
precision, to become the laureate of violence—a myth-maker, an
anthropologist of ritual killing, an apologist for 'the situation', in the
last resort, a mystifer.[11]

It might be said in Heaney's defence that he is employing his myth neutrally, as it were, as explanatory of the pathology of violence, not as in any sense an endorsement or an explaining *away* of the violence. Certainly the beautiful poem 'The Strand at Lough Beg' (in *Field Work*), in its poignant direct confrontation with the horror of the murder of his cousin ('blood and roadside muck in your hair and eyes') suggests the temporary nature of Heaney's embrace of myth. Further evidence that, as with Yeats, so Heaney's poetry constantly develops and pits conflicting attitudes against each other in a rich dialectic, is that, in *Station Island* (p.83), 'The Strand at Lough Beg' is itself held up for (surely over-harsh) inspection. The murdered cousin speaks:

> 'The Protestant who shot me through the head
> I accuse directly, but indirectly, you
> who now atone perhaps upon this bed
> for the way you whitewashed ugliness and drew
> the lovely blinds of the *Purgatorio*
> and saccharined my death with morning dew'.

Finally, it should be said that not all the poems, even in *North*, celebrate unambiguously the dark rituals of blood-sacrifice: 'Strange Fruit', for example, 'had ended at first with a kind of reverence, and the voice that came in when I revised was a rebuke to the literary quality of that reverent emotion'. [12] Here, the emotional patterning of 'The Grauballe Man' (corpse into aesthetic icon) is reversed:

> Murdered, forgotten, nameless, terrible
> Beheaded girl, outstaring axe
> And beatification, outstaring
> What had begun to feel like reverence.

Despite the sturdy defence Heaney has made elsewhere of 'the obstinate voice of rationalist humanism', [13] his reverence for and exploitation of the myth of the fierce territorial goddess in the 'bog poems' show how even this most compassionate and sensitive of imaginations can fail victim—even if temporarily—to the temptation (perhaps especially potent for a Catholic religious sensibility) of myth-making. The virtuous philosopher must register his perturbation in the face of this ritualised obeisance to a fatalistic historicism, in which we must all bend low and bow and kiss the quiet feet of the goddess. He must register alarm the more urgently because of the very power of the poems which mediate Heaney's atavistic vision.

The work of another fine poet, John Montague, illustrates—
notably in *The Rough Field*—the cultural paradigms which make
the province a difficult place in which to live. *The Rough Field*
(1972) is an ambitious attempt to integrate the poet's memories
of and feelings about his family and his own small townland,
Garvaghey in Co. Tyrone, with more general meditations on the
disasters of Irish history from the breaking of the power of the
O'Neills in 1603 to the siege of the Bogside in 1969. Montague
writes most movingly here, and in his recent volume, *The Dead
Kingdom* (1984), of his personal and family life; *The Rough Field*
is always eloquent, and has not only a kind of epic sweep, but
some of the unfussed density of detail more frequently
associated with the novel form. [14] It is, however, less compelling
as an interpretation of the North to itself. Opening with the
description of a bus journey from Belfast to Garvaghey, the
poet's distate for the industrial, for the urban and suburban is
immediately apparent: the station is a 'symbol of Belfast in its
iron bleakness', there are 'narrow huckster streets', 'a
wilderness of cinemas and shops', the 'shabby through-
otherness of outskirts'. This evidence of Montague's nostalgic
primitivism is amply buttressed by the rest of the poem.
Discussing the general problem of attitude exemplified here,
Derek Mahon remarks pertinently:

The suburbs of Belfast have a peculiar relationship to the Irish cultural
situation inasmuch as they are the final anathema for the traditional
Irish imagination. A lot of people who are regarded as important in
Irish poetry cannot accept that the Protestant suburbs in Belfast are a
part of Ireland ... At an aesthetic level they can't accept that. [15]

For Montague, things do not get better outside Befast:

> Through half of Ulster that Royal Road ran
> Through Lisburn, Lurgan, Portadown,
> Solid British towns, lacking local grace.
> Headscarved housewives in bulky floral skirts
> Hugged market baskets on the rexine seats
> Although it was near the borders of Tyrone—
> End of a Pale, beginning of O'Neill—
> Before a stranger turned a friendly face.
> Yarning politics in Ulster monotone.

Nobody, of course, has to love the suburbs of Belfast, or the
'solid British towns'. What is disquieting is Montague's
tendency to dismiss as 'unpersons' the people who live in these

places. *People* begin, as it were, on the borders of Tyrone. In
'The Bread God', Montague's Catholics have all the tradition,
associated with the mass rock and Christmas morning
congregations 'from Altcloghfin, Beltany, Rarogan': the only
Protestant exemplar is a Paisleyite bigot ranting in a hate-sheet.

This imaginative blank in the poem is probably itself a product
of Montague's ideology of the landscape as the repository of
truth. Underlying *The Rough Field* and *The Dead Kingdom* is the
ancient Irish genre of *dinnseanchas*, the poetry and lore of place.
Montague's poetry eschews the dynamic myths of Kathleen ni
Houlihan or the murderous Goddess of the Bog. He
appropriates history, however, in a related if different way, by
freezing it into landscape. The beautiful poem 'Like dolmens
round my childhood, the old people' (section 5 of 'Home Again'
in *The Rough Field*) embodies a striking metamorphosis in its
impressive conclusion:

> Ancient Ireland, indeed! I was reared by her bedside,
> The rune and the chant, evil eye and averted head,
> Fomorian fierceness of family and local feud.
> Gaunt figures of fear and of friendliness,
> For years they trespassed on my dreams,
> Until once, in a standing circle of stones,
> I felt their shadows pass
>
> Into that dark permanence of ancient forms.

Here is a characteristic strategy, in which a demythologised
Ireland is subtly re-mythologised. Montague's imagination pays
full tribute and allegiance to that 'dark permanence', which for
him is most obvious in the Irish landscape with its place-names,
'shards of a lost tradition' as he refers to them in 'A Severed
Head':

> All around, shards of a lost tradition:
> From the Rough Field I went to school
> In the Glen of the Hazels. Close by
> Was the bishopric of the Golden Stone;
> The cairn of Carleton's homesick poem.
>
> Scattered over the hills, tribal
> And placenames, uncultivated pearls . . .
>
> The whole landscape a manuscript
> We had lost the skill to read,
> A part of our past disinherited;
> But fumbled, like a blind man,
> Along the fingertips of instinct.

'The Irish landscape', remarks Montague, 'is a kind of primal Gaeltacht'[18]—which does not readily accommodate the place-names brought or imposed by the planters, English or Scots. It is in this sense that Montague petrifies history. Divisions are written in—almost literally—to the landscape, and are consequently naturalised. Onomastic distinctions become natural distinctions, and the people of the 'solid British towns' do not—cannot—fit into this spatialised history, this primal Irish landscape.

### III

It is an apparently universally accepted truism that the Irish, north and south, live too much in the past, are obsessed by history. Whatever the truth of this in terms of the nationalist tradition, it requires some modification with regard to the Ulster Protestant sensibility. Maurice Craig in his popular ballad may say

> It's to hell with the future and live in the past:
> May the Lord in his mercy be kind to Belfast.

If the evidence of the poems of Tom Paulin and Derek Mahon is accepted, however, it would have to be said that the Protestant Northern Irish imagination feels deprived of a history, does not have enough past of its own in which to live. There are of course a few triggering dates, 1688, 1690, 1912, and—as Tom Paulin, particularly, emphasises—the United Irishmen of the 1790s were strong in the North; but, all in all, the landscape of 'Protestant history' is perceived as rather featureless. This sense that history has more or less stopped, or at least passed by, which affects the Protestant imagination, has interesting analogues in Scotland. There, too, Scottish history 'stopped', or was absorbed into the larger English or British imperial history after the failure of 1745. This can be seen very clearly in the novels of Sir Walter Scott—paradoxically the father of the historical novel in Europe—whose greatest works show history as happening 'back there'; the Hanoverian triumph ushered in the modern world, of commerce and progress, and this modern world is, for Scott, essentially a storyless environment.[17]

The links between Scotland and Northern Ireland are well known, and something of that Scottish sense of the suspension of history has affected the Ulster Protestant imagination. Tom Paulin,[18] for instance, sees Northern Ireland as *a Strange*

*Museum,* the title of his second collection, and in it speaks of 'the long lulled pause/before history happens'. ('Before History'). Access to history seems open to him only on a purely personal level, as when he describes riffling through his grandmother's belongings, and concludes bleakly:

> There is so little history,
> We must remember who we are. ('After the Summit').

For Paulin, 'public' history begins to happen again only in the form of violent intrusion, when what he sees as the icy stasis of Northern Ireland is shattered by the events from 1968 onwards. 'A Partial State' is characteristic, and incidentally reveals the male-female city-country polarities which also inform the mythic and racial landscapes of Heaney and Montague:

> The chosen, having broken
> their enemies, scattered them
> in backstreets and tight estates.
>
> Patriarch and matriarch,
> industry and green hills, no
> balance of power. Just safety.
>
> Stillness, without history;
> until leviathan spouts,
> bursting through manhole covers
>
> in the streets, making phones ring on
> bare desks. 'The minister is
> playing golf, please try later'.

Paulin's imagination constantly reverts to these images—his 'Trotsky in Finland' for example, emblematically 'crosses the frontier' and is seen 'plunging from stillness into history'.

If Northern Ireland, then, is felt to have no history, no continuous narrative, no shaped drama, the corollary of this feeling is an intuition that Irish history really happened 'down there', in the south. An anonymous reviewer of Robert Kee's popular history *The Green Flag* (1972) unconsciously put his finger on a deeply rooted if often unrecognised attitude lurking in the Protestant imagination. Contrasting the spectacular drama of nationalist history to the apparently flat and monotonous stasis of the Protestant North, the reviewer speaks of

the superior attraction for the cultivated mind of the winding caravan of Irish nationalism with its poets, assassins, scholars, crackpots, parlour revolutionaries, windbags, mythopoeic essayists, traitors, orators from the scaffold, men of action, emerging from so long and so great suffering of the people to impart an almost mystic quality to their often futile and often brutal deeds—the superior attraction of that to the hard, assertive, obsessive, successful self-reliance of the Ulster Protestant which has about it as much poetical imagination as is contained in a bowler hat.[19]

What happens then is that the Protestant poet, lacking access to the dynamism of nationalist history, or entrée to a racial landscape such as John Montague's, sees his own culture as oppressively unredeemable, and is forced back on a loveless repetition—admittedly powerfully expressed—of clichés about the sterilities and narrowness of the Calvinist statelet. The very titles of Paulin's poems are indicative—'Still Century', 'In the Lost Province', 'A Partial State', 'Cadaver Politic', 'A Just State'. A recent, very powerful, poem 'Desertmartin'—the name has its appropriate resonance to Paulin's mind—sums up in its imagery his defining attitudes:

> At noon, in the dead centre of a faith,
> Between Draperstown and Magherafelt,
> This bitter village shows the flag
> In a baked absolute September light.
> Here the word has withered to a few
> Parched certainties, and the charred stubble
> Tightens like a black belt, a crop of Bibles ...
>
> These are the places where the spirit dies.
> And now, in Desertmartin's sandy light,
> I see a culture of twigs and bird-shit
> Waving a gaudy flag it loves and curses.

The poem enacts an inferiority complex which has both historical and aesthetic aspects. These harsh asperities on the soured, bitter culture of twigs, bird-shit and Bibles of the North is—though it has its truth—a partial truth. In a sense, this vision of the North is itself a mythological construction generated in complex and subtle ways by the nationalist mythology. Though Paulin's *Liberty Tree* as a whole takes a more forgiving attitude to his culture, fastening particularly on the vigour of the Northern colloquial speech and dialect, he—and others—might look more considerately and more consideringly under that bowler hat. The Northern Protestant culture badly needs its own Patrick Kavanagh.

Derek Mahon's poetry[20] is the most impressive work to come from 'the Protestant imagination', and though there are parallels with Paulin's work, Mahon's is ultimately not only more complex but more compassionate. Like Paulin, Mahon excoriates the Old Testament dourness, the Mosaic imperatives which cramp Northern Irish culture, as in 'Ecclesiastes'— 'the/dank churches, the empty streets,/the shipyard silence, the tied-up swings'. Like Paulin, too, he registers the theatrical appeal of nationalist mythology, as in the poem 'As It Should Be', in which the 'mad bastard'—the Spectre of Irish History itself—is shot down, but in which the modern demystified world which results is seen as rather flat and anonymous. The nicely judged ambivalence of this poem, however, gives evidence of Mahon's possession of 'wit', in the sense of the word as T.S. Eliot famously applied it to the poetry of Andrew Marvell: 'It involves . . . a recognition, implicit in the expression of every experience, of other kinds of experience which are possible . . .'[21] The elegance and poise of Mahon's stance, reflected in his lucid style and in his touches of humour, indicate a more inclusive and balanced attitude than Paulin's, a wider perspective. Contrasting the mythic past with the mundane present, he is kinder to his own tradition than Paulin, as in the poem 'Glengormley', which speaks of the heroes of the past, 'the unreconciled', strangling 'on lamp-posts in the dawn rain' and admits that 'much dies with them'. Nevertheless, for all the ironic obliquity of tone, the poem celebrates an alternative:

> Wonders are many and none is more wonderful than man
> Who has tamed the terrier, trimmed the hedge
> And grasped the principle of the watering can.

In the superb 'Courtyards in Delft', in which the bourgeois perfection and the 'trim composure' of Pieter de Hooch's portraits of Dutch life clearly function as an analogue of Belfast suburbia, Mahon in part laments the somewhat anaemic spareness of the life:

> Nothing is random, nothing goes to waste:
> We miss the dirty dog, the fiery gin.

But another voice will not be silenced, a voice which balances against the appeal of the Dionysiac and the mythic the claims of a lovingly detailed reality:

Yet this is life too, and the cracked
Out-house door a verifiable fact
As vividly mnemonic as the sunlit
Railings that front the houses opposite.
I lived there as a boy and know the coal
Glittering in its shed, late-afternoon
Lambency informing the deal table,
The ceiling cradled in a radiant spoon.

Significantly, even in this tender poem, Mahon ends (Paulin-like) with a wish that the Maenads might enter, 'smashing crockery, with fire and sword'.

The watermark of Mahon's sensibility is not, however, a craving for the brutal irruption of history. On the contrary: he constantly hungers for, and creates, places of the mind beyond time, out of time. His desire seems to be that of 'The Last of The Fire Kings', to be 'through with history',

Perfecting my cold dreams
Of a place out of time,
A palace of porcelain

Where the frugivorous
Inheritors recline
In their rich fabrics
Far from the sea.

Mahon hungers for the world of art, to be gathered into the artifice of enternity as a refuge from the nightmare of history. 'The Snow Party' is both fine example, and fine poem:

BASHÓ, coming
To the city of Nagoya,
Is asked to a snow party.

There is a tinkling of china
And tea into china,
There are introductions.

Then everyone
Crowds to the window
To watch the falling snow ...

Elsewhere they are burning
Witches and heretics
In the boiling squares,

Thousands have died since dawn
In the service
Of barbarous kings—

But there is silence
In the houses of Nagoya
And the hills of Ise.

In one sense, this ceremonious stasis, as in a Japanese print, is the logical *ultima thule* of the Protestant sense of extrusion from Irish history. Mahon's humanism will not, however, allow him to forget or to dismiss history—'the boiling squares' *will* intrude, the Last Fire King finds it difficult or impossible to perfect his cold dream:

But the fire-loving
People, rightly perhaps,
Will not countenance this,

Demanding that I inhabit,
Like them, a world of
Sirens, bin-lids
And bricked-up windows ...

This humane balancing of attitudes is itself testimony to the width and depth of perspective which Mahon brings to bear on experience. His is a sensibility with resemblances to Beckett's, or even Pascal's. The hot furious struggles of Ireland are distanced by an imagination prone to the cosmic view, so that even the city where the recent troubles initially exploded is seen now as 'tranquil, its desolation almost peace':

Here it began, and here at least
It fades into the finite past
Or seems to ... ('Derry Morning')

There is, however, nothing cold or minimalist in Mahon's detachment. The most appealing quality of his poetry is its tenderness, a tenderness towards the silent, the lost and inanimate and dispossessed things of the world, the tongueless victims of history or of human carelessness. He writes of 'The Apotheosis of Tins', of 'A Garage in Co. Cork', of a motorbike which 'disintegrates/With rusty iron gates/In some abandoned stable', and belonged to 'a tentatively romantic/Figure once', who became 'Merely an old lady' ('An Old Lady'). The justly praised 'A Disused Shed in Co. Wexford' is the definitive example of Mahon's willingness to reach out to rescue the lost history of the victimised and of the forgotten. The mushrooms of the poem have waited a half-century, without visitors, in the dark, since the last Irish civil war:

> Once a day, perhaps, they have heard something—
> A trickle of masonry, a shout from the blue
> Or a lorry changing gear at the end of the lane.

The door is opened on them, but it may be shut again:

> They are begging us, you see, in their wordless way,
> To do something, to speak on their behalf
> Or at least not to close the door again.
> Lost people of Treblinka and Pompeii!
> Save us, save us, they seem to say,
> Let the god not abandon us
> Who have come so far in darkness and in pain.
> We too had our lives to live.

It would be barbarously reductive of a fine poem to identify these mushrooms with the Protestant community of Northern Ireland, but the veiled analogy is there. Mahon perhaps suggests, without rancour, that his own 'lost people' in their 'wordless way' are in a sense victims, the flotsam of history.

## IV

To generalise so sweepingly about 'the Catholic and Protestant imaginations', to omit consideration of so many other fine poets from Northern Ireland (Hewitt, Longley, Simmons, Deane are only the most obvious omissions), is worse than a crime, it is an error. Neverless, and despite the overfree rein given to the 'virtuous philosopher' (read 'interferring moralist'), it seems worthwhile to explore, however inadequately, what may be called the deep structure of the Northern problem, of those levels perhaps below consciousness which shape cultural and political predispositions. Among these, then, are the Catholic imaginative obsession with mythological history and racial landscapes, and the Protestant imagination's sense of its lack of history and its consequence deprivations.

NOTES

1.  Cited in A. T. Q. Stewart, *The Narrow Ground*. London: Faber (1977).
2.  Richard Kearney, *Myth and Motherland*. Derry: Field Day Pamphlets (1984), p.22.
3.  *Collected Pruse*. London: MacGibbon and Kee (1967), p.19.
4.  From *Mules*. London: Faber, 1977, p.11.
5.  *Preoccupations*. London: Faber (1980), p.56.
6.  Heaney's major publications, all published by Faber, London, are: *Death of a Naturalist* (1966), *Door into the Dark* (1969), *Wintering Out* (1972), *North* (1975), *Field Work* (1979) and *Station Island* (1984).
7.  *The Listener*, 26 April 1973.
8.  *Preoccupations*, p.57.
9.  'North: "Inner Emigre" or "Artful Voyeur"?' in Tony Curtis, ed. *The Art of Seamus Heaney*. Poetry Wales Press (1982), p.76.
10. Discussing the ritual blood-letting of the Iron Age, Heaney says somewhat chillingly: 'It seems to me that there are satisfactory imaginative parallels between this religion and time and our own time. They are observed with amazement and a kind of civilised tut-tut by Tacitus in the first century AD and by leader-writers in the *Daily Telegraph* in the 20th century'. 'Mother Ireland', *The Listener*, 7 December 1972.
11. 'Escaped from the Massacre?' review of *North*, *The Honest Ulsterman*, 50 (Winter 1975).
12. John Haffenden, *Viewpoints: Poets in Conversation*. London: Faber (1981), p.61.
13. See Seamus Deane's 'Interview with Seamus Heaney', *The Crane Bag*, I (Spring 1977).
14. See Terence Brown, *Northern Voices: Poets from Ulster*. Dublin: Gill and Macmillan (1975), p.169.
15. *Irish Times*, 17 January 1973.
16. *Irish Times*, 30 July 1970.
17. See Cairns Craig, 'The Body in the Kit Bag: History and the Scottish Novel', *Cencrastus*, 1 (1979), pp.18-22.
18. Paulin's major publications, all by Faber of London, are: *A State of Justice* (1977), *The Strange Museum* (1980) and *Liberty Tree* (1983). 'A Just State' and 'Cadaver Politic' are from *A State of Justice*; 'Before History', 'A Partial State', 'Trotsky in Finland', 'Still Century', and 'In the Lost Province' from *A Strange Museum*; 'After the Summit' and 'Desertmartin' from *Liberty Tree*.
19. *Times Literary Supplement*, 26 May 1972.
20. Derek Mahon's major collections, all published by Oxford University Press, London, are: *Night Crossing* (1968), *Lives* (1972), *The Snow Party* (1975), *The Hunt by Night* (1982). 'Glengormley' is from *Night Crossing*; 'Ecclesiastes' and 'As It Should Be' from *Lives*; 'The Snow Party', 'The Last of the Fire Kings', 'The Apotheosis of Tins' and 'A Disused Shed in Co. Wexford' from *The Snow Party*; 'Courtyards in Delft', 'An Old Lady', 'Derry Morning' and 'A Garage in Co. Cork' from *The Hunt by Night*.
21. 'Andrew Marvell' in *Selected Essays*. London: Faber, 3rd edition (1951), p.303.

# SOME THOUGHTS ON WRITING
# A COMPANION TO IRISH LITERATURE[1]

ROBERT WELCH

In the twelfth century *Acallam na Senórach* (*The Colloquy of the Ancients*), which is a compendium of the lore relating to Fionn mac Cumhail and the Fianna, there is a powerful passage which describes the death of Cael and Créd at the Battle of Ventry. Cael has won Créd, a fairy woman whose rath is under the mountains called 'The Paps' in County Kerry, by reciting to her a poem he has learnt from his foster-mother in the tumulus at Newgrange on the Boyne in County Meath. They are at Ventry fighting with Fionn, because Ireland is threatened by invasion. Créd heals the wounded but on the last day of the battle Cael is drowned, and his fairy wife dies stretched beside him, after she has recited one of the most intense poems in the Irish language:

> The bay roars above
> the mad stream of Reenavere.
> the wave breaking on the shore
> laments the drowning of the warrior

We sense in this tale, brief and skeletal though this rehearsal of it is, that we are in the presence of a view of things which is very old, very Irish, and also, somehow, very true. Créd is the female healer, associated with the land itself. Her house is under the Paps, and in that house there is a great vat of sweet beer, 'tangy malt', over which bends an apple tree, laden with heavy fruit. The symbolism is strong. The love match betwen Créd and Cael is linked to the well-being of the country itself, and it is no accident that she should accompany her man to Ventry when he goes with Fionn to fight against the foreigners, the interlopers, '*na h-allmhúraigh*'—those outside the wall, those beyond the ramparts. To read a story like this and then to take up, say, Yeats's play *Cathleen ni Houlihan* (1902) is to realise that, while the arts of story and of literature are products of specific times and places, they also respond to clusters of emotion, significance, and symbol which human language is always seeking to revise and reshape. Though theosophised and decked out in the occult symbolism of the Golden Dawn Yeats's Cathleen is energised by a combination of nationalism and devoted love (Maud Gonne played the leading role in 1902). Yeats's play also contains a very old feeling that the land is presided over by a female entity, and that she wants to protect it from the strangers who would rob it of its central core of meaning.

There is often a good deal of discussion about Yeats's 'Irishness': whether he can really be thought of as an Irish writer, coming, as he did, from Anglo-Irish stock. The argument here often takes the line that the real Ireland is that which Yeats took it upon himself to despise: the Ireland of shopkeepers and small farmers, whose systems of values, commercial, respectable and conservative, was antithetical to Yeats's espousal of a proud, indignant and aloof ideal of the supremacy of the imagination. But Yeats's emphasis upon vision, though deeply anti-democratic, led him into a reading of the old codes inherent in Gaelic literature; and his version of these, though politicised by nationalism, and affected by the late nineteenth century revulsion against materialism and modernisation, is very accurate indeed. We should not only look for Yeats's translation of the Gaelic world into modern Anglo-Irish literature purely in terms of details of syntax or rhythms, or in the fact that he went for much of his content to the old legends and sagas: we should rather look at the way in which his writing continually represents the patterns of symbolic meaning as these have to do with the *relationships* between visible and invisible, landscape and emotion, intelligence and difficulty, as these manifest themselves in Gaelic literature. These relationships are not static: Gaelic literature has its own way of perceiving them. It has its own networks of significances: for example, specific places accumulate around themselves complicated encrustations of historical and legendary association; a certain kind of episode, in a tale (a death, maybe), will activate appropriate formal developments. It all adds up to a quality of density of reference. To read Gaelic literature is to cross-read; it is to be 're-memorised' (a word that Austin Clarke uses superbly in his poem about the trouble and joy of memory. 'Mnemosyne Lay in Dust').

It was a peculiarly fortunate stroke of fate that Yeats should come along when he did, with the particular depth and breadth of mind with which he was gifted. Schooled in the learning of the Renaissance Platonists, who saw the mind as the storehouse of human memory, he read Gaelic literature, in translation, not primarily for nationalist or opportunist reasons, but because his own style of enquiry was exactly the one needed to re-activate the memory codes of the Gaelic World. He wanted to re-collect and re-invigorate those relationships between emotion and landscape, the individual mind and exterior fate, a man's energy and his 'doom', that Gaelic literature transacts in its particular ways. He is in touch, imaginatively, with the Gaelic world, and it is a very limited view of how a culture transmits itself that disallows his connections with that world simply because he did not learn the Irish language.

Yeats is taken as an example here, because he—along with Joyce—is the pre-eminent Irish writer of this century. One of the convictions that led to the writing of a *Companion to Irish Literature* was that the work of these writers, set in the context of the entire body of Irish literature, in all its languages (including Latin and Norman French), would be seen to belong to that literature, in its entirety. This is not an attempt to claim them back from world literature, but merely to emphasise that it is a very difficult thing to prevent a culture from continuing to emit its identifying signals, even when the language in which the signals are transmitted is changed. Nor is it an attempt to diminish the individuality of these writers; rather to say that a writer discovers his individuality when he finds ways of entry into the mother-lodes. There his work acquires, then, both fling ('*sprezzatura*') and coherence, something that Yeats, Joyce and Seamus Heaney have found, but Ezra Pound, for example, did not.

The mother-lode has been mentioned, and there is a need for caution in terminology of this kind, but, even if we take such a rebellious theologian as Joyce, we see how deep his transactions were with the basic codings of Irish literature. In 'A Mother' he has great fun with the meanness and the pathetic exclusivities of the Gaelic revival at the turn of the century. Mrs Kearney is a frantically ambitious and pushy mother, who has to deal with the self-satisfied and inept Hoppy Holohan, the concert organiser, when she negotiates a contract for her daughter, Kathleen, to play the piano in the Antient Concert Rooms at an Eire Abu evening. Yeats's Cathleen ni Houlihan is split in two, and the Kearneys, in the end, fall out with Holohan over money: the plot of Yeats's *The Countess Kathleen*, where

Ireland's soul is saved from the evil of materialism, symbolised in gold, is totally ripped apart. This could be read as a deliberately revolutionary or destructive strategy by Joyce, gleefully tearing open the fabrications of cultural nationalism to show the meanness within. But that is only part of the story, because Joyce, a deeply humane writer, shows the profound sadness involved in the rift between Kathleen and Holohan. 'I'm not done with you yet' the mother says; to which Hoppy replies: 'But I'm done with you'. They have lost the faith. Créd and Cael are separate again.

One of Joyce's themes (indeed it is a basic element in his method) is the return to the body. To return to the body is to return to that activity of the senses which comes to us out of the past, out of all the molecules and the genetic interconnections that result in us having our being here and now. Language, for Joyce, was the means by which that sensing of our past is made conscious and articulate. More than that, his style, or styles, rather, are increasingly ambitious attempts to make his readers conscious of language itself as a storehouse of accumulated experience. We are prevented from seeing language in this way by the myopia of custom. Joyce's rhetoric breaks custom to reveal all the complications inherent in the languages the human body has developed to express its desires and longings. For Joyce language, in literature, can be a return to what has made us what we are; it is Finn again. And he is awake. There is no doubt that the complex of interwoven experience to which Joyce returns again and again is Ireland, her history, her past, her languages. Again, as with Yeats, this is not simply a matter of theme: it has to do with the voices he sets talking, and the way they create, in their speech, interacting relationships between, say, a singificant event in a story and the art of formal expression to which it can give rise.

One of the devices to which Joyce returns again and again is the keen (*Caoineadh* in Gaelic). Place his extraordinary passage in *Finnegans Wake* where Anna Livia Plurabella recalls her father lifting her up on his shoulders at the fair, and the way Joyce's language opens up the emotion of that scene, alongside the account Humphrey O'Sullivan gives in his Gaelic diary of the deaths of the Callan blacksmith and all his family during a food shortage in July 1830, and we can see that the twentieth century writer is at his most modern, his writing packed with most surprise, when he allows that voice to surface which has a formal and dignified way of dealing with loss:

And it's old and old it's sad and old it's sad and weary I go back to you, my cold father, my cold mad father, my cold mad feary father, till the near sight of the mere size of him, the moyles and moyles of it, moananoaning, makes me seasilt saltsick and I rush, my only, into your arms. I see them rising! Save me from those therrble prongs! Two more. One two moremens more. So. Avelaval. My leaves have drifted from me. All. But one clings still. I'll bear it on me. To remind me of. Lff! So soft this morning, ours. Yes. Carry me along, taddy, like you done through the toy fair! If I seen him bearing down on me now under whitespread wings like he'd come from Arkangels, I sink I'd die down over his feet, humbly dumbly, only to washup. Yes, tid. There's where. First.[2]

It was well his wife and child went with him, and that they didn't stay behind in loneliness and sorrow, seeing the forge implements with no hand to use them to provide their daily bread. The music of his sledge or hammer striking red-hot on the anvil will never again be heard. Dark beads of perspiration will never again be seen on his cheeks. His long arm will never again hold the tongs over a fire, blown into bright flames by the large bellows, puffing and blowing, expanding and contracting in turn. His all-powerful arm will never again put a shoe on a neighing stallion, a skittish mare, a shaggy gelding, nor a lively kicking colt.

The three coffins, covered with white sheets, were side by side in a cart. Men, heads bent, were drawing the cart with ropes to the final resting place, where the smith was buried deep down on the windward side, his dear wife beside him, and the little child in her arms, as they used to lie together in their marriage bed.[3]

All literatures will have their formal means of dealing with grief, but the ways in which those formalities emerge will be different. What is remarkable in Irish literature is that its most achieved writers in its most recent, English phase, are at their best when they are drawing upon the system of meaning and patterns of relationship that belong to Gaelic literature. When a writer writes in Irish, there is not, or at least there does not appear to be, a difficulty about his access to the structures and codings of Gaelic literature, and yet there are writers in Gaelic, modern ones, such as, for example, Breandán Ó h-Eithir, who, though excellent and competent practitioners of Gaelic, are much *less* Gaelic than either Joyce or Yeats. This is not perverse: because of the capaciousness of their minds, their restless interrogation of experience, their total absorption into what it means to seek to make relationships between language and its memories, they are continually finding access to what is stored in the collective information systems of Irish culture, and that goes right back to the mother-lode. Mairtín Ó Cadhain and Joyce have much in common; so too do Bishop Berkeley and Eriugena; so too do Thomas Kinsella and Giolla Bridhde Mac Con Midhe writing a poem to God, imploring him, as if he were a chieftain, to bless him with the tangible evidences of love. Again, *A Companion to Irish Literature*, embracing all the literature of Ireland, will point to the continuity of Irish tradition; or, rather, to the *persistence* of certain modes of apprehension, certain formalities, certain relationships between different areas of experience, which survive the shift from one language into another. Indeed, it could be argued that this shift, far from occluding the Gaelic strata of Irish culture, made writers all the more anxious to search them out. It is the 'fascination of what's difficult' that rouses the will to full intensity, in defiance of all that exterior fate snatches away. An initial loss uncovers fullness:

> 'I am of Ireland
> And the Holy Land of Ireland,
> And time runs on', cried she.
> 'Come out of charity,
> Come dance with me in Ireland'.

Our century is one in which, from its beginning, we have been preoccupied by origins, from Frazer through to Freud, to Jung and to Lévi Strauss, up to Heidegger, Eliade, Casteneda, and, yes, even Derrida. It is again the peculiar fortune of Irish literature that it is, in all its phases, totally absorbed by origins. In its most recent, English phase, it is obsessed with them, because the inherent native tradition of origin-hunting (as evidenced in the *Lebhor Gabhala*, *The Book of Invasions*, which tracks the different inhabitants of Ireland back to the Flood), became allied to the question of national identity in the latter stages of its colonial history. This alliance marks Irish literature as the paradigm for all the nationalist literatures in the post-colonial phase of world history.

A *Companion to Irish Literaure* will help to make the reader conscious of the opportunities and dangers attendant upon the politicisations inherent in the notion of indigenous culture, by showing how reactions to specific events are coloured by the prejudices and expectations of people who feel the way they do for specific reasons and motives. The Playboy riots are a good example of how people will want to believe, from time to time, that their interpretation of what is authentic must hold, and that anything else is mere apologetic shoneenism or just downright betrayal. The quest for origins can become a stiff-legged strut of defiance. The manifold nature of Irish literary tradition, if that is set forth in a rational, ordered and impartial manner, will act against the tendency to appropriate the 'National Being' for political or sectarian objectives. A *Companion to Irish Literature*, then, should aspire to that condition of impartial account.

This was the objective of Sanuel Ferguson, of Douglas Hyde, and of many of their successors in the field of Irish and Celtic Studies. But mention of Hyde returns us to a difficulty—and it is an inescapable one, however much may be said about the continuity of Irish tradition, or the persistence of certain modes of apprehension. This is the fact that one of the two languages of Irish literature has virtually disappeared as a language of everyday communication. This is a simplification, and there are many now who use Irish in their everyday lives who were not native speakers, and their number will probably increase as the century goes on. But still there remains the awesome fact that the Irish are one of those races, who, for all kinds of complicated reasons, committed 'linguistic suicide', in David Greene's disturbing phrase. What happens to a people when they lose their language? And what happens to their sense of themselves when they live in the aftermath of that loss? These are questions to which there are no ready answers, but one thing is clear: Ireland did not cease to produce literature when the language of the great majority of its people became English. On the contrary, it would seem as if the virtual disappearance of Gaelic intensified the sensitivity of the Irish people towards language, so that English as it is spoken and written in Ireland became a subtle and capacious instrument, associated with the loss of the language it was replacing, but also carrying with it the promise of an audience and a readership that was extensive, modern, and accustomed to the idea that language could be used to articulate complex states of mind and conditions of men.

English was, then, a challenge and an opportunity. There is, surely, in a writer like Edmund Burke, the sense that he is relishing his mastery of highly orchestrated cadence, not just for the musicianship of it, but because he realises that English can perform very difficult co-ordinations of argument and passion, and that these are necessary if he is to interpret the rational order and justice (as he sees them and feels them), of English constitutional liberty. He sees them and feels them so keenly because he is very conscious that communal civilisation, which sanctions individual freedom, is something which evolves slowly, and that that evolution is intrinsically linked with the ability a language has to display, interpret and indeed enact the interplay between freedom and order, passion and intelligence, on which a sane society grounds itself. That is the Burke is a master of English; he wanted and achieved that mastery because, being Irish, he knew that a complicated society needs to acknowledge linguistic mastery if it is not to degenerate into faction, fanaticism, and delinquent strife. The Irish are often praised for their oratorical power, but the real reason why they revel in the turns and subtleties of English syntax is that they want to approach and apprehend the order and power which it represents. This is not the gift of the gab, but the deep need to absorb, personalise, and make familiar that which is foreign, out there, and strange. That is the way the English language presents itself to the Irish writer. It is a web of absorbing difficulty, carrying in its interlocking strands an active information system that refers to sanctions, liberties, restraints, orders and passions that have been thought about, refined, ordered, redefined and challenged ceaselessly since the time of Shakespeare and even further back. A line such as 'And broils root out the work of masonry' shows us many things, but among its achievements are the kinds of things it can take for granted: that the Roman idea of the constructed city can be threatened by the frightening propensity men display to undo what they have done. Furthermore the use of 'work' in combination with 'broils' setst the familiarity of the everyday against the terror of war, emphasise in the peculiar plural 'broils'. This oddness is carried forward into the inversion of the normal meaning of 'root', here applied to 'rooting out'. And so on. What we see in this line is how English, in Shakespeare's hands, is charged with very English notions of stability and order, and how it gives a writer the confidence to say these kinds of things. Furthermore, though this is from one of Shakespeare's sonnets, and probably not meant for publication, the fact that Shakespeare was a dramatist meant that his working of the language, as a complex medium for conveying movements of apprehension, imprinted itself on the English mind, thereby enriching it by making it aware of the possibilities the language could afford for variation, depth, and tactile suddenness of effect. Shakespeare, in other words, is one of the determining factors of modern English culture, and the English were peculiarly fortunate to have, at their first stage of colonial expansion, a writer who would expand the language inwards, while opening up depths of interior life and thought.

This was the complex instrument for which the Irish decided, in the end, to opt, abandoning, in Samuel Beckett's half mocking, half-sorrowing phrase their own 'poor dear Gaelic'. In going for English they were forsaking a language with its own great powers and capacities, but one not exercised by the movements of modern, that is to say, post-Renaissance, consciousness. Daniel Corkery was wrong about some things, but he was surely right when he said that the Renaissance did not come to Ireland. Scepticism, doubt, the power of modern reason—Gaelic does not really know any of them, until the twentieth century, when they flood into the poetry of Séan Ó Ríordáin and the prose of Mairtín Ó Cadhain.

For an Irish writer, such as Burke, to write English was to venture into a foreign network, one associated with the supremacy that a colonial power exercises and enjoys. To master that was to gain access to reserves of authority which the English, would seem, to an Irishman, to enjoy as a birthright. There is a Cornish proverb which goes: 'Those without speech gets their lands took'—and the Irish knew how true that was. The Anglo-Irish, too, knew that however they might be regarded by the native Catholic Irish, in London their accent, manners and general demeanour would mark them off as Irish. To master the writing of English, to develop oratorical powers, was to gain access to the hidden codes on which the English view of life was based (there is an old link between mastery and mystery); having lost their own mystery (and the Anglo-Irish, too, were affected by that loss) they found satisfaction in taking on themselves the 'mystery of things' as enshrined in the master language. Because of their loss they would probably— and naturally—have been all the more anxious to lay claim to English. The colonial language, then, was colonised by those who had themselves been colonised. And not only that, the Irish writers sought ways of making English respond to the codes and modes of apprehension which were once in the keeping of Irish, but which, from about 1800, began to be without a language. English was being seeded by instincts of life not its own. This interaction, which was often opposition, lies at the heart of what we call Anglo-Irish literature. We have Burke's vibrant style, full of alertness and wide-awake intellectual tension, as he seeks to interpret, better than any Englishman has done before or since, the nature of English constitutional liberty; and we have Thomas Moore's Irish Melodies, that seek to attune English to the 'breath' (his word) of Irish song. Burke and Moore, unlikely allies, are both engaged in a kind of invasion of English. And Shaw, in times nearer to our own, relished expounding the folly of the English to the English in a language bristling with irony and supremely conscious of its author's mastery. This arrogance of Shaw's, which is primarily linguistic, may be why he is not entirely liked in England—or in Ireland either for that matter—because his mockery spares no-one.

Samuel Beckett opted out of the whole colonial interchange when he wrote in French. Or did he?

A *Companion to Irish Literature*, which attends to the literature of the two main languages of Ireland, must raise questions in the reader's mind about the interplay between these two languages and languages systems, and the oppositions between them. Synge's speech was deeply affected by the sense that there underlay the English spoken in Ireland, another linguistic set of arrangements that troubled that English language, stretched it, and made it new. The energy of Synge's language, its quality of strange and immediate realisation, owes much to the intense concentration he brings to English, in order to force it to open up to soundings, associations, grammatical patterns, that belong to another language system. This thought occurs when it is realised that, in an alphabetically arranged *Companion*, there must be, quite near to the entry on Synge, one on Spenser, who pushed the English language of his own time into a recovery of other Englishes that had passed, and also tried, anticipating Milton, to give it Latin gravity and force, and an Italian rapidity.

There is a sense in which all really good writers are trying to write other languages *through* their own, native, one. The writer is in search of the gift of tongues, though often he may not be a very good linguist. Shakespeare tries to write Latin in English, and make it part of all the Englishes of England; what Milton is up to is obvious, and the same can be said of Wordsworth. Shelley tries to write Greek; Carlyle German, and so on. Irish literature in English is in a peculiar situation, in that the language system that persistently calls to it, since 1800 in any case, when it began to be displaced, is Irish. Irish writers are often seeking to write through to Irish in their English. Sometimes this is painfully obvious, and it can become stage-Irish (of the-mist-does-be-on-the-bog kind) and (even worse) American-Irish. But sometimes, too, the language becomes tense with expectation, restraint and attentiveness, as the writer strives to push his English as far as it will go towards an original otherness. Yeats's Crazy Jane poems are a case in point; or Joyce's great cadences of lament; or Thomas Kinsella's stark, bardic rigour; or Montague's syllabic finesse; or Brendan Kennelly's accentual passions and meditations. Always Gaelic is there, whether actually on the page or not. There is no question of the Irishness of these writers, despite the clamant pieties of nationalist exclusivity. Irish writing is now mostly in the English language, but an English continually trying to remember the other language in itself. And this happens, whether the writer knows Irish or not, simply because to be an Irish writer is to be involved with Ireland and all the old codings she emits. There is a passage in the preface to Seán Ó Ríordáin's *Eireaball Spideoige* (1952) that puts this points very clearly. Ó Ríordáin, probably the best Irish poet since Yeats, and one of the most intelligent poets of modern Europe, describes the activity of poetry as follows:

> . . . *is minic a bhraitheas gnó neamhchoiteann a bheith idir lámha agam agus mé á gcumadh; gnó seachas scríbhneoireacht nó ceapadóireacht, gnó a bhí níos comhgaraí do ghlanadh. Measaim go rabhas i riocht duine a bheadh ag glanadh meirge nó clúimh léith d'íomháigh agus ag lorg agus ag athnuachaint na bundeilbhe—ag lorg grinneall-dhromchla. Má cuirtear an glanadh seo, an tóch seo, i gcomórtas le casach-taigh le linn slaghdáin, is féidir an bhundealbh a shamhlú le scamhóig. Nó is féidir an gnó a shamhlú le dall ag léamh Braille. Is aithnid dúinn go léir an dromchla, an fhoirm seo a scagadh ó gach foirm eile; ní fios conas is aithnid; agus is eol dúinn é a bheith seanda, bunúsach, údarásach, buan, álainn agus ní féidir teagmháil leis gan geit áthais.*[4]

Often I felt that I was engaged upon an extraordinary activity when I was creating; an activity other than writing or inventing; an activity that was closer to cleansing. I think I was like someone cleansing rust or dust off an image, looking for and renewing the basic pattern— looking for the patterns on the seafloor. If this cleansing, this, this scouring, is compared to a cough during a cold, then the basic pattern can be imagined as a lung. Or the activity can be thought of as a blind man reading Braille. We all know the pattern, this form which has been separated out from all other forms; we do not know how we know it; but we know it as being old, basic, authoritative, persistent, beautiful, and it is not possible to contact it without experiencing a thrust of joy.[5]

Even more subtly, Ó Ríordáin goes on to argue that a person or a thing cannot experience a thrust of joy in himself or itself: there must be a searching out of a pattern other than one's own. When one contacts that pattern, thoroughly experiences it, then one realises and experiences one's own. A culture cannot realise its own patterns; it needs us and our language to discover them. When we discover them we are brought into a realisation of our own selves and our attachments to language, culture, patterns and meanings. In Ireland there are two languages in the cultural matrix, which creates all kinds of problems, but it also means that there are two modes of enquiry, two stores of power, each of which discovers and expresses the potential of the other for realisation and surprise. Our loss is our gain. Surely one of the reasons why there has been so much good Irish writing in the last one hundred years has to do with the fact that the transactions between Irish and English have not disappeared, nor do they show any signs of so doing, as Brian Friel's *Translations* displays so well.

This is why it has seemed appropriate to undertake the writing of a *Companion to Irish Literature* which will attempt to provide, for the first time, a systematic account of the single body of Irish tradition in its two separate but interdependent lives, in Irish and in English.

NOTES

1. The present author is completing a *Companion to Irish Literature*, to be published by Colin Smythe Ltd, Gerrards Cross.
2. James Joyce, *Finnegans Wake*. London: Faber (1966), pp.627-8.
3. *The Diary of Humphrey O'Sullivan*, tr. and ed. Tourái de Sholdrasthe. Cork: Mercier Press (1974), pp.88-9.
4. Seán Ó Ríordáin, *Eireaball Spideoige*. Dublin: Sáirseál agus Dill (1952), p.12.
5. Translation by the present author.

# CONTRIBUTORS

DAVID BURLEIGH was born in Northern Ireland in 1950 and grew up in Portrush. He was educated at Coleraine Institute and at the New University of Ulster. He has lived for six years in London and six in Tokyo. Before coming to Japan he worked for a charity organisation that gave advice to the homeless in London. He currently teaches English at a crammer school in Tokyo and also at Waseda University. He contributes articles to a variety of journals and is interested in poetry. His own poems have appeared in publications in Ireland, England and, more recently, in Japan. He has also collaborated on translations of Japanese poetry.

JOAN COLDWELL, Professor of English at McMaster University, has served on the executive of the Canadian Association for Irish Studies. She has published widely on Irish and Canadian literature and on Romantic poetry and is the author of *Charles Lamb on Shakespeare*.

MAURICE HARMON is a Professor and Director of Modern Irish Studies at University College, Dublin, a former Chairman of IASAIL and a founder member of the American Committee for Irish Studies. He has written several studies of Modern Irish Literature in the English language. These include *Sean O'Faolain; a critical introduction* (1966, rev. ed., 1984), *J.M. Synge Centenary Papers* (1972), and *The Poetry of Thomas Kinsella* (1974). He has compiled a *Select Bibliography for the Study of Anglo-Irish Literature and its Backgrounds. An Irish Studies Handbook* (1977)—and an anthology *Irish Poetry after Yeats* (1979). He edits the *Irish University Review: a Journal of Irish Studies*.

A. NORMAN JEFFARES is Life President of IASAIL. He has written *A History of Anglo-Irish Literature* (1982). His biography *W.B. Yeats: man and poet*, first published in 1949, is still in print, and his *New Commentary on the Poems of W. B. Yeats* (1984) succeeds his earlier *Commentary* on Yeats's *Collected Poems*

237

(1968). He has edited twenty-four plays for the Folio Society in *Restoration Drama* (4 vols, 1974) as well as editing, and writing on, the work of many Irish authors. He has held posts at Trinity College, Dublin and the universities of Groningen, Edinburgh, Adelaide and Leeds; and he is now teaching at the University of Stirling, Scotland. A former Vice-Chairman of the Scottish Arts Council and member of the Arts Council of Great Britain he is now chairman of the National Book League (Scotland).

BRENDAN KENNELLY was educated at St. Ita's College, Tarbert, County Kerry, and at Trinity College, Dublin and the University of Leeds. He is a Fellow of Trinity College, Dublin, where he is Professor of Modern Literature; he has taught at Swarthmore College, Pennsylvania and Barnard College, New York. He was awarded the AE Memorial Prize for poetry in 1967. He has written two novels; edited *The Penguin Book of Irish Verse* (1970; enlarged edition, 1981); and written 28 volumes of poetry (4 of them in collaboration with Rudi Holzapfelmes); these include *My Dark Fathers* (1965); *Selected Poems* (1969, 1971); *New and Selected Poems* (1976, 1978); *Shelley in Dublin* (2nd edition, 1982); *Cromwell* (1983, 1984). In addition to three books written in collaboration with Seoirse Bodley he has also written the text of *The Real Ireland* (1984). His latest volume of poems is *Moloney Up and At It* (1984).

DECLAN KIBERD lectures in English at University College Dublin. He was formerly Lecturer in Irish at Trinity College Dublin, and Lecturer in English and American Literature at the University of Kent at Canterbury. His book *Synge and the Irish Language* appeared in 1979, and another study, *Men and Feminism*, will be published by Macmillan of London in 1984. He is currently writing a book entitled *Revival or Revolution?: The Selling of Irish Literature*. He has recently written the script for the RTE feature film *Samuel Beckett: Silence to Silence* and presents a weekly arts programme on Irish television. He is the current Director of the Yeats Summer School.

ALASDAIR D. F. MACRAE is a graduate of the University of Edinburgh. He was a lecturer in the University of Khartoum, Sudan, for five years, and has been a lecturer in English at the University of Stirling since 1969. His main area of interest lies in poetry in English of the nineteenth and twentieth centuries and his specialist work is in Shelley, Yeats and Edwin Muir. He has written studies of Shakespeare's *Macbeth*, Shelley's *Selected Poetry*, and Eliot's *The Waste Land* for Longman/York Press. Coming from a Scottish Gaelic background, he has in recent years developed an interest in Irish literature both in English and Irish.

AUGUSTINE MARTIN was educated at Cistercian College, Roscrea, and University College, Dublin, where he is now Professor of Anglo-Irish Literature and Drama, having previously been a lecturer in English and then Professor and Head of Combined English Departments. He was a Senator of the Irish Republic (1973-80), Director of the Yeats International Summer School at Sligo (1978-81) and Vice-Chairman of the Irish Cultural Relations Committee of the Department of Foreign Affairs (1979-82). He was appointed to the Board of Directors of the Abbey, the National Theatre of Ireland in 1983. He has lectured in Britain, America, Canada, France, Denmark, Belgium, Lebanon, Singapore and Japan. His publications include *Anglo-Irish Literature, a History; James Stephens, a Critical Study;* and a biography of William Butler Yeats, and he was the Editor of *The Genius of Irish Prose*.

JOHN MONTAGUE was born in Brooklyn, New York, and brought up on a farm in County Tyrone, Northern Ireland. He was educated at Armagh and University College, Dublin. He has published many books of poetry, *Poisoned Lands* (1961), *A Chosen Light* (1967), *Tides* (1970), *The Rough Field* (1972), *A Slow Dance* (1975), *The Great Cloak* (1978) and *The Dead Kingdom* (1984), as well as a book of stories, *Death of a Chieftain* (1964). He edited *The Faber Book of Irish Verse* (1974). He is at present working on another book of stories, a selection of essays and more lyrics. He has received many prizes in Ireland, England and the United States, including a Guggenheim award. He is President of *Poetry Ireland*.

A. C. PARTRIDGE, who is Emeritus Professor at the University of the Witwatersrand, Johannesburg, was Dominion Fellow at St. John's College, Cambridge in 1950. He has written sixteen books for English publishers, for the Language Library of André Deutsch, for Bowes and Bowes, for Edward Arnold and others. His latest book is *Language and Society in Anglo-Irish Literature* (1984). He has been visiting Lecturer at the University of Keele, Staffordshire, and at the University of Alberta, Edmonton, and is presently a member of the International Shakespeare Association. He has published articles on Shakespeare for *Poetica* in Tokyo.

ANN SADDLEMYER, Professor of English and Drama at the University of Toronto and past Chairman of IASAIL, has published extensively on Irish drama. Her most recent books are *Theatre Business, The Correspondence of the First Abbey Theatre Directors* and *The Collected Letters of John Millington Synge* in two volumes; she is also co-Editor of the journal *Theatre History in Canada*.

MASARU SEKINE teaches English at Waseda University, Tokyo. He studied English literature and drama at Waseda University and the universities of Manchester and Stirling, and he is also a trained Noh actor and dancer. He is a Director of Academic Advisory Services Ltd, and Representative of IASAIL-JAPAN. He was formerly a research curator at Waseda University's Theatre Museum and has been a visiting Lecturer at Darlington Hall. He has written on various aspects of modern drama; his translation of *Pippin* was produced at the Imperial Theatre, Tokyo, in 1976; and his book *Ze-Ami and His Theories of Noh Drama* is being published by Colin Smythe Ltd in 1985. He is at present writing a book (in Japanese) on Irish drama for a Japanese publisher.

FRANK TUOHY was born in 1925. He graduated from King's College, Cambridge. He has worked for the British Council in various countries, including Brazil and Poland, which are the settings of his novels *The Animal Game* (1957), *The Warm Nights of January* (1960) and *The Ice Saints* (1964). The last won the James Tait Black and Geoffrey Faber prizes. He has written three collections of short stories, republished as *The Collected Stores* (1984). His biography of W.B. Yeats was published in 1976, and he has contributed articles and book reviews to the *Times Literary Supplement, Encounter, The Spectator* and other journals. He is at present teaching in Tokyo.

GEORGE WATSON was born in County Armagh in Northern Ireland, and educated at St. Patrick's College, Armagh, Queen's University, Belfast, and Wadham College, Oxford. He is a Senior Lecturer in English at the University of Aberdeen, and is the author of *Irish Identity and the Literary Revival: Synge, Yeats,*

Joyce and O'Casey (1979), and of various articles on Irish writing. His most recent book is *Drama: An Introduction*, London: Macmillan, 1983. He has lectured at universities in the U.S.A., Spain, Denmark and Ireland.

ROBERT WELCH was educated at University College, Cork and the University of Leeds. He is Professor of English at the University of Ulster, having previously taught at University College, Cork, the University of Ife, Nigeria, and the University of Leeds. He is the author of studies of nineteenth century poetry and of translations from the Irish. He is completing *A Companion to Irish Literature*, which will deal with the two literatures of Ireland, that in Irish and that in English. He is married and divides his time between Portstewart and West Cork.

# INDEX

*Note.* In the listing of titles under individual writers the words 'A' and 'The' have been disregarded so far as alphabetical arrangement is concerned.

243